A Fair Distance

Lois Boblett's Western Memoir
1851-1922

L. Darlene Spargo

Columbine Ink
publishing words and images of the West

Denver, Colorado

>⊷ ⊶<

ISBN 978-0-9821740-7-4

>⊷ ⊶<

A Fair Distance is an original publication. It is published by
Columbine Ink, LLC by arrangement with the author.

Columbine Ink

5560 East Dickenson Place
Denver, Colorado 80222-6202
303-756-1106 • 303-484-3293 fax
peg@columbineink.com
www.columbineink.com

A Fair Distance is available through your bookstore.
or by visiting www.columbineink.com.

>⊷ ⊶<

Printed in the USA

>⊷ ⊶<

For

Judy Artley Sandbloom: without her vision, research, and encouragement
this book would not have become a reality.

And for

Dorothy M. Stanley, who always believed.

Preface

When Judy Artley Sandbloom brought me a copy of Lois Whitcomb Boblett's memoir, I couldn't put it down.

Most of the women's stories I had read revolved around a single episode, such as a journey on the Oregon Trail. Lois's story covered most of her life, half the country, and many of the important events of the Western migration.

We couldn't help but wonder if it was all true.

Judy and I decided to see if we could prove her story, and our research began in earnest. Every location, every event, every person she mentioned became a subject for research, and time after time, Lois's story was correct in every detail. Often, she added information to what was already in the record.

Lois Whitcomb Boblett was both a woman of her time and a woman ahead of her time. She had no time for politics, current events, or gossip. Her world was a day-to-day struggle. Throughout the seven decades of her memoir, Lois tells us about moving to new places and starting over.

In sharing Lois's story, we wanted to place her in a historical context so we could understand the unique challenges and hardships she faced. The events swirling around Lois affected her decisions, the way she lived, her opportunities, and restrictions. Lois lived on the frontier, and decisions made in the East had a direct impact on her and her family.

How Lois dealt with the trials and tribulations she faced – in her own words – is fascinating.

Contents

Contents (concluded)

Figures

Acknowledgments

First, my thanks to Judy Artley Sandbloom who fulfilled her role superbly in providing research for this book, who was instrumental in documenting Lois's story, and who will always have my admiration and gratitude.

I wish to thank the special people who assisted both Judy and me in our search to find and know Lois Whitcomb Boblett.

If Lois's family hadn't treasured and saved her story throughout the years, it would have been lost forever and we would be the poorer for its loss. Dolores Clark, Robert and Beth Mix, Lois E. McNaught, and Kathleen Pasta are some of the family members who kept Lois's story alive.

I also wish to express my appreciation to all the local historians who gave of their time and expertise in assisting us in our research, including:

> *Colorado: Mike Sinnwell, Jeffrey A. Lockwood, and Richard Gehling.*
> *Arizona: Ryan Flahive, Bill Lynam, Fred B. Nelson, and Dan Messersmith.*
> *Connecticut: Theodore P. Kaye.*
> *California: Col. Herbert M. Hart and Ruth E. Mather.*
> *Washington: Noel V. Bourasaw, James R. Warren, and Kraig Anderson.*
> *Idaho: Linda Hackbarth, Ann Ferguson, Ellen Larsen, Kevin Knight, and Chuck A. Peterson.*
> *Yukon Territory: Murray Lundberg, Alan Taylor, Claire Rudolf Murphy, and Jane G. Haigh.*

And to others who added to the book:

> *Photographers: Mike Sinnwell, Murray Lundberg, Judy Wight Branson.*
> *First reader and historian: Jim Bailey, Wenatchee, Washington.*

My deepest appreciation goes to Columbine Ink's Peg Williams and Anne Justen, who turned our draft into the book we had only dreamed it could be.

And finally, a special thank you to my husband and Judy's husband who gave us the time, encouragement, and support to bring our vision to life.

L. Darlene Spargo

Introduction

$\mathcal{L}$ois Almena Whitcomb Boblett was both a woman of her time and a woman ahead of her time.

Although she kept journals, we have been unable to locate them; perhaps they are lost forever. Fortunately for us, a family member sat down with Lois in 1922 and typed her memoirs and the family passed copies around among themselves. One of these copies came to our attention, and for a year we studied it and discussed the possibility of publishing the memoir. At times, Lois's story seemed too good to be true. We decided to document her story and our research began in earnest. Every location, every event, every person she mentioned became a subject for research, and time after time, her story was correct in every detail. Often, she added additional information to what was already in the record.

What Lois didn't say was as interesting as what she did say. She seemed to have no time to waste on politics or current events or gossip. Her world was confined to the day-to-day struggle for survival and the pursuit of a better, stable future for her children. We share the same goals today, but while we are fighting traffic, she was fighting Indians.

When we imagine a home of our own, we take many things for granted: power, indoor plumbing, and food in the cupboards. She fought to have her dirt floors covered with stone and had to grow her family's food. Time and again, circumstances conspired to force Lois to start over, which she did with little more than an ironic shrug. *If you had to do something, you might as well just get started and do it.*

In telling Lois's story, I endeavored to place her in history, as no one lives in a vacuum. Events swirling around Lois affected her decisions, her mode of living, her opportunities, and limitations. Even though Lois lived on the frontier, decisions made on the other side of the country affected her and her family directly. How Lois dealt with the trials and tribulations she faced is truly fascinating reading.

As you read the book, please note that Lois's story is written in regular type and the historical additions are in shaded sidebars. As a service to the reader, I have added chapters and subheads. The chapters reflect the moves, starting from Lois's birth in Wisconsin, to new United States territories, states, and districts and Canada's British Columbia and Yukon Territory. Some of Lois's long paragraphs have been split into two or more paragraphs. However, throughout Chapters 1-13, her words are printed as written, misspellings and all.

The photographs and illustrations, of course, were added by the author and provide another dimension in understanding Lois's journey across the continent.

For Lois Almena Whitcomb, moving on was a way of life. Her parents, Aretas and Lydia Priest Whitcomb, had already moved from New Hampshire to Pennsylvania to Wisconsin prior to Lois's birth in Milwaukee. Aretas always meant to stay in each new place, but something inevitably disrupted his plans: an offer too good to pass up;

a more promising gold field down the road; troubles with the Indians; and finally, the desire to live out his remaining years near his children.

As frontier historian Ray Allen Billington remarked, "Whether men went west in search of adventure or wealth, they were driven by impulses that failed to motivate their neighbors who stayed behind. In every pioneer there was a touch of the gambler. Those who did not respond to the lure of the frontier were the contented, the cautious, and the secure. Wealth and poverty were not the deciding factors; the cost of migrating kept the very poor at home, while many with fortunes responded to the lure of the setting sun."

Leaving "civilization" behind was not an easy decision, but the lure of gold and land, as well as adventure, drove the emigrants. From 1848 to 1853, more than 250,000 prospectors flooded into California, Nevada, Utah, and Colorado. By 1900 nearly 600,000 settlers took advantage of the Homestead Act to file claims on more than 80 million acres. In 1890 the U.S. Census office declared the country settled and the frontier a thing of the past. The westward migration was the most dynamic phase in the nation's history. Never before, or since, have so many people moved into and settled such a vast area so quickly.

Who Came and Why

One needs to consider certain points in order to understand the migration. Migration did not proceed in an orderly fashion. Not everyone came out at the same time or or to the same place. Migration was very selective. Who migrated was often based on age, economic status, ambition, and personal attitudes. The poor did not emigrate. They couldn't afford the equipment and supplies needed. Moving West was not an easy proposition. It required planning and skill. The settlers had to confront the immediate challenge of providing shelter, food, health, and protection. Only after those needs were met could they turn their attention to the task of building communities, schools, churches, and social networks.

Among the reasons people left the East were:
- increased industrialization, which depressed job opportunities among skilled craftsmen;
- overcrowding, with most of the land already under the plow;
- the end of the Civil War with its resultant upheaval of newly discharged men; and
- the perceived or real persecution felt by religious, political, or cultural groups, such as the Mormons.

Families that went and did well wrote home and encouraged others to join them. Inter-related families often formed groups that remained together as they traveled west, searching for new opportunities. They were able to protect and support each other, combine resources when times were bad, and stave off the terrible loneliness that plagued many of the early settlers.

The earliest incentive to emigrate was the promise of instant wealth in the gold fields. That dream was quickly replaced by the real promise of free land.

Aretas Whitcomb was one of the first to take advantage of the new homestead law. Congress approved the Preemption Act in 1841, under which a settler could file on a 160-acre claim and purchase the land for $1.25 per acre after erecting a dwelling and meeting certain conditions. The Donation Land Acts of 1854 regulated the price of land based on quality, with some parcels selling for as little as $0.125 per acre. Free land was offered to settlers to encourage them to move to the new territories and begin farming. The 1862 Homestead Act allowed men and women to claim up to 160 acres of land. The qualifications were:

- be 21 years old or head of a family;
- be a U.S. citizen or be in the process of becoming one; and
- to never have fought in a war against the United States.

The settler would have to live on the claim for at least six months of the year for five years and improve the land. For those not wanting to wait five years, title could be obtained under the process of preemption for $1.25 per acre.

Another avenue to land ownership was the 1873 Timber Culture Act, which provided for settlers to secure title to an additional 160 acres of ground if they planted and maintained 40 acres of trees for eight years. This requirement was lowered from 40 to 10 acres in 1878. Any type of tree could be planted, including fruit trees.

The men loaded up wagons, and the land rush was under way. The majority of women who moved west traveled over the Oregon Trail or the Mormon Trail in wagon trains comprised of a number of families. These women created support groups among themselves and often settled in the same communities at the end of the trail.

The Whitcomb and Boblett Families' Journeys
Instead of joining the westward push, the Whitcomb family headed south and west from Nebraska Territory to the mines around Pike's Peak. Women were scarce in the mines, and early towns that seemed to spring up overnight and disappear just as quickly.

Lois learned from an early age to be independent and self-reliant. She had a strong role model in her mother, who simply dealt with whatever happened and made the best of it. Lois was not a fatalist; rather she was a realist. Lois and Ed Boblett's marriage appears to be more of a partnership than many marriages at that time, when women had few legal rights and lived under strict social constraints. She often said, "Where my husband can go, I can go," not "I have to go." She was determined to keep up with him, and often she was the one to decide when it was time to give up and move on to something new.

Lois regretted her lack of formal education and wanted more for her children. Her courage, resilience, and faith allowed her to continue on under sometimes horrific circumstances. If the women who settled the West were to survive, they had to learn to cope with illness, the death of loved ones, fire, famine, storms, and isolation. Many women like Lois dealt with the isolation by writing diaries and journals. Lois wrote of being the only woman and wishing there were others nearby. In fact, there were other women in the mining towns, but they were usually prostitutes and did not have contact with "respectable" women like Lois.

In many ways, Lois's story and experiences were the same as those of all women who crossed the Plains. She was responsible for preparing food, laundry, setting up camp, caring for children, tending livestock, planting and harvesting, sewing clothing for the family, and educating the children. Her story is unique in that she traveled a different path, taking a man's part as well as a woman's, proving that she could indeed go where her husband went, and she did it as his equal when she married Edward Alexander Boblett.

Ed was twice Lois's age when they married, but nowhere in her writings does she imply that he treated her as anything but a full partner in life. This was unusual for the times, as women had few rights to themselves. Any property they owned at marriage became their husbands'. Women could not vote. If a woman left her husband, she might lose custody of the children. If he deserted her, she had few if any legal remedies.

Historian Ruth Mather explored the subject of violence against women in her book, *Scandal of the West*, including the story of Lucinda Bohall. Lucinda married John E. Vedder June 1, 1855, in Sacramento, California, when she was a teenager. He promptly informed her that her duties were to clean, sew, and cook, while he announced that as a man he could stay out all night, refuse to provide treatment for her if she fell ill, and "stomp" her if she gave him any trouble. Both had fiery tempers and passersby often heard them fighting. Vedder would sometimes pick her up and toss her into her wedding trunk and tell her to leave and take her daughter with her.

The local Marshall, Henry Plummer, finally intervened and helped Lucinda find a lawyer and secure a divorce. Plummer arranged for a guard for Lucinda until she could make arrangements to leave town. On the night that Lucinda was to catch the 2 a.m. stage, Plummer stood guard himself.

Vedder was furiously jealous and forced his way into the house before she could finish packing. He crept up the stairs and fired two shots, both missing Plummer. Plummer's answering shot found its target. Vedder died in Lucinda's arms.

When the prosecutor learned that Lucinda had lived with a man before her marriage, thus soiling her reputation, he charged Plummer with murdering Vedder. The fact that Lucinda and Plummer barely knew each other didn't matter. After two trials, the jury decided that anyone sending a lawyer to help dissolve a marriage must be a seducer and found Plummer guilty of second-degree murder. He served time in San Quentin before being set free by Governor John Weller in response to a petition signed by 100 city and county officials. However, Weller didn't exonerate Plummer; he pardoned him on the grounds of "imminent dangers of death from consumption."

Lucinda's father-in-law kidnapped her daughter and filed for custody claiming that Lucinda's new "disrepute" rendered her an unfit mother. He denied her visitation rights unless he could sleep at her house and be "somewhat intimate with her." Lucinda's child died, and Lucinda quietly disappeared with her reputation in shreds.

Plummer eventually moved to Idaho Territory and then to Montana Territory, where he continued his career as a sheriff. He married, built the first jail, and attempted to put a stop to vigilante hangings. A crime wave swept through the area: a murder, two stage robberies, and the attempted robbery of a freight caravan. Not content to wait for Plummer to find the outlaws, a vigilante group formed. In a month-long hanging spree, vigilantes hanged 21 men suspected of belonging to gangs. One of those was Plummer himself, who left his sickbed to try to stop a lynching. Unarmed, he was marched up the gulch to the pine gallows and strung up. Immediately, the vigilantes spread the word that he had been the leader of a vicious gang called the "Innocents" that was responsible for 100 murders and robberies. Mather joins other modern historians in believing that Plummer was an innocent victim of vigilante justice.

American Women in the 19th Century
Equality laws were slowly being implemented by individual states. Laws allowing married women to own their own

property separate from their husbands were passed in Mississippi in 1839, New York in 1848, and Massachusetts in 1854.

Divorce law still allowed the divorced husband legal control of both children and property. The end of the Civil War brought about changes in the way women saw themselves. Widows inherited land, money, and family possessions and became a force to be reckoned with. Things were changing for women, but slowly and not without a fight from men and even some women, who felt their roles in life were threatened by the "new" women.

In the first half of the 19th century, women were constantly exposed to an idealized vision of the "true" woman in sermons, religious tracts, and secular literature. Although Lois considered herself a religious woman, she did not subscribe to the idea that a woman's place was on a pedestal. One of the most popular publications of the time was *Godey's Lady's Book*, with a circulation of 150,000 by 1865. Many women, and men, looked to *Godey's* for advice and guidance in everyday life, and the magazine editorials reflected the views of the day.

One example of the ideal woman appeared in the *Editor's Table* section of the magazine in 1851:

"We are not intending to enlarge on this theme, which will be better done by abler pens. We only allude to it here, in order to draw the attention of our readers to one curious fact, which those who are aiming to place women in the workshop, to compete with men, should consider: namely, that one, or very few specimens of female ingenuity or industry will be found in the world's greatest show-shop. The female mind has as yet manifested very little of the kind of genius termed mechanical, or inventive. Nor is it the lack of learning which has caused this uniform lack of constructive talent. Many ignorant men have studied out and made curious inventions of mechanical skill; women never. We are constrained to say we do not believe woman would ever have invented the compass, the printing-press, the steam-engine, or even a loom. The differences between the mental power of the two sexes, as it is distinctly traced in Holy Writ and human history, we have described and illustrated in a work soon to be published. We trust this will prove of importance in settling the question of what woman's province really is, and where her station should be in the onward march of civilization. It is not mechanical, but moral power which is now needed. That woman was endowed with moral goodness superior to that possessed by man is the doctrine of the bible; and this moral power she must be trained to use for the promotion of goodness, and purity, and holiness in men. There is no need that she should help him in his task of subduing the world. He has the strong arm and the ingenious mind to understand and grapple with things of earth; but he needs her aid in subduing himself, his own selfish passions, and animal propensities.

"But the elevation of the sex will not consist in becoming like man, in doing man's work, or striving for the domination of the world. The true woman cannot work with materials of earth, build up cities, mould marble forms, or discover new mechanical inventions to aid physical improvement. She has a higher and holier vocation. She works in the elements of human nature; her orders of architecture are formed in the soul. Obedience, temperance, truth, love, piety, these she must build up in the character of her children. Often, too, she is called to repair the ravages and beautify the waste places which sin, care, and the desolating storms of life leave in the mind and heart of the husband she reverences and obeys. This task she should perform faithfully but with humility, remembering that it was for woman's sake Eden was forfeited, because Adam loved his wife more than his Creator, and that man's nature has to contend with a degree of depravity, or temptation to sin, which the female, by the grace of God, has never experienced. Yes, the wife is dependent on her husband for the position she holds in society; she must rely on him for protection and support; she should look up to him with reverence as her earthly guardian, the 'saviour of the body,' as St. Paul says, and be obedient. Does any wife say her husband is not worthy of this honor? Then render it to the office with which God has invested him as head of the family; but use your privilege of motherhood so to train your son that he may be worthy of the reverence and obedience from his wife. Thus through your sufferings the world may be made better; every faithful performance of private duty adds to the stock of public virtues."

The opening of the West meant that women were removed from their social and familial circles, and they found themselves accepting responsibilities previously handled by men but without any increase in rights. With most professions closed to women, *Godey's Lady's Book* printed an editorial in 1856 by Sarah J. Hale that advocated teaching as a profession for women:

"Thanks to the spirit of Christian freedom, women in our land are favored above the sex in any other nation . . . The Homestead laws, and the security given that the property of a married woman shall remain in her own possession, are great safeguard of domestic comfort. The efforts made to open new channels of industry and profitable professions for those women who have to support themselves are deserving of much praise; but one greater act of public justice yet remains undone. Government, national or State, have never yet provided suitably for the education of women. Girls, as well as boys, have the advantages of the free school system; but no public provision has been made, no college or university endowed where young women may have similar advantages of instruction now open to young men in every State of the Union."

The editorial lists the reasons women should be considered as teachers:

"That while, as a general rule, women are not expected to support families, nor pay from their earnings to support the State, they can afford to teach for a smaller compensation than men; and, therefore, earn funds bestowed to educated female teachers gratuitously will in the end prove a measure of economy, and at the same time will render education more universal and more elevated by securing the best class of teachers at a moderate expense. That those most willing to teach are chiefly found in the industrial class, which as yet has received few favors from National or State Legislatures. That by providing for such gratuitous advantages for women to act as educators will secure a vast number of well-educated teachers, not by instituting a class of celibates, by employing the unoccupied energies of thousands of young women from their school-days to the period of marriage, while, at the same time, they will thus be qualifying themselves for the most arduous duties of their future domestic relations." Even educated women were expected to eventually settle down and marry.

The shortage of women in the West gave women the power to choose their husbands and at the same time, divorce was easier in the territories. Lois lived at a time that placed her at the forefront of important and critical junctures in American history even though she was not aware of them.

Chapter 1
Iowa
1851-1856

I, Lois A. Whitcomb, was born in Milwaukee, Wisconsin, in 1844. My mother, Lydia Whitcomb, cooked in the first hotel in Milwaukee. My parents were born in New Hampshire. They married there and lived there some time; two children being born, Josiah and Eliza. Then they moved to Pennsylvania, where another girl, Sally Ann, was born. Next they moved to Wisconsin where the subject of this narrative saw the light of day in Wisconsin February 1, 1844. They then moved to Dain County, near Madison, leaving there when I was seven years old.

Iowa – The First Move West, 1851
My father, Aretas Whitcomb, being of a roving disposition, sold his farm, hitched up his horses and started for Iowa. While living near Madison, sister Eliza married a man by the name of Amos Dexter. He sold out too, and he and father hired a man by the name of Freeman to help drive the stock of horses, cattle, sheep and hogs. The first day we had a good deal of trouble with the hogs as they would not drive good. Father said you can not drive a hog but could coax him. So he got a bucket of corn and told the man that by dropping a grain at a time they could coax them from the ranch. They did this and after that they drove quite as well as the cattle.

We camped out most of the way, but it being late in the fall we sometimes put up at a roadhouse. I remember one in particular. We saw they were dirty people and Father did not want to go into the house, but he finally went in and engaged our board and came back to the wagon for us to go to the house. We were glad for it was cold and snowing. We went into the house and there was no fire except that in the kitchen and there were a lot of chickens over the stove and several children playing around and they were about as dirty as the chickens. There were some slats over head for a loft with some hay scattered over them. It smelled so badly that we could not stay in the house, so we went back to the wagon. Just then Mr. Freeman said, "This will never do; we will have to go further on." So, pretending to be sorry, we climbed back into the wagon, thankful to get away.

I do not remember much else that happened till we got to the Mississippi River. I had never seen such a large river and I thought it a grand sight. We crossed the river by a ferry drawn by a rope. One of our cattle backed off the boat when about in the middle of the river, swimming back to the shore but Father followed her, bringing her back tied to the boat. It frightened me; of course, I could not bear to see it drown, so I screamed and cried as though it were one of the family. This was at Dubuque.

When we got to Iowa, there were a lot of wolves. As the women of those days had to do the spinning and weaving of cloth for clothes, we had to keep sheep. We had thirty or forty head, so sister Sally and I had to keep the sheep near home until Father and Josiah cleared and fenced the farm, putting up the necessary buildings. We became very much attached to the sheep, especially the lambs. There was a large spring on our place and quite a branch ran out from it. When the lambs were young, they did not like the cold water so we took them in our arms and carried them over. They soon learned this trick and they would run to us to take them in our arms, and when tired they would come to have us carry them. One sheep died leaving a lamb and we were wondering what to do with it, when we thought of a very gentle cow we had. We took [the lamb] to her and taught it to suck her. It was amusing to see a cow claim a lamb for her own and the lamb claim the cow as her mother. Father had about a dozen cattle. My brother and we girls used to milk them and Mother made butter and cheese.

One time there was a peddler came to our place. He stayed all night with us. He had a heavy black moustache. I had never seen a man with a moustache before and I thought he was a devil. I was very much afraid of him. In the evening, the folks went to the barn to do the chores and left me in the house to see that everything was all right. I climbed up in a chair and went to sleep and I suppose he thought it would be fun to kiss me, so he did. I was frightened, ran out to the barn screaming with all my might and said the "devil" kissed me. I never heard the last of it.

Mother made a loom and used to take in weaving. She wove coverlids and it was lots of work.

The third summer there was a school. Sister and I had to go and we got up early and helped Brother milk the cows. I was the smallest so they gave me the easiest cows to milk, but I milked my five cows.

> Lois might have been fortunate that she had to milk only five cows. Gender roles were strictly defined, as illustrated by Daniel Drake's quote in Cathy Luchetti's book, *Men of the West*:
>
> "Liz was taught [milking] . . . as early as possible, seeing that it was held by the whole neighborhood to be quite too girlish for a boy to milk, and mother, quite as much as myself, would have been mortified if any neighboring boy or man had caught me at it."

Mother got breakfast and we did up the work and then went to school. It was two miles and a half to school. We trotted part of the way and ran the rest. There was a large hornet's nest on the road. One day we got a number of the scholars to go with us to club [the nest]. I carried the clubs and the rest thew them. My sister threw one and we were watching to see how near it came to the nest. It went pretty close and a hornet flew like a bullet and hit her between the eyes and she fell as though she had been shot. She was soon nearly blind. It frightened us so that we went back to school. We went home that night and told our brother and he took his gun and shot the nest down. We were very glad to get it out of the way.

Father said he was always going to stay there [Iowa] but that fall a man came along and wanted to stay all night. Our house was as large as a hotel and he told him he could stay. We had a nice large frame barn and were going to build a nice house the next year. This man talked to Father and wanted to know what he would take for the farm. He told him he would not sell, but finally, thinking that he would put the price so high that he would be in no danger in being taken up, he named the price. The man had Father draw up the deed and gave him the money immediately.

We sold the sheep and part of the cows and then moved to Mitchell County, Osage, Iowa. My brother-in-law [Amos Dexter] had a farm adjoining Fayette County. This joined Father's farm. When Father sold out, Mr. Dexter put his place up for sale, and after selling came to Mitchell County. Here, he and Father got adjoining places again, buying government land at a government sale.

Here they broke prairie land for themselves and others. Sally and I had no sheep to care for and there was no school, and having nothing in particular to do, we planted corn. This was a novelty to us, but being trained to do as we were told, we set to work. We had to plant every fourth furrow by taking an old axe and chopping down through the sod to make a place to drop the corn. Then we chopped at the side of it to cover it. The men started breaking a team of four yoke of oxen, so Sally and I with our corn and axe would plant as soon as they came to the fourth row. There were a lot of striped gophers taking out the corn as we planted it. Our brother, Josiah, taught Sally to shoot; Sally and I thought we could fix the gophers. As the team went around, we hunted gophers, shooting them so we had a good crop of corn.

We had a pair of oxen as gentle as cows, and Sally and I would yoke them up and go out in the field and gather a load of corn and haul it in. Brother Josiah had a spell of lung fever that left him very weak, so Sally and I had both girl's and boy's work.

At Osage, we had no water for the house or stock so Father thought that he would dig a well. There was a river [probably the Cedar River] not far from the house and Father thought he could get water, so he got men to dig a well. They got down about sixty feet and they saw that it was not safe. While we were eating dinner, we heard an awful rumbling. We went to see what it was and saw that the well had caved in. Father abandoned it. This was before the days of artesian wells. From that time on, Father was dissatisfied there, for he never liked to haul water.

There was a branch [of the river] not far away, but it was always dry in the summer. One spring there was about two feet of snow on the ground. It was Sunday. Pa, Ma and Josiah went to church three miles away to a town called Mitchell Center. They crossed this branch river just where it came into the timber. It turned warm and the snow melted very fast on the prairie. They expected to stay all day and come home after church at night, but when the morning services were over they hurried home. We all got into the wagon and drove down into the branch in the timber and it was a sight. A hundred yards above was a body of water I should judge to be four feet high and where we were there was none. Soon there came a little stream like a long black snake darting along by us. It would run over the top of the snow in the ravine and where there were big holes, the water would shoot clear through and beyond as the main body of water would rush on crushing the snow as it went.

Chapter 2
Nebraska Territory
1856-1859

*F*ather had a chance to sell out and he sold again, getting a good price. Mr. Dexter sold out too, and between them they bought a grist mill and saw mill. They hitched up a span of horses and started off to hunt a location. They traveled around considerably, going into Minnesota and northern Iowa, down to Sioux City. There they crossed over into Nebraska and settled in Dixon County on a small stream called the Aowa Creek in the Missouri River bottom. They returned to get us at Osage and we packed up to move again. They had just started school about two weeks before we left, but as we were going away, Mother said it was no use for us to start.

According to oral family history, Lois named the creek the Aowa, its present-day name. The first settlers into Dixon County, Nebraska, arrived around 1856. They were John, Solomon B., and Jacob Stough; two brothers by the name of Brown; C.F. Putnam; and W.H. Jones, who located on the west branch of Aowa Creek; and John Paschal, who located in Aowa Valley. In the same year Amos Dexter and Aretas and Josiah Whitcomb settled in the Missouri bottom, where they built the first saw mill in the county. Hard financial times swept through the territory in 1857 and 1858, gold and silver disappeared, and paper script of the "wild cat" species became utterly worthless. Many settlers became discouraged and left, returning to the East or heading to the Pike's Peak gold rush in 1859.

The three plagues of the Plains were fires, blizzards and locusts.

Prairies existed because of the annual fires, not in spite of them. The great, level sweep of the land encouraged fires to race across it. A full-blown prairie fire could move at the speed of 65 miles a day.

One story was told of a couple in a buggy who drove wildly ahead of the fire for 65 miles before they were able to escape. When they stopped, the poor horses dropped dead in their traces.

There were few trees on the prairie because fires suppressed them, while native grasses depended on fire to destroy the old dry tops so new sprouts could arise from the roots. As fires were suppressed by farming and settlement, trees began to encroach on the open land. Although fires were good for the prairie, they were terrifying and often fatal to the settlers.

Father went to St. Louis to get the mill and Mr. Dexter and wife went with him. Ma, Sally, two hired men, and myself started to our new home with teams again and our cattle, not having any sheep or hogs. We reached our destination in due time and in good condition.

It was a very dry fall and a fire going through there had killed a great deal of timber, and it had grown up with thistles, six to eight feet in height and as thick as could be. There had been a frost and killed everything, and it being so dry, made it rather unpleasant to look at. The folks took a scythe and mowed down the thistles around camp.

They made our camp of logs, putting them up about six feet high and stretched our wagon sheets for the roof, taking common cloth for the gable ends. We had a rag carpet and Mother cut it and the men put grass down covering it with the carpet. They made some double pole bedsteads, one above the other. Then we filled ticks and put them on above and below. We knew that we would need a lot of extra beds when Pa came with the millhands so we saved hay. Then the men put up a lot of hay for the stock and Mr. Dexter bought loads of corn and hauled it in to feed when they were putting in the mill.

Fire – The First Plague, Fall 1856

One day Mr. Dexter went out on a horse to one of our neighbors for something and he set the hired men to cutting saw logs. The wind was blowing quite hard and we were getting dinner ready when we saw a smoke start up on the prairie. The wind was just right to bring it to where we were, so we called the men to come and set back fires, but they laughed at us and told us not to be afraid, they could take care of the fire when it got there; but we went to carrying water and filled everything with water that we could, and then threw water around as fast as we could.

Our camp was about three quarters of a mile from the Mississippi River. There was a sand bar a mile wide next to us, so when I saw they could not get the backfire started, I got frightened and thought we would all be burned to death, so I ran toward the sand bar thinking I would save myself. I didn't say any-thing to anyone but started to go. I went across the branch that we were camped on, crossing a log. No one saw me. If they had, they would have called me back. As I got across the branch, I looked back and could see the fire close to camp and I saw no chance to escape. I saw the men cutting the horses loose. I just threw up my hands and said, "Lord, what shall I do?" I heard a voice say, "Go back and help fight the fire and do the best that you can." I looked around and supposed I would see some one, but I saw no one and I knew that God had answered my prayer. I went back as fast as I could and went to work, but before I could get to the camp, which was only a few steps from where I stood, it was all on flames as far as I could see. I could not have gotten to the sand bar, but would have been burned to death.

> When pioneers reminisced about the "old days," stories of prairie fires were among the first to be told. Examples abound in the *Federal Writers' Project, American Memory Archives* in the Library of Congress.
>
> Mrs. Ross was 19 years old when she moved to Iowa with her husband and two little boys. She was typical of the strong, hard-working women that settled the frontier.
>
> "We didn't get lonesome, too busy picking up chips and running after cattle. We staked our cows out but had to tend them with water, and move them to fresh pickin, that was at first.
>
> "There was lots of hard work never worked so hard in all my life as I did in them hills. We homesteaded just south east of the Myrtle school house then after we proved up and living 8 years in all there we bought a place and moved 1 [1/2?] miles. We lived up in there 31 years in all, then we moved down here (North Platte) between the rivers.
>
> "I boarded 13 teachers and milked 18 to 20 cows besides my other work. We always had plenty of meat and potatoes and bread and butter and eggs, we never went hungry in them hills. We always had hogs at our place. They boys always went hunting after they got up big enough.
>
> "The Mr. got his hands burned in a prairie fire and then he couldn't help anymore with the milking. Prairie fire was the worst thing out there and this was a bad one and he was burning fire guards for the neighbors, they was new in there and I guess didn't know how or something, and the fire got away from them when the wind changed and they was OVERTAK-EN AND BURNT. Him and the oldest boy was took to Gandi and stayed there a long time being treated for the burns. We lost a horse from burns in that prairie fire, he died about a month later."

George W. Bates was another pioneer interviewed by the *Federal Writers' Project* of 1936-1940.

"Once, while he and quite a few other men were surveying at what is now Riverside [Iowa, 1853] a prairie fire came. The prairie fires would travel as fast as a horse could run, or faster, as the grass was so high and dry, it just went. There was a little creek near where they were surveying and someone said for them to wet their blankets and wrap themselves in the wet blankets and lie on the bank of the creek. They all did that but one man who wouldn't wet his blanket. He got badly burned and had to doctor all winter, but finally, in the spring he died from the effects of the burns."

Sometimes the women had to deal with several catastrophes at a time. Mrs. Will H. Burger recalled one such time.

"The next spring father and mother were away working and Mrs. J.W. Davis stayed to look after the baby. While they were gone a prairie fire came, but they had plowed up around the house and barn and weren't damaged. The next day a snow storm came up; they had a cellar under the house and took the horse and cow down cellar and kept them from freezing. The next year they had grasshoppers, but stayed on the homestead until mother died."

I promised God then I would be a Christian as soon as I knew how, but I am sorry to say I have not always lived as close to Him as I should have, yet I have never denied Him, and how could I when He spoke to me so plainly? Two men came just then and my brother-in-law, full speed on a swift horse. He got there just in time, and as he came, yelled to us to backfire, just as we had told the men to do. They had never seen fire running and knew nothing about it. Mother and Sister had fought for their lives and therefore knew.

By this time, the trees were falling all around us. With the wind blowing, they tried to start the backfire only to have it put out, with the main fire coming on us with lightening speed. The ground and the thistles were so dry and the wind blowing so hard that the flames would set the very tops of the tallest trees on fire. In the meantime, the wind blew off our tents and things were getting on fire inside.

The men ran into the place where the corn was stored and where the horses were tied, cutting them loose and by some means saved them. Then the men rushed back to the tent where Sally and I were doing our best to put out the fire with the water we had stored for the occasion. We had stuffed hay between the logs to keep out the weather and this soon caught fire. Sally and I would wet them down and we often had to throw water on one another to save ourselves from getting on fire. The men pulled out the hay from the outside and this we wet down. In order to breathe, we would put our aprons in water the men would bring to us and them to our mouths. Mother and Eliza gave out and they were told to go down under the bank of the creek. They said the flames swept right over them! We worked from eleven-thirty till three without stopping to eat or rest. The main part of the fire having passed, the old dead trees kept scattering fire about us until the wind died down.

Oh dear, what a plight everything was in! Mother's carpet was burned so badly that we could not do anything with it, and the straw ticks we had filled were all burned and the feather beds were also burned. The ground was so dry that the fire extended down the tree roots some three or four feet. It was not safe to travel for a long time. We next gave our attention to the horses and cattle. They all came home badly burned. One cow had a place on her back as large as my two hands, burned nearly to the bone. As soon as they were safe, the men, without stopping to eat, ran to our hay and just barely saved it. One of the men through exhaustion came near to dying, going so long without eating and working so hard in the heat.

Not long after this it began to rain and it continued until the ground was soaked. Shortly, Pa came home with the mill. The Missouri was low, and it being so late in the fall, they were afraid to come farther than Sioux City, twenty-five miles below us on the Iowa side, so we had to get men and teams to haul the mill that distance. Under the conditions, it was a real undertaking.

Blizzard – The Second Plague, 1858

Brother Josiah at this time was in Osage. As soon as Pa could get the mill home, he left Dexter to boss the mill while he went back after another load of our goods. At this time, Brother's wife had a baby girl born to them. As soon as she was able to travel, he took her to Auburn to her parents and left her there until spring, while he and Pa started with their load of goods.

They got within eight miles of a town called Sack City and there came up one of those awful Iowa blizzards; the snow hiding the roads and they could not tell where they were. They concluded the best thing they could do was to unhitch, getting on the horses and do the best they could to reach town before the snow fell so heavily they could not travel. They reached the town all right, and if they had kept on with the load, they possibly could have made it too. They thought that they would go back the next morning after the things, but the storm lasted for four days and where it was level, there was at least four feet of snow. It had drifted in immense drifts and it was impossible to get the things. After a time, they thought it pos-

Blizzards would sweep across the plains and were as dangerous as the fires. J.W. Hartman's story included all three of the dangers facing early Plains pioneers:

"Our greatest scares those days were Indians and the great prairie fires, as the rolling land was not yet settled and it all was a vast prairie. All settlers were along the streams where they had their wood and poles for their dugout and sheds. Coal was not available in those days. I remember the great Easter storm of [1873?], one of the most disastrous in Nebraska up to that time. It snowed and blowed for three days so hard that [you could?] not leave the house. The snow was deep and it froze in the face of the cattle. The cattle drifted with the wind and snow and consequently were smothered to death in the snow. Many homesteaders lost all of their stock this way. It was also terrible on wild life. Prairie chicken, quail, birds, were destroyed. We found, after the storm, many flocks of quail that had smothered."

Emma Mackey's experience with a blizzard, as written in the *American Memory Project*, was typical. The speed at which the storm could arrive was one of its most frightening aspects.

"It was so nice that forenoon (December 12th) and the hired man said he was 'so happy as a sunflower.' The men went to the river bottom for hay. All at once the wind came up from the northwest like a big black cloud and seemed to go right around the house, freezing the windows up with frost so thick you couldn't see through them any more than you could see through a board. The men could hardly find their way to the house; the hired man wanted to go with the wind and if they had they would have been frozen to death, but my husband knew the way and finally reached the house; he knew the windmill was between the barn and house. They had a basket of corn and the hired man pulled one way and my husband the other; couldn't see any more than you could see through a wall. It lasted about three days; it didn't snow so much but the air seemed full of snow on account of the high wind. Had a baby ten days old and had two other children. As it happened there was a big windbrakes on the place and the cattle took shelter there. Some of the neighbors had lots of cattle that froze."

13

One of the most tragic blizzards to strike the plains occurred in 1888 and was called the School Children's Blizzard. It sped across the Dakotas, Nebraska and Kansas, striking just as some schools were releasing the children. A number of the teachers and children never reached home.

Lizzie Lockwood was one of the teachers caught in the storm in Nebraska, and her story is included in the *American Memory Project.*

"I taught there at the time of the blizzard of 1888, and stayed in the school house all night with seven of my pupils. My father had always told us that in case of a blizzard never to go out of the house looking for anyone else. The blizzard started in Dixon County about 1:15 in the afternoon. It got so dark we had to put our penmanship away as we couldn't see. My father sent my oldest brother, Martin (better known as Pat) after us. He wandered about until 7 in the evening and finally came to Will Benedict's house; he had passed right near the school house several times and didn't know it as he couldn't see on account of the blizzard. He had two horses and my sister was to ride one of them and I was to ride the other. He had a [scarf?] around his face but it was so cold that his face froze and all the skin came off. We were about out of fuel and all we had to eat was what remained from our noon lunch, which wasn't very much. We kept our coats and overshoes on all night; had no light except by keeping the door of the stove open; I read to the children and we played games. We weren't worried until my father came in the morning and wanted to know where Pat was. Father brought a big pail full of biscuits and molasses. Mr. Benedict got to the school house around noon and told us that Pat was at his house. The parents came after their children in sleighs."

The first school in Dixon County, Nebraska, was taught by Miss Margaret Gorman, in Daniel Donlin's house in 1857. It isn't known if Lois attended, but perhaps she did. She certainly knew how to read and write; in fact, girls often had more education at this time than boys because the boys were needed on the farm. Many chil-

dren were taught at home by their mothers.

Most of the early teachers were women. It was one of the few occupations open to women which were considered respectable. She generally began teaching at 16 or 17 and was forced to quit if she married. Although she could marry, it was not always encouraged. In June of 1870, the San Francisco Board of Education voted to "discharge any female teacher who may commit the crime of marriage." Her pay was often by subscription, with parents paying $1 or $2 each month per pupil. If she did not live nearby, she would board with one of the families, sometimes moving to a different home each term.

Lizzie Lockwood taught in Dixon County after Lois moved away, but things would have changed very little from the time Lois was living there.

"I never went to school until I was 10 years old, then I taught the same school where I went to school, for seven years. The first school near Allen, Dixon County, was held in a granary; a sister of mine taught there six weeks; I learned my letters on the stove; taught when I was seventeen, and taught for seventeen years, and never went above the Eighth grade; my brothers went to school to me after they were 21. There were only four families who had children in school in a private house where I went to school. I didn't see a blackboard until one or two years before I started to teach. Mothers wouldn't think of sending their children to school without a slate rag any more than they would now without a handkerchief.

"I remember when I was little there was only one lead pencil in the neighborhood and the neighbors used to borrow it back and forth. When a child was sent to the neighbor for the pencil they were cautioned to be sure and not fall and break the lead off the pencil. The pencil was always wrapped in paper and very carefully guarded.

"The first school at Harmony Hill, near Allen, Dixon County, about one and one-half miles from my home, was built in about 1878. It was a sod school house and had windows that slid from side to side. Our school always had the name of having the best programs sible with the aid of some men and ox teams to get to the wagon. They got about half way and came back, thinking they could make it the next day, but that night the wind blew and covered their tracks so that no one could determine the way. They tried again and again but with the same results. At last they gave up and the wagon stayed there all winter until the roads settled in the spring.

Dexter got the mill up and some lumber cut and a small house built for us to live in and it was a very hard winter. It was the winter of 1855-56, if I remember that right. We could not hear anything from Pa and Josiah, as there was no traveling at all. Realizing the terrible winter, we began to think they had perished. It was either Christmas or New Years that Josiah came home on snow shoes. He had camped out on the prairie one night. He had a big knife and a hatchet with him and he had crawled down in a ravine and cut drifted snow and built himself a snow house. The next night he got to Sioux City and then home. The winter following the one described was also very cold. We lived here for three years.

Nebraska Indian Encounters, 1859

The Sioux Indians were camped near us and they used to come to our house for cornmeal. Pa gave it to them and said it always paid to be kind to them. One evening, Pa invited a number of the young Indians to come in to dance for us. They went through all their different dances and we enjoyed it very much. When they were through, Mother gave them a lot of bread and butter with sugar on it. They went to their tents singing and laughing. One time, we went to their tents to see how they lived and one old squaw asked me to marry her son, but I told her in Sioux language that I did not want a man that had no beard, so she cut off a piece of a long-haired buffalo robe, and holding it to his face said, "Now he has a nice beard." But I told her it was no good. That evening he came up to the house with a beard and moustache painted on his face. He laughed and said, "Now am I all right?" I told him again it was no good and would wash off, so then he went away.

I remember that Pa had a man cutting cord wood and he wanted to marry one of the young squaws, but she told him he was too lazy. He was the laziest man I ever saw. The Indian girls would go out and race with him at cutting wood and they always bested him. Sally and I were both young and had learned to talk pretty well with them and we had lots of fun teasing them, but they had too much sense to want such a man as he.

This same winter, there was an Indian who froze his foot while he was out hunting. The game was killed out of the woods there so the Indians had to move on. They went up the river on the ice and our men went out to see if they were all gone when they saw an Indian sitting by a few coals.

It proved to be the one who had frozen his foot. They came to the house and told Pa and he gave his consent to bring him in. We washed and dressed his foot and gave him his supper together with some old clothes and fixed him up all nice, furnishing him a nice bed and he was contented.

After about six weeks, his father and two half-brothers came to bury him. They went out to where they had left him to die and looked around but could not find him. Then they came to the house and Indian style came in without knocking. They saw the Indian sitting by the fire and hurrying to him, they kissed and hugged him, saying never a word.

We were overcome too and wept in joy also. We kept them for a day or two and they went away. The one with the frozen foot could not go yet so they went without him. When the old Indian started away, he and his sons knelt at the door and prayed for at least five minutes before leaving. In about six weeks, his old squaw came with a pony after him and he went away. We gave him some salve and liniment to take with him, but, unfortunately, he broke the liniment bottle, lamenting as he went.

Just across the river was Dakota. It still belonged to the Indians, but they did not stay there, and some men went over and cut some logs and brought them to Father, wanting to sell them, but he said he did not want logs that were stolen from the Indians. They took them down the river. Some time after that, the Indians discovered that their trees had been cut down and, knowing that Father had a mill, they thought that he had taken them. They came and demanded money for the logs, but Father told them that some men had been there to sell but he would not take the logs and they had gone down the river with them. However, one night they came and burned the mill. They could not get to the ones who had taken the logs, but Indian like, they burned our mill knowing at the time that the logs had not been cut there.

Chapter 3
Kansas Territory – Colorado
1859-1862

*F*ather, Josiah, and Mr. Dexter tried to repair it but with little success. Soon after this the gold excitement broke out in Colorado and we caught the fever. Meantime, Sally was married to a man by the name of Preston Hotchkiss, and Josiah's wife gave birth to another baby girl. Josiah did not want to take them out in the wilds, so he took them back to Iowa.

> Lois refers to Colorado, but in 1859 Pike's Peak was actually in Kansas Territory. Colorado was split from Kansas and became its own territory February 1861.

On the way back [from Iowa], Josiah met some men that had started going by the old Oregon Trail to Fort Laramie. They wanted us to join their party. We did and I believe there were about twelve teams; eighteen men and five women with one little boy of five years. As the Indians were peaceable, we had no fear of them, so we started on. We went about fifty miles when we lost the trail. The party stopped. There were so many buffalo tracks it was impossible to follow the trail. The party stopped and camped for dinner and discussed whether to turn back and go by Omaha and up the Platte River or go across the country. One of the party picked up a chip and, as it was damp on the underside, it was suggested that we toss it up and if the dry side turned up, we would go ahead, and if the wet side turned up, we would turn back. This was agreed to and in the test the dry side won.

All went well until we got about a hundred miles from the settlement. The cook killed all the deer and antelope that we wanted. Here we came to a beautiful stream called Elkhorn. There were many beaver swimming about in the water and the men wasted a good many shots only to fail to get a beaver. We learned afterward that a beaver would sink when killed.

About an hour before sundown, my brother with another fellow started up the river to hunt for deer. Seeing no sign of deer, they commenced shooting at a mark. At camp we thought they were finding plenty of game, so Pa and Dexter took their guns, which were always ready, and went to help get some game. They were probably about one hundred yards from camp when we heard an awful yell. The Indians were coming at us all painted for war, bearing their arrows, shields and spears. Among them were two chiefs that wore crowns on their heads, made from buffalo horns and bright colored feathers. The also carried banners made from deer hide, covered with porcupine quills brilliantly colored. Around the edge of the banners was a fringe of buckskin strung with bell-shaped pieces of tin. These banners were about six feet long and one foot wide. They were coming over the hills, giving the war whoop at every jump. There were some seventy-five of them and they looked like so many devils.

They reached Pa and Dexter first, but recognizing them, threw down their arms, rode up, shook hands and declared themselves friends. The Indians coming in this manner had frightened the horses and they had run away. However, the Indians caught them and next morning brought them back save a very fine

William B. Parsons wrote a guide book in 1859 titled *The New Gold Mines of Western Kansas: Being a Complete Description of the Newly Discovered Gold Mines, the Different Routes, Camping Places, Tools and Outfit, and Containing Everything Important for the Emigrant and Miner to Know, by Wm. B. Parsons, Who passed the Summer of 1858 on the Plains and in the Mines.* Without a doubt, Mr. Parsons succeeded in this endeavor. His listing of supplies considered necessary for the trip is quite extensive:

Article	Weight-lbs	Cost
Three yoke of oxen		$180.00
One wagon (wooden axletree)		100.00
10 sacks flour	1,000	20.00
200 lbs sugar	200	35.00
600 lbs bacon	600	60.00
80 lbs coffee	80	12.00
80 lbs rice	80	5.20
10 lbs tea	10	7.00
7 lbs saleratus	7	1.20
4 lbs tartaric acid	4	1.75
40 lbs tobacco	40	12.50
25 lbs powder	25	8.50
100 lbs lead	100	10.00
100 lbs dried apples	100	9.00
10 lbs dried peaches	20	9.00
80 lbs salt	80	2.50
5 lbs pepper	5	1.25
4 bushel beans	240	8.00
1/2 bbl. Crackers	40	3.00
1 10-gal. water keg	15	1.50
10 glls. vinegar	100	2.50
1 coffee mill		.60
2,000 gun and pistol caps (Eyel's water proof)	1.25	
4 gross matches		1.00
1 box pickles	60	7.00
25 lbs soap	25	2.00
1 box candles	40	10.00
4 picks	30	5.00
4 shovels	20	6.00
2 axes	8	2.50
4 pans	5	1.00
2 chisels	2	2.00
2 augers	2	1.25
1 saw	3	1.50
1 frower	4	1.25
1 draw knife	1	1.25
1 skillet	10	1.75
2 coffee pots		1.00
8 tin plates		.50
8 tin cups		.50
2 frying pans	8	1.50
4 butcher knives		3.50
12 knives and forks		3.00
12 pairs blankets		40.00
? bbl. Whiskey	175	8.00
4 water buckets		1.00
2 small tin buckets		1.25
4 gold pans	10	3.00
60 feet rope	8	1.50
2 sheets iron	20	3.00
Totals	3,173	$603.00

mare which they said had fallen and broken her neck. Our men told them that they knew better and that she must be brought back by noon, and she was. We had thirty head of horses in the train and they all ran away, but the Indians gathered them up for us. They said it took them all night to catch them and we thought so by their looks.

When the Indians came, nearly every man was cleaning his gun and had the locks to pieces. We were at their mercy, but the treatment we had given to the poor frozen Indian [at Aowa Creek, Nebraska] was what had saved the lives of the party. After it was all over, the men attempted to poke fun at the women saying we were very foolish to get so excited, but we found out one of the men loaded his horse pistol, which was nearly two feet long, with a double load, and we returned the jibe that somebody got more excited than the women.

Water From an Unexpected Source, July 1859

We made it a rule to fill our water kegs at night. Pa and Dexter had filled theirs before the rail but none of the rest of the party had. After the return of the horses and all had shaken hands with the Indians, we broke camp and started.

This was in July of 1859. We

Parsons notes that this is not everything a miner needs. He recommends buying "four mules to pull the wagon rather than oxen or horses, as they are faster and more valuable at the end of the trip. However, at $400, the mules are twice as expensive as oxen. Horses are considered too weak for the purpose."

Other items he considered necessary were rifles, fishhooks, sewing supplies, writing supplies, and common medicines since doctors were rare. Enough clothing should be carried to last six months and should be simple. He recommends leaving home the "white Marseilles shirt, fancy gaiters, and kids."

Several of the items on the list might not be familiar today. A **frower,** or **froe**, was a wood-splitting tool. Blacksmiths made a chisel-shaped blade that was attached to a wood handle. The blade was struck on the top with a mallet or hammer, driving it into the wood, with the handle serving as a lever. With this tool, a man could quickly cut shingles and barrel staves from blocks of wood.

Saleratus is sodium bicarbonate, today's baking soda. It was collected from the shoreline of alkaline lakes. Sometimes the saleratus imparted a bitter taste to the bread, and occasionally turned the bread a green color. The **crackers** referred to in the list are actually hardtack. Hardtack was also called sailor's biscuits or pilot bread. It was a staple of a sailor's diet and was issued to Civil War soldiers as part of their daily rations, usually a pound a day. Also known as "teeth dullers," "worm castles," or "sheet iron crackers," the crackers were so hard that they were usually dipped in a liquid or sucked on for a while until they became soft enough to chew. Stones or rifle butts were often used to crush the crackers, which were then mixed into coffee, soup, beans, or bacon grease and fried for breakfast. Hundreds of recipes existed for hardtack, using any type or combination of flour, oats, or cornmeal with the addition of a little salt or sugar if it was available. The flour was mixed with a little water and then baked, usually twice, to render the cracker dry enough to last for months without spoiling. The crackers were carried in knapsacks and pockets to provide a quick, portable meal while on the trail or out working.

Candles were made from tallow, animal fat. An excerpt from the Lewis and Clark journals tells of another use for candles:

"Killed nothing in these mountains of stone."
"The Party reduced and much weakened from the want of food."
"Passed on the side of rocks where one false step of a horse would be certain destruction."
"Men without sox wrapped rags on their feet."
"We laid down and slept, wet hungry and cold."
"We dined [on] a little bears oil and about 20 pounds of candles from our stock of provisions."

Twenty pounds of candles for 31 men, plus one woman, Sacajawea, with a nursing baby, was not a feast.

Considering the wagons of the time were about four feet by 12 feet, it is truly amazing what the emigrants and miners were able to pack into one.

Lois and her family carried a cook stove, large tents, churns, and basic farming tools as well as many of the supplies listed in Parson's book. Unfortunately, these wagons were a treasure trove to some Indians. Good sense dictated that people form into companies. A raiding party was much less likely to attack a large party than two or three wagons traveling together.

traveled until night and found we were on a sandy desert with only two ten-gallon kegs of water in our train. Thinking it would not be far to water, we had not been saving and for twenty-five people and the weather being hot, it did not last very long. After we started the next morning, we only stopped long enough to rest the horses and cattle; so we traveled for three days. One man's tongue was swollen out of his mouth. One of the teamsters that was a distance ahead found a little water in a buffalo track and

Parsons didn't include a map of the trails, choosing instead to giving stop-by-stop directions to the mines. He broke the routes into categories: Northern, Southern, and Santa Fe. His description of the route Lois and her family traveled is not complete, but the last portion of his Northern Route matches her description of their trip.

"Starting at convergence of the road from Fort Laramie:

Cottonwood Cr'k		6 miles
Little Sandy	12	18 miles
Rock Creek	17	35
Patterson's	18	53
McDowell's	20	73
Russell's Ranche	24	97
Hume's	24	121
31-Mile Creek	12	133
5-Mile Creek	26	159
Fort Kearny	5	164
17-Mile Point	17	181
Plum Creek	18	199
Cottonwood Sp'g	40	239
Fremont Spring	40	279
O'Fallon's Bluff	5	284
Cross'g S Platte	40	324
Fort St. Vrain	200	524
Cherry Creek	40	564
Mines	6	570

Total Miles from Laramie Rd.

Parsons adds one piece of advice:

"And here, in starting, let me mention the rule – Always cross a creek before camping. The streams rise so rapidly upon the plains that a slight shower at night might prevent crossing in the morning, but would be no hindrance to travel on the prairie beyond."

drank it. Evidently there had been a rain a short time before, but we searched and found none.

We came to a dry branch of a river with cottonwood trees and bushes on the bank. The men thought if they should dig here they would surely find water, but the deeper they dug the drier it seemed to be. We women had also been searching and one, in passing alongside of the men, brushed her skirt on his hand. He declared we had been in water somewhere. We denied having been in any, nor had we seen any. Our clothes were wet however. We had camped on the bottom land where the grass was waist high. There was a heavy dew on the grass. It seemed as though God's hand was in it and sent the heavy dew for our benefit. We spread out a number of clean tablecloths and sheets and, before long, we had all the water we wanted and several buckets ahead for the next morning.

The next morning, they started out to hunt for water and found a river. I believe it is now called Loup Fork. When the stock came within five or six miles, they threw up their heads and started running. The nearer they got, the faster they went until they came to the bank and they piled over each other to reach the water, which was low. Nothing could be done with them until they had a drink. After the kegs were filled and the cows had fed for a time, the men came back to camp. The next morning, we broke camp and started for the river. We rested there for three days, washed our clothes, baked, and set our wagon tires, which were in very bad condition.

Buffalo, July 1859

On a knoll not very far away, we saw some Indians. We beckoned for them to come as they seemed friend-ly, but they were not. One of our men started towards them and they sent a man to meet him. After these two conferred for a time, all the Indians came into our camp. They told us we must leave as there was a band of Pawnees and Omahas coming and they would surely kill us. We were ready to start by the next morning. We had to travel a number of miles down the river before we could cross. Here we found the Indians, several thousand in number.

The Indians seemed friendly and there were some Frenchmen who were with them, and they told us they were out on a buffalo hunt and that we must go with them because they were afraid we would scare the buffalo. We traveled with them two weeks, then decided that they only wanted us along so that we could furnish them with milk and butter. One of the Indians told Pa the white man was like squaw and would not fight. At this, Pa jumped up and walked away. He called some of the party and told them he was going to hitch up and pull out. My brother and brother-in-law said they were ready. While the whole party was anxious to leave the Indians, yet, they waited to see how Pa fared after he had hitched and started. It was not long until they were all with us.

The Indians surrounded a herd of about one hundred buffalo near us. They were on a sloping hill when seen grazing. One of them nearly killed all of us. One of the buffalo turned on his pursuer, killing the horse and throwing the Indian. They drove one close to our camp and asked one of our men to shoot it with a rifle. Mr. Hotchkiss, Sally's husband,

James Griffing joined the steady stream of emigrants heading across the plains in the spring of 1859. He wrote a four-page letter to the *Oswego Times*, [New York] describing the trip and offering advice for those thinking of heading West. He experienced first-hand the problems of crossing a river.

"Topeka July 27th 1859
Mr Editor
    "In crossing ravines it is generally best to keep the well beaten tracks, for there stones & brush are thrown in to prevent miring, at other points your team or waggon may sink so deep that extraction may seem next to impossible, and thru its very sticking to ones nature to wade into some bottomless mirehole to lift for hours at a time on some sunken waggon. I well remember an illustration of this fact in our attempt to cross the old Indian ferry at the mouth of the Kansas. The family waggon was landed safely on the opposite Shore the horses were brought back to help the heavier waggon up the bank. We had just gone down into the boat with the heavy waggon and four horses and were all crowded safely when water was fast seen rushing over the End board under the false bottom, there was no chance to retreat and in a very few moments must sink. Our propelling power was an old rope attached to trees on Each bank which was seized by the Indians and the boat moved by pulling hand over hand. No Sooner was our danger perceived than the cry arose 'All hands to the rope,' which was quickly obeyed and the old scow went plowing the waters with great rapidity. When we had reached about the centre of the stream the false bottom commenced flopping about the horses legs. So that we were obliged to drop the rope to liberate the horses from the waggon, this left us at the mercy of the current, but the momentum already given caused one corner of the boat to touch the Shore about 15 rods below the ferry before she went down. The horses had already pitched out of the boat and were floundering in the bottomless sediment abounding at the mouth of this river, and could not possibly reach terra firma. From ten Oclock until sundown, it took our company aided by about twenty Indians to Extricate ourselves.
    "The present year has far surpassed any former, in the vast amount of travel through & in this territory. Some days the road would be lined from morning until night, bound Either for Pike's Peak, California, or Oregon, and not a few to settle in the territory. A great Share of the Pike's Peak Emigration returned before getting there, Especially those not "Counting the cost" before starting. Reliable reports are beginning to come in but none very flattering as yet, that in a few diggings, some are taking out at the rate of a hundred dollars a day, and that hundreds were working for their board, that much was being done by way of prospecting and they still lived in hope. My sheet is full -
    Yours J. S. G."

The Whitcomb group began their journey in Dixon County, Nebraska, and traveled generally southward toward the Oregon Trail, which began in Council Bluffs, Iowa. There is no way of knowing how far they wandered across land before they picked up the trail again, but a generally south direction would have taken them down to the Platte River, which they could then follow into Fort Kearny, covering about 180 miles. The entire trip to the mines would have been at least 580 miles.

Morton and Watkins' *History of Nebraska* quotes the *Dakota City Herald*, providing a good illustration of the importance the northern route from Omaha by way of the Loup Fork Crossing had assumed by 1859:
"The secretary of the Columbus Ferry Company at Loup Fork informs the Omaha *Nebraskian* that the emigration across the Plains, up to June 25, was as follows: 1,807 wagons, 20 hand carts, 5,401 men, 424 women, 480 children, 1,610 horses, 406 mules, 6,010 oxen. And 6,000 sheep had crossed this ferry at that point. This statement includes no portion of the Mormon emigration but embraces merely California, Oregon, and Pike's Peak emigrants and their stock, all going westward. The returning emigration cross at Shinn's ferry, some fifteen miles below the confluence of the Loup Fork with the Platte. Many of the outward bound emigrants also crossed at the same point so that it is probable that not less than 4,000 wagons have passed over the military road westward from this city since the 20th of March."

An 1860 editorial in the *Nebraskian* noted that a traveler met 700 teams in one day between Loup Fork (Columbus) and the Elkhorn River. About 500 of these kept the north route and crossed the Loup at Columbus; the other 200 crossed the Platte by Shinn's ferry and took the tortuous route on the other side of the river. By 1865, this route had become involved in Civil War politics. The *Advertiser*, a fervently loyal paper, insisted in an 1865 editorial that traffic should be diverted from Nebraska City as a punishment for disloyalty to the cause of the Union.

Figure 2: Loup Fork Ferry. Library of Congress Prints and Photographs Division, LC-USZ62-7781.

thought he could shoot it in the heart, but he missed the shot. Oh, how they laughed! We saw thousands of buffalo, and the men killed and jerked all we wanted.

We came to a small branch river to get some water but found the bank lined with dead and dying buffalo in all stages of decay. As we were camping here, it was use this water or have none. Again we were two days without water except what we had in our kegs. The next water we came to was a small pond a few hundred feet across. Before we came to this, several head of cattle again struck out to hunt water for themselves. We hunted them but could not find them. They had gotten mixed up with the buffalo.

From this on we saw no more Indians until we crossed the Platte River. When once we had driven into the river, we dared not stop until we had crossed on account of the quick sand. The wagons would rattle like they were going over a very rocky bottom. We crossed the river all right just below Fort Kearny. I tell you we were a happy crew when we got into the road where white people traveled. I almost felt like getting down and kissing the road.

We were now meeting people all the time, some going for supplies, or, being discouraged, were
continued on page 25

The Whitcombs were fortunate to see the mighty herds of bison. They couldn't have known that millions of bison would disappear in an astonishingly short time. A headline in the December 26, 1884, issue of the *New York Time*s read: "The End of the Buffalo, How The Mighty Herds Have Been Exterminated From The Great Plains." The article was written in Fort Keogh, Montana.

"The harvest of furs in the Northwest is about ended, for the buffalo are on the eve of final extinction. Hunters who are engaged in the business of hunting the buffalo are returning daily from the ranges on the north and south sides of the Yellowstone River and report not a bison to be found in a country where they formerly roamed in myriads. Men who have hitherto been hunters by profession are now compelled to turn their attention to something else, as there is nothing left for them to hunt.

"The year the Northern Pacific Railroad was completed, there were no less than 5000 hunters scattered along the line of that road, engaged in slaughtering bison and other animals for their fur. Glendive alone shipped no less than 100,000 robes, and from many other points in the Northwest great quantities of robes and hides were sent to market. In days gone by the Laramie Plains – in fact, the extensive prairies of Wyoming, Nebraska, Colorado and Utah – were black with the numerous herds of buffalo which roamed over that fertile country, and it is worthy of note that, notwithstanding these animals were the main sustenance of the Indians, and were hunted by the redskins for their hides and meat, nevertheless, this representative American animal did not begin to numerically decline till the white hunter got on his trail. The Indians realized that the buffalo was the mainstay of their lives, and therefore they were not wasteful nor improvident in the destruction of game. The commerce in buffalo skins has only sprung up in the past 40 years, and no mortal will ever know how many noble bison have been sacrificed during that period for the hides they wore. There are many people now living who remember very well when vast herds of buffalo roamed over the plains bounded by the Missouri River on the east and the Rocky Mountains on the west. Many of these people

were no doubt travelers on Wells, Fargo & Co.'s buckboards that sometimes traveled for days without being at any time during daylight out of the sight of buffalo herds.

"In 1859 St. Joseph was the western terminus of railroad communication. Beyond, the stage coach, the saddle horse, and the ox trains were the only means of commerce and communication with the Rocky Mountains and the Pacific slope. The wild riders of the Pony Express told wonderful stories of the myriads of buffalo migrating north and south in the great valley with the changing seasons, which stories were looked upon in those days as the fabrications of over-fertile imaginations, but which have since turned out to be facts. When commerce first began to ask for bison hides there were plenty of indolent men in the East who took upon themselves the profession of hunter as an easy and pleasant method of gaining a livelihood. When the Pacific Coast became somewhat settled the buffalo found themselves walled in between the enemy, who began to encroach on the buffalo country by pushing trading posts far out on the ranges and establishing a traffic with the Indians for hides and robes. Before that time the red man had simply looked upon the buffalo as a means of sustenance, the flesh being used for meat and the hides for clothing and housing; but when the white traders asked for the robes and offered the Indians beads, shells, paint and other trinkets in exchange, a regular system of barter sprang up between the two races which has only come to a conclusion by the utter extinction of the animal.

"The first great transcontinental railroad in 1868 divided the buffalo into two great bands and put an end to their migration. The railroad also let in the hide hunters, who went at the thing in a businesslike way. One good shooter in the employ of some trader would have eight of ten skinners following in his wake while he went on ahead and did the slaughtering. Each hunter was pretty sure to drop 90 to 100 animals a day, and each hide secured was worth 75 cents to $1 each in its raw, untanned state. The skinners received the meat as their portion, but as they generally selected the tenderloins and tongues, the remainder of the meat was left to rot on the prairie.

"The writer remembers, in the fall of 1881, while passing over the country tributary to the Little Missouri River in southeastern Montana, of meeting on the knoll or rise in the prairie, a hunter lying comfortably on his back with his long-range rifle resting between his legs, pumping shot after shot into an acre or so of buffalo some twelve or thirteen hundred yards away. The gentleman was not a hunter, but rather a sportsman, a well-known long range shot on the Creedmoor rifle range on Long Island and had come west on a pleasure excursion. He had the regulation Remington Creedmoor long-range riffle with peep and globe sights, vernier scale and spirit level, and was trying what effect his fine-sighted target rifle would have on the buffalo at long range. He had evidently found the true windage and correct elevation, for after every shot I could see a visible commotion in the herd, which told that the bullet had hit something. The distance being so great, the animals had not heard the noise of the discharge, and consequently did not take fright until the sportsman tired of his sport. Then for some reason they bestirred themselves and rolled off over the prairie in the wake of an old bull, who seemed to be the leader. Our friend had dropped exactly 45 buffalo in all, but what to do with them he did not know, and so they remained—hide, hoof, horns, and all—to rot where they had fallen.

"The division of the buffalo by the Union Pacific and the Kansas Pacific Railroad had left two great bands of them, one on the north and the other on the south side of the tracks. Those on the south side in Texas, New Mexico, and Arizona have long since disappeared from the ranges, their places being taken by the herds of domestic cattle and of numerous flocks of sheep. The disappearance of the buffalo from the Northwest dates from the conquest of Sitting Bull. When the military drove that great Indian warrior from the hunting grounds of his tribe, the buffalo went with the red man. In the country were thousands upon thousands of buffalo that fell beneath the bullets of the soldiers when there were no Indians to shoot at. It was grand sport for the soldiers but it was death to the buffalo. Upon the prairies of Dakota and Montana, where they once wandered in thousands, not a single one is now to be found. The only remnants of these mighty herds that once thronged the Northwest are a few hundred animals scattered in the vicinity of Woody Mountain, across the line in British Manitoba. Last year a herd of about 75,000 were corralled in the forks of the Little Missouri, on the south side of the Yellowstone River, but they were rounded up by the Gros Ventres and Crows, who attempted to drive them onto their reservations before the white hunters could get a shot at them. In this they were unsuccessful, for the white hunters did get wind of the affair, and by the time both reds and whites got through with them, not 5,000 of that mighty herd were left to cross the Yellowstone. The remnant which did get over in safety continued their journey into the north, and at last found a refuge near Woody Mountain, in the British territory.

"The prairies of the Northwest are covered with the bleached bones of the countless dead, and here commerce steps in again to ask for something else; the very last remnant of an annihilated race. The white skeletons strewn along the Northern Pacific have hitherto given the tourist a special sense of getting his money's worth of romance as he sped toward the National Park and the Rocky Mountains. That is all over now, for a regular business has sprung up in the buying and selling of buffalo bones. The harvest of furs has come to an end, but the harvest of bones has just begun. Nearly every station along the Northern Pacific has at present a bone buyer, and all over the prairies can be seen, piled up for shipment, the chaotic anatomy of countless thousands of buffalo. Farmers and ranchmen, when they have nothing else to do, harness up their teams and go to gathering buffalo bones. These are hauled to the nearest railway station, where they are paid from $2 to $3 per wagon-load for them. The bones that surveyors have stood up as sightings have been picked up and carried off with the rest. These bone gathers occasionally run across buffalo bones with Indian arrowheads sticking into them. They tell the tale of days gone by, when the red man chased the noble bison unmolested by the whites, and claimed all the western country as their hunting ground."

Figure 3: Crossing the Platte. Illustration in *Harpers's Weekly*, AP2.H32 1859 *Pike's Peak Gold Miners*, Library of Congress, Lot 4392C.

Fort Kearny was a welcome sight to all the travelers along the main branch of the Oregon Trail. Built in 1848 and the only fort between the Missouri River and Rocky Mountains, Fort Kearny's mission was to provide aid and protection to the emigrants. Later it served as a station for the Pony Express and stage coaches.

New arrivals always checked the post office for letters from home and mailed their own letters to their families. Thirty thousand emigrants passed through the fort during its first 18 months in operation. The emigrants took this opportunity to rest livestock, repair wagons, catch up on laundry, bake bread, and replenish their food stocks.

Fort Kearny was located on the Platte River, often described as "one mile wide and one inch deep." Washington Irving declared it "the most magnificent and useless of rivers."

Chalkley J. Hambleton joined the rush to Pike's Peak in 1859 and described the fort in his book, *A Gold Hunter's Experience*:
"The fort consisted of a few buildings surrounded by a high adobe wall for protection; and adjoining was a strong stockade for horses and oxen. There were a few United States troops here. Just outside the fort grounds were some ranches, stores, saloons and trading posts. The two Missourians [in the party] proceeded forthwith to get dead drunk and it took them till next day to sober up. By way of apology, they said the whisky tasted 'so good' after being so long without it. We were now on the main central route of travel from the States to the mountains, Salt Lake, California and Oregon. We saw teams and trains daily going in both directions, and Kearney was a favorite place for them to stop over a day and rest. Our course now lay along the south side of the Platte, clear to Denver."

returning home. One day we met a government train with an escort of soldiers and a company of little children. We were close by. We gave them milk for the babies. They told us the children's parents had been murdered by the Mormons at the Mountain Meadow massacre. I remember one night we camped near here.

One night not long after we had camped for the night, a band of Indians came along. They begged us to buy some buffalo robes. One of the braves threw me a beautiful robe as a present, I supposed. I saw the other Indians look at me and laugh. I was told that if I accepted [the robe], it meant I would be his squaw. I looked at him a few seconds then threw it back at him with all my might and ran to our wagon. How our people laughed at me, but I could not see the funny side. I was scared. I believe these were the Shawnees.

One hundred and fifty years after the Mountain Meadows Massacre, controversy still swirls around the events leading to destruction of the Fancher Party in 1857. Certainly, Mormons, local Paiute Indians, and militiamen participated in the massacre.

The Fancher wagon train could not have chosen a worse time to cross Utah. Joseph Smith, founder of the Church of Jesus Christ of Latter-day Saints, and his brother, Hyrum, were murdered in 1844 by a mob in Carthage, Missouri. Brigham Young assumed leadership and moved his people on a harrowing winter trip to Nebraska and eventually to the Great Salt Lake valley in Utah. In 1850, Young was declared Governor of the Territory of Utah.

By 1857 misunderstandings, prejudice, and politics had created such a state of tension between the U.S. Government and Utah Territory that President Buchanan declared Utah Territory to be in a state of insurrection. The President appointed a non-Mormon as governor and ordered Colonel Albert Sidney Johnston to march with his troops into Utah to stamp out the "rebellion." Young saw this as a declaration of war and prepared accordingly. The distrust of anyone from the outside reached hysterical proportions.

Alexander Fancher unknowingly led his wagon train into this powder keg in August 1857. The train consisted of 62 men, 40 women, and 50 children. It was a rich train, with at least 600 cows, enough oxen to pull 40 to 60 wagons, and a number of horses and mules.

The fact that most of the travelers were from Arkansas and Missouri revived bitter memories of the death of Smith and the ouster from Nauvoo, Illinois, a town established by the Mormons in 1839 after escaping religious persecution in Missouri. Within three years, Nauvoo was one of the largest cities in Illinois and the tenth largest in the U.S. The loss of Smith and continued persecution and distrust forced the Mormons to flee the city in 1846. When rumors spread through the Utah Territory that members of the train were involved with Smith's death or that the train was an attempt by the government to settle Utah with non-believers, the stage was set for disaster.

Disagreements exist over whether the original plan was to annihilate the train or just kill some of the men and steal the cattle. John D. Lee, John M. Higbee, and Isaac Haight are generally credited with the planning. John Lee was a militia major and Indian agent and was well respected by the Paiutes. He was able to enlist their aid in attacking the train. Between 200 and 300 Paiutes and Pahvant Utes agreed to the plan. Alexander Fancher selected the wide, green meadows for a camp. During the night, the attackers were able to quietly scatter or corral much of the train's stock because Fancher neglected to set a guard. At dawn on September 7, shots rang out as the emigrants were making breakfast. Six or seven men died immediately and others were wounded. Fancher ordered the camp into a defensive circle, but the train was left stranded without a water source inside its perimeter.

By September 9, the need for water in the camp had become desperate. An attempt to dig a well proved futile. Fancher made his next mistake; he believed he was under an Indian attack and could obtain help from the Mormons. Two volunteers slipped out of camp under cover of darkness. Fifteen miles from camp, they stopped to water their horses. Seeing some white men approaching, they begged for help. Instead, William C. Stewart, a Mormon priest, shot the first man, William Aiden, dead. The other volunteer was able to return to the camp and give the warning that white men were also involved.

The siege carried over September 10 with conditions in the train deteriorating rapidly because of lack of water. Meanwhile, the attackers were making plans. The emigrants were to be lured from the train and marched through a copse of trees some distance away. There, each militia member would kill the person nearest them and the Indians would kill the women and children.

September 11 dawned hot and dry. When Fancher and his companions saw white men approaching carrying a white flag, they believed they had been saved and cheers filled the air. Lee convinced them that if they laid down their weapons and left their belongings behind for the Indians, they would have safe passage out. He then arranged for the small children, all aged three to nine years old, to be placed in a wagon, followed by a wagon containing 17 injured men. The older children were to walk out, followed by the women and then the men. The militia walked beside them, ostensibly to protect them from the Indians.

The first wagon pulled out and the rest of the party followed. They traveled almost a mile to the Indians' hiding place. Suddenly Major Higbee gave the order: "Halt. Do your duty." As the militia members shot the person assigned them, the Indians joined the attack with knives and clubs.

It was over in minutes. One hundred and twenty emigrants lay dead with only the wagonload of 17 or 18 children surviving. Seven of Fancher's nine children were among the dead. The children were handed over to Mormon families, some paying the Indians in blankets, flour or horses for the children.

By May 1859 the U.S. government had recovered all of the children. They were taken by government train and returned to Arkansas. Nine men were eventually indicted and ordered to stand trial. The first trial ended in acquittal. A second trial, 19 years after the massacre, found John Lee guilty, the only participant held accountable. He denied to the end that he was the mastermind of the massacre and believed he was the chosen scapegoat. Lee calmly faced the firing squad on March 23, 1877, at Mountain Meadows. Two monuments now mark the spot of the massacre.

Denver, August 1859

When we were within fifteen or twenty miles of Denver, we laid over a day or two. We saw a small stream coming down the mountain side. Sister Sally and myself took a shovel and pan, crossed the Platte to this stream and commenced prospecting for gold. We found very little, but did not know for sure until we reached camp that it was gold. One man in our party had been to California in an early day and declared it to be gold. We were very proud to think we were the first of our party to find gold. We went on to Denver. There were only a few dirt-roofed houses that were vacant.

We found some vacant ones [houses] and moved in, but of course we had to do our cooking out of doors. They commenced a hunt for hay for the stock for the winter. My brother and brother-in-law found plenty of grass in the mountains. They cut and stacked the hay and came back for us. Sister Sally had left a churn of cream for us to churn. I went over after breakfast and Lo! I found a skunk in the cream. He could neither upset the churn or jump out. He was doing the churning and in the house everything was scented up in fine shape. We hung the clothes out of doors and cleaned up the best we could, but they could not stay in the house when they returned.

We soon packed up and went to where they were making hay. We built a log cabin for the winter. After considerable discussion, Dexter and Eliza (sister) went back to Nebraska to look after things there. They came back in the spring bringing three heifers, two of theirs and one that Father gave me when it was small, providing I would raise it without milk. I would boil hay, making a strong tea and thickening it with graham flour. When spring came, my calf was a beauty and later made a fine cow. I will tell more about her later.

Mr. and Mrs. Hotchkiss, [sister Sally and husband], built a cabin near us. All we had to do was eat, sleep and take care of the cows. It was very lonely until one day a company consisting of four men, one

Lois was 15 years old when her family arrived in Denver. She would find it a vastly different world from the rural faming communities of the plains. One of the differences was the scarcity of women in the mining camps. Although only a sentence long, James Sayre Griffing's description of this woman's experience in Denver is telling in several ways: white women were extremely scarce and generally young, they were educated, they were settling in to stay, and there was at this time no apparent fear of Indians.

"A young lady of this neighborhood writing to her father, says she has seen but three white women Since she left the settlement, that her husband has started a bakery in Denver city, that about 800 Indians are camped within a few rods of the house that more than half a dozen squaws are looking over her shoulder whilst writing."

Figure 4: Pike's Peak – Street in Denver City, Kansas Territory. #102926, #FC6.DE*4, Special Collections Acquisitions, Library/Archives. Kansas State Historical Society.

Women remained scarce in the West for some years. In 1864, there were 183,856 men in California and only 48,149 women. Men were driven to advertise in newspapers for brides. One man described himself in Frank Leslie's *Illustrated Newspaper*, March 5, 1859, as

"A trifle over 24 years of age, wears spectacles solely for the preservation of his eyes, neither squints nor uses tobacco, admires flowers, 'tater patches, ladies and large pumpkins, and is the owner of a double-edged rapier and a military uniform with two rows of buttons on each side."

If a woman was interested, the man would send her a train or stage ticket, and the happy couple would marry as soon as she arrived in town.

Men weren't the only ones to advertise. The Civil War left many women in the East widowed or without hopes of marriage because of a shortage of local men. The following correspondence to the *Blaine Journal*, Blaine, Washington Territory, is self-explanatory:

"Zanesville, Ohio September 5, 1888
Mr. Postmaster, Delta, Wash. Ter.:
Kind Sir:

"Having seen a notice in the Roseville, Ohio paper stating that there was a number of marriageable gentlemen in Delta, I decided to write. I am a young lady 24 years of age, medium height, rather stout build, dark brown hair and eyes, neat form. I am a good housekeeper, have some knowledge of music. I desire to correspond with a gentleman with a view to an early marriage. I am not seeking beauty or wealth, but a kind husband is my object. Please insert this in your paper. Please address Miss Lutella SMITH, Zanesville, Ohio, 4 Vine Street, Seventh Ward."

The odds of finding a mate were, of course, much higher from women than men. Lois would have attracted a great deal of attention in the camps and would have had numerous admirers. On average, women in the West married later than their sisters in the East, but Lois married Ed when she was 16, the result of a mixture of loneliness and proximity. Ed was about 15 years older than Lois, but the marriage was a success.

Women were scarce, but Denver was booming. Chalkley Hambleton wrote in **A Gold Hunter's Experience**,

"Denver was at that time a lively place, with a few dozen frame and log buildings, and probably a thousand or more people. Most of them lived and did business in tents and wagons. A Mr. Forrest, whom I had known in Chicago, was doing a banking business here in a tent. The town seemed to be full of wagons and merchandise, consisting of food, clothing and all kinds of tools and articles used in mining."

Denver had its share of characters. Jeff Smith earned the nickname of "Soapy" when he made a fortune selling soap by turning it into a game of chance. He would wrap a $100 bill inside a bar of soap, mix it in a tub with other bars, and take bids on randomly picked soap bars. The problem was that no one ever seemed to find the bar containing the money. This scam worked for Soapy for 20 years. Soapy branched out into other scams and shady business deals, surrounding himself with a gang of associates. Eventually, when Soapy began rigging Denver elections, he and his pals were shown the road leading out of town.

One of the booming businesses in Denver was the stagecoach. Up to nine passengers could be seated inside the coach and six or more could ride on top, along with the luggage. Stagecoach journeys were long, dusty and hard. As the number of passengers grew, Wells-Fargo was obliged to draw up a list of rules for proper stagecoach etiquette.

1. Abstinence from liquor is requested, but if you must drink, share the bottle. To do otherwise makes you appear selfish and unneighborly.

2. If ladies are present, gentlemen are urged to forego smoking cigars and pipes as the odor of same is repugnant to the Gentle Sex. Chewing tobacco is permitted but spit WITH the wind, not against it.

3. Gentlemen must refrain from the use of rough language in the presence of ladies and children.

4. Buffalo robes are provided for your comfort during cold weather. Hogging robes will not be tolerated and the offender will be made to ride with the driver.

5. Don't snore loudly while sleeping or use your fellow passenger's shoulder for a pillow; he or she may not understand and friction may result.

6. Firearms may be kept on your person for use in emergencies. Do not fire them for pleasure or shoot at wild animals as the sound riles the horses.

7. In the event of runaway horses, remain calm. Leaping from the coach in panic will leave you injured, at the mercy of the elements, hostile Indians and hungry coyotes.

8. Forbidden topics of discussion are stagecoach robberies and Indian uprisings.

9. Gents guilty of unchivalrous behavior toward lady passengers will be put off the stage. It's a long walk back. A word to the wise is sufficient.

An editorial attributed to the *Omaha Herald*, 1877, included some of the same suggestions while adding additional words of advice.

"The best seat inside a stagecoach is the one next to the driver. You will have to ride with back to the horses, which with some people produces an illness not unlike seasickness, but in a long journey this will wear off, and you will get more rest with less than half the bumps and jars than on any other seat…[When anyone] who traveled thousands of miles on coaches offers, through sympathy, to exchange his back or middle seat with you, don't do it…Bathe your feet before starting in cold weather and wear loose overshoes and gloves two or three sizes too large. When the driver asks you to get off and walk, do it without grumbling. He will not request it unless absolutely necessary.

"If a team runs away, sit still and take your chances; if you jump, nine times out of ten you will be hurt. In very cold weather abstain entirely from liquor while one the road; a man will freeze twice as quick while under its influence. Don't growl at food at stations; stage companies generally provide the best they can get. Don't keep the stage waiting; many a virtuous man has lost his character by so doing. Don't smoke a strong pipe inside especially early in the morning; spit on the leeward side of the coach. If you have anything to take in a bottle, pass it around; a man who drinks by himself in such a case is lost to all human feeling. Provide stimulants before starting; ranch whiskey is not always nectar. Be sure and take two heavy blankets with you; you will need them. Don't swear, nor lop over onto your neighbor when sleeping. Don't ask how far it is to the next station until you get there. Take small change to pay expenses. Never attempt to fire a gun or pistol while one the road; it may frighten the team and the careless handling and cocking of the weapon makes nervous people nervous. Don't discuss politics or religion, nor point out places on the road where horrible murders have been committed, if delicate women are among the passengers. Don't linger too long at the pewter washbasin at the station. Don't grease your hair before starting or dust will stick there in sufficient quantities to make a respectable 'tater' patch. Tie a silk handkerchief around your neck to keep out dust and prevent sunburns…Don't imagine for a moment you are going on a picnic; expect annoyance, discomfort and some hardships. If you are disappointed, thank heaven."

woman and a little girl came down out of the mountains to winter. There were two young men and two married men. Three were brothers and one was a cousin. There were lots of large flat rocks near us and as one of the brothers was a stone mason, a floor of rocks was laid in their cabin. Now, we had only a dirt floor and had to keep wetting it to keep the dust down. I wanted Pa to haul the rock for us for a floor, but he didn't think it would pay for so short a time, but he told me I could have the oxen. I think they were the largest cattle I ever saw; they must have been over five feet tall. Their yokes were so heavy I could not lift it to their necks, so when the stone mason and his cousin saw me, they came out and yoked them for me. The oxen were very gentle. Pa saw that I meant business, so he came out and hauled the rock. Jake [one of the three brothers] laid the floor for us.

When Sister and I went to call on the family of cousins, we asked their name. I guess I must have laughed when she said Boblett because she said, "You better not laugh for it may be your name some day, you cannot tell." I said, "I will never wear that name." But this cousin was a nice looking young fellow and I was about sixteen years old and the only young lady there. Of course we were together considerably as I had to take milk to their house. We often invited them all over for dinner. My father was no hunter and there was lots of game there, and they would kill deer and antelope and give it to us. My mother was a good cook and they all enjoyed coming over, especially Ed the Cousin, as we all called him.

My brother Josiah was away nearly all the time. He carried the mail from Denver to a mining camp called Tarryall. It rained all winter and when it began to break away in the spring, he had to quit for a while, so he came home.

Ed, Josiah and myself thought we would try climbing a mountain, as I had never had an opportunity before. It was Sunday so they took no guns. We took our lunch with us and, as we were eating, a crow lit in a little vine close to where we were. Ed jumped up with a handful of rocks and he commenced to throw at it, and down came the crow. We all had a good laugh. From that time Ed was a regular visitor every week and on Sunday evenings, so the winter soon passed. Soon after, Ed and his cousin went away to the Gregory mines. Pa thought it was too soon for him to go with his cows, so he went up in February and stayed until April. I thought, "I am too far away for him to come to see me," and I was very lonely as Sally and her husband had moved to Denver, Colorado, leaving me with Pa and Ma alone.

The Whitcombs, Dexters, and Bobletts had plenty of company in their search for gold. From the time that John Gregory located his first mining claim on May 6, 1859, and early June, the population of miners in the area jumped from 20 to over 3,000. First called Gregory's Diggings, the town was soon renamed Mountain City. It would also become known as the "Richest Square Mile on Earth."

The following item appeared In the June 11, 1859, issue of the *Rocky Mountain News*:
"When we entered the diggings on the 20th of May, there were about 20 men in that vicinity, only two quartz leads had been opened and but three claims on one of those and two on the other. In two weeks from that time more than 3,000 men were at work, at least 30 leads satisfactorily prospected, and several hundred claims opened and profitably worked."

One day I was so lonesome, I did not know what to do, so in the evening I strolled out and went up on a hedge bank just back of our house. I walked along for a time, then sat down and wondered if Ed was thinking of me. Just then I saw a man coming down and I wondered who it could be, and something kept

The first newspaper published in the mountains was the *Rocky Mountain Gold Reporter and Mountain City Herald*. Mountain City was the subject of an article in its first issue, dated August 13, 1859:

"Although not three months old, it contains already some 300 buildings substantially erected, with a population of between 2,800 and 3,000, nearly all of whom are miners. Yet the arts and trades are well represented, we have about 25 stores, 2 jewelry shops, 3 tailor shops, blacksmiths, shoemakers, and painters."

Fortunes were indeed being made in those early days of the gold rush. The December 21, 1859, issue of the *Rocky Mountain News* declared:

"From a million and a half to two millions of dollars in dust has been taken out, which has found its way to all parts of the Atlantic States and Territories…" With the price of gold fixed by the U.S. Government at $20.67 troy ounce, one and one-half to two million dollars worth of gold at that price would weight between 90,000 and 125,000 ounces. In February 1860 there was a report of a six pound gold nugget found near Gregory's Gulch. The owner refused an offer of $16 an ounce for the nugget."

Another local paper, the *Daily Central City Register* printed an article on December 3, 1874, and described the living conditions:

"By the first of June 1859, Gregory Gulch from North Clear Creek to the confluence of Eureka, Nevada and Spring Gulches was literally crowded with human beings huddled together in tents, wagons, log cabins, dugouts, houses made of brush, and of every conceivable material that promised shelter."

The *Rocky Mountain News* reported on April 25, 1860:
"The emigration is coming in at the rate of over one hundred men each day, and constantly increasing."

After the Western Stage Co. began running a stage in June 1860 from Mountain City to Denver, travel became faster and easier. A trip that had taken three for four days now took seven or eight hours.

By the end of May, the *News* reported that emigrants were arriving at the rate of a thousand a day. The rush was on in earnest as gold was discovered in other gulches, quickly followed by the establishment of mining camps. Some of these camps were Springfield, Bortonsburg, Missouri City, Nevada City, Dog Town, Eureka, Russell Gulch, Lake Gulch, Black Hawk Point, Chase's Gulch and Enterprise City. The Gregory Gulch area had 20,000 to 30,000 inhabitants by the middle of July 1859.

The 1860 U.S. Census located 34,000 people in the mining region. The Whitcomb, Dexter, and Boblett families were counted in Missouri City, a few miles southwest of Central City. Lois's age is given as 16 and her husband Ed's as 32. Everyone listed their occupation as "miner," even Lois and her mother, Lydia.

Figure 5: USGS Historic Trail Map of the Denver 1x2 Quadrangle, Central Colorado, 1861. Glenn R. Scott, 1999.

Missouri City existed as a town with a post office for just three years, and then was abandoned as were many mining towns. This map shows Missouri City and Whitcomb in 1861.

Ed and brothers Louis W. and Reuben Borton formed the Borton and Boblett Mining Co. in Missouri Flats and Illinois Gulch in the summer of 1859.

Borton was a member of the first Constitutional Convention from Illinois Precinct, and was a candidate for Associate Justice of the Supreme Court under the Provisional Government also in 1859. Reuben removed to Golden City and in January 1860 was Justice of the Peace there.

Reuben Borton filed a claim for farming lands, Jefferson County, Jefferson Territory, in Table Mountain Canyon, at a point where the spur of the mountain runs to the creek line near Eli Carter's claim.

The town next to Missouri City was called Whitcomb for a time.

Aretas Whitcomb operated his quartz mill there until selling it to James Peck in 1860. The town's name changed to Nevadaville.

Figure 6: Present-day Nevadaville. Photo by Mike Sinnwell, Rocky Mountain Profiles.

saying that it walks like Ed, so I sat there for awhile until he got close enough that I could tell the color of his clothes, then I knew it was he. Down the mountain I went and got along side of him and walked to the house. Of course I was not so lonely any more. He stayed a couple of days and went back, but not until he had asked Father and Mother for me and gotten their consent. He never said he would come again.

My brother's wife's brother, Mr. Miller, had come out to Colorado and was with us, and he wanted to know what that fellow was after. I told him he came to see Pa and Josiah on business. He tried every way to get me to tell something, but I always avoided a straight answer. He told my brother he could not tell whether I was easily plagued or whether I did not care for him. While Ed was last with us, it was decided we should start in two weeks, so of course he did not come, I went to him.

How many men of today would walk one hundred miles and back twice to see their girl, making four hundred miles in all? Well, the time came for us to start, so we packed our goods and started and followed the mountains along for over twenty-five miles to a town called Golden Gate. There we struck the road from Denver to the mines and camped for the night. Got supper and soon there came some men from Denver and camped. After they had supper, they commenced singing a song, the chorus I shall never forget. It commenced this way: "We took our flight in the middle of the night, and off to the peak we started." The rest corresponded with it.

The next day we started for the mountains. It was our first trip. Ma and I walked nearly all the time, for we thought it was safer. I do not remember how long it took us, but we were several days. We got into camp after the men were through with their work, and I never saw men who seemed to enjoy themselves in such queer ways. They would holler, "Oh Joe," and listen to the echoes that seemed to come from innumerable throats.

They would mock roosters crowing, horses neighing, and anything they could think of. It was quite a change from the quiet nook where we had just come from.

The first Sabbath we were there, Pa heard of a man who was going to preach some two miles away, so he struck out and the rest followed. When we got there, we were very much astonished to find it was our old friend Mr. Alonzo Gifford. In the afternoon, Ed and I and his married cousin and his wife went up on Quartz Hill to see some of the rich quartz mines. They kept a guard there. They were not at work. The rock looked like it was half gold, and it was the grandest site I ever saw. Ed and I decided we would not get married until my sister Eliza and her husband got back from Nebraska and until we got a house built.

Father, Josiah and Ed were preparing to build a double house and Mother and I were going to keep boarders. Josiah would mine, while Pa would look after the stock, get wood, and do the chores around the house.

Lois Marries Ed Boblett, June 17, 1860
The second Sabbath, we all went over to hear our friend again and from then on we went regularly until he went away in June. When we learned the preacher was going away, we made ready for the wedding. The miners were intending to make a time of it, saying we were to give them a ten-gallon keg of liquor. So we said nothing to any one, save our relatives, and the preacher who was to marry us on Sunday night. It so happened, we had company that night and we had to wait until they had gone before the ceremony could proceed. It was between 10 and 11:00 o'clock that night when the preacher came to our tent, and we were married. No

> The miners were probably planning to throw Lois and Ed a chivaree. After the newly wedded couple settled down for the night, the neighbors would pay them a call, making as much noise outside the house as possible, banging pans and drums and ringing bells. Sometimes the partiers could be convinced to leave if the groom paid them a bribe, but other times the groom might be kidnapped and hidden away for the rest of the night. The chivaree was usually just noisy fun, but it could become dangerous if revelers drank too much and began shooting their guns into the air.

one but our relatives knew of the secret for a week, when a brother-in-law of Mr. Boblett's, by the name of Rosebrough, was on his way to our place, ran across the preacher and asked him if he had gotten acquainted with a man by the name of Boblett. He laughed and said, "I guess I did. I tied him to a woman the night before I left." He came up to our place and the first thing he did was to tell me the news of our wedding.

We stayed all winter then we took a claim about a mile away, but it being dry and no water for irrigation save what we could get from a very small stream. Ed built a good log house but we had no lumber for the floors or doors. We also built a pole chicken house as we had some chickens. One day, Ed went to Denver with a load of wood, and I was there all alone and there came a big drove of Texas steers to our spring. They began to paw the ground and they tore our chicken house all to pieces, even to the bottom poles. I really thought they would try our house but they finally went off and I went over to Father's.

Locust – The Third Plague, 1861
The first year, we did not get very much land cleared or a ditch to irrigate our crop, nevertheless, we had a very fine garden. Just as the corn was ripe enough to cook, one day there seemed to be a big cloud

The cattle that invaded Lois's farm might have been driven by Charles Goodnight or Oliver Loving. Goodnight started a cattle business in Texas and was a member of a local militia that fought against Comanche raiders before joining the Texas Rangers in 1857. He drove cattle as far as Denver prior to the Civil War, but quit to fight for the Confederacy. At the end of the War, he returned to Texas and rounded up his cattle who had wandered free for four years. Needing to find a market for them, he decided to drive his herd to New Mexico and Colorado even though it meant crossing the barren waste of West Texas.

Goodnight's partner was Oliver Loving, an old rancher who made his money selling beef to the Confederate Army and had also run some to Colorado earlier. They set out in 1866 with 2,000 head of cattle for Fort Sumner, New Mexico, blazing what became known as the Goodnight-Loving Trail. On reaching New Mexico, Loving continued on with the herd and Goodnight went back for another herd. They made $12,000 on the enterprise.

Loving was killed by the Comanches in 1867 while taking another herd to New Mexico. Honoring Loving's dying wish, Goodnight left the drive to return Loving's body to Texas for burial. The trail they established became one of the most heavily traveled in the Southwest.

Goodnight sought to breed cattle that could stand up to the drives. He was successful in breeding the rangy, tough Texas longhorn to Herefords. He also crossed buffalo with cattle to produce the first "cattalo." As Lois knew from experience, if the cattle had been without water for a while, nothing could keep them from the stream once they had caught its scent.

coming up. This was about noon and we watched the cloud. It seemed so low and it darkened the sun like a heavy shower was coming, but presently down came the grasshoppers. Before night the leaves and lots of the ears of corn were all eaten up and the rest of our garden ruined the same way. We took brush in our hands and fought them off and saved quite a lot of our garden. We did this every day for two or three weeks. Finally they all raised and passed on, then we were all right once more. We raised enough corn so we had seed, and plenty of potatoes for winter and seed for a large patch in the spring.

We all worked and got a number of acres in crops the next year and the first we knew there were little mites of grasshoppers, and in order to save anything that year, we had to fight them till they grew up and got their wings. We would scatter dry hay around in small patches, then took brush in each hand, driving the little pests on the hay, setting fire to it and killing bushels of them that way. Our hay began to give out, so the men would go out and dig trenches, driving them in and burying them so they would bother no more. We were on the Platte River and some one said to drive them into the water. We tried it and it worked fine; we fed many a bushel of grasshoppers to the fish that way. We raised quite a good crop of potatoes however and sold them. If I remember rightly, this was in the year 1861. In the valley, the potatoes sold for four cents a pound, but Mr. Boblett and my brother-in-law [Hotchkiss] took the most of ours to the Rarell Mines and received nine cents a pound.

While we were living on this ranch, we had no stove so we built a sort of furnace out of doors to cook on. There were lots of large flat stones, so Sister and I took a coal chisel and drilled four holes large enough to set the kettles in; this as a stove top with a chimney built to it did fairly well. We had tin reflectors to bake in. We fixed the front of our stove so we could use one of the reflectors, and it worked fine.

Locust swarms often appeared as massive, greenish clouds before sweeping down to devour everything in their path, including clothing and leather goods. One swarm recorded in Central City, Colorado's newspaper, the *Miner's Register*, September 7, 1864, would have looked like the one that fell to earth on Lois and Ed's ranch.

"The immense clouds of grasshoppers which passed over the city yesterday were a sight, we believe, has never before been witnessed in the Territory. By looking towards the sun they could be seen in a dense cloud like a swarm of bees. They appeared to be coming from the western slope and going eastward to the plains. There were very high up, probably 2,000 feet, as they were flying entirely above all the mountains about here. A few straggling ones lighted here, but the vast majority of them passed over. We should expect to see everything swept before them wherever they go."

Settlers quickly learned that the locusts weren't choosy about their diet. Lizzie Lockwood recalled a swarm that swept through the family farm in Nebraska:

"The grasshoppers used to come in clouds; my father always wore shirts made out of ladies' cloth, which mother made for him, and he was always careful of them because they were so nice. One day mother had washed; it began to get dark and father came running in from the field and told mother to take in his shirts as the grasshoppers were coming, and they would eat holes in his shirts."

The biblical plague of locusts is the best-known incident of locust infestations, but was certainly not the only one to sweep the land clean.

Locusts are related to grasshoppers and look similar but differ in one important way. If conditions are right, locusts enter a behavioral phase called the gregarious phase. When the perfect combination of water and plant growth promotes breeding, the colony becomes overcrowded. If the locusts' hind legs are rubbing against each other at the rate of several contacts per minute over a four-hour period, the locusts enter into the gregarious phrase and swarm.

Lois probably dealt with the Rocky Mountain swarm, which may have produced larger swarms than any other type of locust. According to *The Guinness Book of Records*, the swarm of 1874 covered 198,000 square miles and must have contained at least 12.5 trillion insects with a total weight of 27.5 million tons. Amazingly, the Rocky Mountain locust was extinct within 30 years.

The locusts thrived in the Rocky Mountain valleys. They needed a hot, dry climate, with sandy soil and just the right amount of moisture, such as the many streams that drained the Rockies. Drought concentrated the sugars in the native prairie plants and this diet, combined with the heat, accelerated the locusts' growth. The locusts were aided in their flight by the low-level jet stream that flows over North America.

The years 1873 and 1874 were peaks for the Rocky Mountain swarm, when locusts stripped the land of vegetation from Alberta to Arkansas, and caused $200 million in crop losses. Farmers fought the locusts any way possible. When locusts spread across eastern Washington State, farmers built a fence to check them. It was made by standing one-foot rough boards topped with about three inches of tin, one edge nailed to the top and the other turned down to prevent the locusts from hopping over. Deep holes or ditches were dug and, when these became full, either dirt was shoveled on them or kerosene was poured over the locusts and set on fire. The stench was terrible. The fence ran north and south for a distance of nine or 10 miles. The fence worked and the farms were saved.

Thomas J. Hartnett was a victim of the swarm but kept his sense of humor:

"In 1873 the grass hoppers came in such droves as to shade the sun. They came in here and in two hours would strip a corn field. They tell a story about a man who was plowing in a field; he took off his vest, with his watch in the pocket and hung it on a post. When he had plowed around the field once and got back to where he had left his vest, all that was there was his watch. The grass hoppers had eaten the vest. They tell, too, about a man who left his team in the field while he went to the house. When he came back the team and wagon had been eaten up by the grass hoppers and they were playing horseshoe with the shoes the horses had worn. The people would make trenches and drag the grass hoppers in the trenches and burn them."

Entomologist and nature writer Jeffrey A. Lockwood believes he has solved the mystery of the sudden collapse of the Rocky Mountain swarm. He credits settlers' activities in the Rocky Mountain valleys. Miners and farmers poured into the valleys, plowing up the egg-containing soil and diverting water from the streams to mining and irrigation. Prairie plants were replaced with crops and cattle and horses were put out to graze, which compacted the soil. In a few short years, the locusts' nursery was destroyed and their life cycle was fatally interrupted. Lockwood makes the case that destruction of the swarm changed the course of the development of the western half of America. Such rapid development would not have been possible in the face of periodic, devastating destruction of the crops.

The nymph stage of the locust life cycle is the hopper stage. Before its wings are formed, they can only hop. These are the ones Lois swept into the river. If Lockwood's theory is correct, Lois and her family were participants in the destruction of one of the largest and most lethal of the world's locust swarms.

One morning as we were doing our work, Father was grubbing out some brush not far from the house. Ed and Amos had gone to Denver with a couple loads of wood and to bring home supplies. We heard queer noises and looking up, there stood the largest elk with the largest horns I ever saw, right within fifteen feet of us. We were so surprised we never thought to shout at him, and he stood and looked at us for quite a bit, then gave a big snort and started off across the river. Then we thought of the gun. I took it and carried it to Father and he followed him for some time but did not find him.

Chapter 4
Iowa
1862-1863

*T*hen we sold our ranch and my cow that my parents gave me. We sold her for $50 dollars, with the privilege of buying her back at the same price, and we all returned to the States. Father, Mother and my sister Sally went to Dakota, and Ed and I and two cousins and a brother-in-law went to Panora, Iowa.

We traveled all the way with oxen and camped all the way with the exception of two or three nights. One night, soon after we camped, an old Indian came along and wanted to stay all night. First he wanted buffalo meat, but we had none. We gave him his supper.

It was a bitter cold night and the wind blew hard. The men could hardly get our tent stretched, but they did the best they could. Jake and Ike Boblett, Ed's cousins, and Mike Rosebrough had a tent and they could get it up easily. They took the old Indian in with them. The wind rose almost a gale in the night, blowing our tent down but did not blow it away, so it kept us comfortable till morning. In the morning, what a time we had dressing ourselves, the tent all down flat on us, and the wind blowing hard, and Oh! so cold and frozen. When the old Indian got up, he laughed and said, "Big tent heap no good, blow down." We all finally got dressed, but it was so cold the men decided we could not cook there, so they hitched up and started. We traveled until about nine o'clock when we came to a ranch and stopped there until the next day. Before we got there, it commenced to snow. Next morning, there was about six inches of snow. We were traveling down the Platte River from the foot of the mountains. As I have before stated, our ranch was where the Platte River comes out of the mountains.

Where the South Platte comes out of the mountains southwest of Denver, just below Littleton, Colorado, a town named Pike's Peak City was laid out during the fall and winter of 1858.

Pikes Peak City was founded at the mouth of Plum Creek by a group of German emigrants, who had come to the diggings with David Kellogg's party from Kansas City. Kellogg was one of the early "townbuilders" who arrived in the area and set about platting new towns. He was involved with laying out townsites named Arapahoe City, Santa Fe, Nonpareil City, and Pike's Peak City. In the rush to settle the country and bring in investors from the East, many townsites, or "paper towns," were drawn up but few actually became towns and some never had any residents.

Shortly after erecting their own 18 x 20-foot cabin on the South Platte, the Germans set about making the acquaintance of Americans in the neighborhood. "We fell in with a company among whom resides the only surveyor in this far distant country," wrote a German named Bluesche. "We took a trip up the river, where we found a beautiful situation for a town. The place is at the mouth of Plumb (Plum) creek on the South Platte, in a most magnificent valley, at the entrance to the mountains. Our company surveyed a piece of land one square mile, and we have already laid the foundations for several houses."

One of the Germans' American friends, Dr. G.N. Woodward, helped to promote the new town. In a letter to Messrs. Van Horn and Abeel of Kansas City,

Woodward wrote:

"This company have located and laid out a town or city, at the junction of Plumb creek with the South Platte, and named it Pike's Peak City . . . we intend building at our new location this winter. All the trade from the mountain miners must be done at this point, and if your friends wish to bring out goods in the spring, this is the point to sell them at."

Historian Richard Gehling believes that Lois's and Ed's farm was possibly near this new settlement.

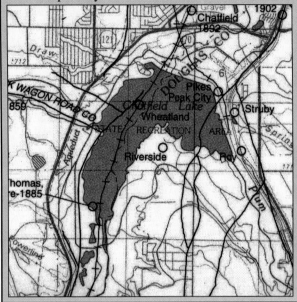

Today, the trip from Council Bluffs, Iowa, to Guthrie Center takes less than two hours, and Panora is just seven miles farther.

That last seven miles turned into a day-long trip for Ed and Lois. Guthrie Center was only four years old when the Bobletts visited Ed's family.

According to the 1860 U.S. Census for Panora, Iowa, the family consisted of Peter Boblett, age 69; his wife, Elisabeth; and children Elisabeth, Charles, and Frances. Peter's three other daughters were Emaline, Almera, and Amanda. Peter Boblett was not afraid to strike out into new country, either. He was born in Virginia, moved his family to Ohio, where two children were born, then on to Elkhart, Indiana, by 1850, to Panora, Iowa, by 1860, and in 1880, he was living in Cass, Iowa.

Lois and Ed stayed in Panora for less than six months before heading back to Colorado. If they took the most direct route between Denver and Panora, it was a trip of at least 600 miles each way, with the return trip to Denver taking two months.

Figure 7: Pikes Peak City: Probable Location of the Boblett/ Whitcomb Ranch. USGS Historic Trail Map of the Denver 1x2 Quadrangle, Central Colorado, Glenn R. Scott, 1999.

We traveled down the river to the mouth at Omaha and camped all the way with the exception of a night now and then. It was late in the fall of 1862. We stopped a couple of days at Council Bluffs. Here, Father and Mother, Mr. and Mrs. Whitcomb, and my sister and brother-in-law, Mr. and Mrs. Dexter turned up the Missouri River to Dakota and the rest of us went to Iowa. We ate our Thanksgiving dinner together the day before we left Council Bluffs, then started again camping out nights when the weather would permit. One place I remember, we had to lay over three or four days on account of the weather and the last night before we got to Ed's father's place, we traveled till long after midnight so as to get through the next day.

While we were traveling along, the Northern Lights appeared; the most beautiful I ever saw. It made the whole surrounding almost as light as day. It flashed up over our heads like streamers of fire till we got near a town called Guthrie Center, then they all disappeared and we could hardly keep in the road. When we got to Guthrie Center, we put up for the night at a hotel. Here the women were asking me where we came from and I told them.

They said, "Why law me, there isn't a decent woman ever go there, there seems to be something in the air that makes them bad." I said, "Oh? I never noticed anything wrong in that way." I said, "A woman can behave herself there as well as here if she only desire." They said, "They would not like to go there for fear of not getting back." I said, "Well, I would advise you not to go for it might be a bad place for you, but I am not afraid to go anywhere my husband goes."

The next day we started on and reached Panora a little after dark, a day or two before Christmas. Of course, we had a nice supper. We were all glad to get to a stopping place. We stayed here till the next June.

While we were in Panora, the Methodist Church held protracted meetings, and I joined on probation, but we left there before the six months were out, so they gave me a probationer's letter, but when we got to Colorado, we were not within reach of a church. I had done my best to fulfill the promise I made when I was a girl in [Aowa] Nebraska in that terrible fire. They did not take people in the Methodist Church and give them catechism to study and as soon as they could answer the questions, take them in full connection. I think it is better, because the old way often they would think, well, I am not a member so will just drop out, but it was not so with me as I will tell you later on.

When we went back, we thought we would stay there with Ed's people, but we had not been there long till Ed began to wish he was back in Colorado, so we wrote to Father and Mother telling them we thought of going back to Colorado. They wrote immediately to us to wait for they wanted to go too, but it would be about the first of June before they could go, so we waited. Ed had some lots there before we were married; he sold them that spring and bought cows and heifers and in all we had fifteen head.

Pa came the first part of June and he had several head of cattle, so when we got them together, we had quite a herd. Ed's people did not want us to go. His brother had 160 acres of fine prairie land; he told us he would make us a deed to half of it if we would stay and move on it with him. I saw they felt so bad about our going I tried to persuade Ed not to go, but his mind was made up to go, so when Pa and Ma came we were all ready. We started in a day or two, bidding the dear father and mother and four sisters all good-bye. So we started for Panora, Iowa. Ed's brother, Charles Boblett, went with us the first day out to help us drive the stock till they got clear away from their old range. We had ox teams, so the loose cattle could easily keep up. In the morning, Charles said he wished he was going with us. We told him if he would come we would wait till he could pick up and get ready, but he said, "No, Pa and Ma need me and I will stay and take care of them."

There on the broad prairie we said good-bye to brother Charles.

Chapter 5
Colorado Territory
1863-1864

We started now in earnest for Pikes Peak, taking turns driving the cattle. I do not remember just how long we were on the road, but I think we were two months. We had several little calves come on the plains and we sometimes had to lay up for a day or two with them, and sometimes we would take the little fellows in the wagons and haul them some distance. One night we camped at a beautiful camping place and were going to lay over for two or three days, but the next day one of Pa's yearlings was sick and died, also one of the calves acted queer. We examined them and one leg of each calf was turning black. We now met another party that was coming the other way and they told us to get away from here as soon as possible or we would lose all our stock. We hitched up, taking our calf in the wagon, be we did not get far until it died. However, we had no more trouble with the stock after this. We thought it was something they ate that caused the trouble.

There was a nice little stream coming down from the hills; on the down side of the Platte River there was lots of alkali, so when we saw this stream coming out of the hills we thought it would be cooler than the river, but it was not. Another time, we came to what looked to be a nice stream, but when we came to drink out of it, we could not because it was salty. Some folks say there is no such thing as running salt water, but if they had our experience, they would change their statement.

As we traveled up the Platte one day, there arose a great cloud of smoke and we thought the country round about was on fire; when we came to a nice green bottom, we camped for the night, thinking the fire would soon pass us, but no fire came. The next morning we could see no smoke and we could never understand where the smoke came from unless that it be a forest fire in the mountains.

Lois's memories of the prairie fire she survived no doubt came to mind when she observed the distant cloud of smoke. Forest fires were as fast moving and deadly as prairie fires. The *New York Times* reported on a fire that swept through the Pike's Peak area on June 20, 1859:

"An immense conflagration commenced raging in the mountain pineries on the 20th ult. It originated on the dividing Ridge between Gregory and Jackson diggings and soon had turned hundreds and thousands of acres of pine land into an ocean of fire that swept away everything towards the snow range. A violent wind that prevailed for a few days increased the vehemence of the destructive element. At Denver City the existence of the fire was first announced by dense volumes of smoke that filled the atmosphere from the mountains to Cherry Creek. Many prospecting parties had been cut off from escape and devoured by the devastating flames. Suffocated and cindered bodies have already been discovered. A party of fifteen persons are known to have perished by the flames."

We traveled on and, after going for some days, we came to a country that had been burned over and we had to buy feed for all the stock. We had quite all our money in stock, leaving us little to buy feed for all the stock. People coming down the river told us it was burned clear to the mountains so the people were compelled to buy hay. As we were riding along, we had a chest that fit nicely in front of the wagon, on which we sat letting our feet hang over the front.

As I sat there, I saw something as we passed over it and I said, "Ed, there is a pocketbook, let me get out." He said, "Sit still, it is nothing but an old one someone has thrown away." I persisted and said I was going to get out and see. He stopped and I picked it up and in it was eighteen dollars. There was no name in it so, as we could not find the owner, we had some money to get feed with. Now I said, "Ed, if I had sat still we would have had to sacrifice some of our stock to feed the rest. Are you not glad I was determined to see what was in the old purse?" Of course, he said yes. You know men hate to give up to a woman that he is wrong and she is right. This money lasted until we got to the foothills of the Rockies some three or four miles from where we sold our claims on the Platte River as it emerges from the mountain.

Later in the fall, the feed was getting scarce and we had no home and some others were thinking of driving their stock around the south side of Pikes Peak. We were on the north side. We hitched up and went with them. Of course, we had very little to move – our clothes, cooking utensils and camping dishes. We had tin dishes as earthen ones are too costly broken in moving. Ed always had a gun along for he was a great hunter and many a time I have gone with him. I got so I could locate game as quickly as he. Those days we knew nothing of breech-loading rifles, so he had to load every time he shot at anything; still I have seen him load and shoot three deer and not move out of his tracks. Many a time I have packed home his gun and ammunition so he could pack a deer on his back for miles. We thought nothing of walking ten, fifteen or even twenty miles on a hunting trip.

As we went to the south side of the mountain, the grass was fine and there were thousands of antelope and plenty of deer. They would come right down past our camp, as many as a hundred at a time. Of course, we had plenty of deer meat. One time, I wanted Ed to let me shoot at an antelope or a deer or something of the kind, but he always wanted to do the shooting. Of course, we never hunted only when meat was needed. Once he saw a little faun in a bunch of weeds and he wanted me to shoot it, but I would not do it; it was too small to feed, and it was so innocent looking I could never pull a trigger on it if I never killed anything. A chicken hawk was the largest game I ever killed.

Here we went to work and put up a cabin and made it quite comfortable for all hands. Mother and I did the cooking for the crew. There were four or five men with us and a boy of fifteen years. This boy had run away from home and came to a neighbor's, a poor man with a large family, telling him his parents were dead and he wanted a place to stay. So this man was going to take his stock over with ours and he thought when he got the stock over there, he could leave the boy to look after the stock.

One day when the game was getting shy and scarce, this boy took a gun and struck out. It was rather cold weather but not freezing hard. At nightfall, here comes the boy with an antelope, claiming he had killed it. When it was examined, it was frozen quite hard, so they said, "How come it is frozen so quickly?" He said, "I killed it early this morning." Then they knew he had not killed it at all, so they hung it up and left it for a time. There was a little snow on the ground and soon there came a stranger to our camp and he had tracked the boy from the place where he had hung the antelope the night before.

We had a justice of the peace along with us and he had been over home and just come back that day. While home, he saw a man that knew this boy's father and knew all about his running away. The Justice told the man to say nothing and he would fix it all right and he asked him if he would sell the meat as we were all out. He said he would. The man told how the boy came to be with our party and all the man's family of little girls, and he was afraid he would go back and made trouble for the family. So the justice asked the man to stay all night and he did.

After supper, he called the boy to him. The boy did not mistrust what was up but came right in and the Justice told the boy he had stolen the antelope and he had better own up to it. He said further, "You told your parents were dead, but the other day I saw a man who knows your father and for aught I know he is an honest man." The boy commenced to cry out and said, "My daddy stole before me and that is what's the matter, you know." So the Justice told him he had to go back home the next day and would give him his choice: to go home to his father or down the river to Kansas, as fast as he could travel. He could wait until morning and then make his choice. He said, "I could arrest you and take you to Denver, but as it is the first offence, and if you will promise never to be seen around these parts again or around Mr. Hammors, the man who brought you here, I will let you go this time." In the morning, the boy started out down the Kansas River on the run. Poor fellow, I could not help feeling sorry for him, yet we didn't want him around with us.

I can not remember anything special happening, till we started back over the Divide towards Denver in the early spring. The place where we were stopping was with the man that bought my cow, as I always called her, and we bought her back when we returned. We passed some cattle and one yearling was determined to follow us. There was a farm house on ahead and we stopped there and tried to get the yearling put up, but the corral was all torn down and so the men told the man at the ranch to tell the owner where we would camp and stay over Sunday, and for him to come and get her. It was a Texas yearling and the man was a Texan that owned her, and he brought two other men with him. They were all on horses and had great big spurs on and each man carried a revolver. This was in 1863, in the time of the rebellion. We were all sitting around the fire on logs when they rode up.

Mr. Boblett invited them to get off and take a seat on the log beside him, which they did.

The rebellion was, of course, the Civil War. Although far removed from the battles, many of the miners and settlers held strong opinions about the war. This particular man, like many other Texans at the time, probably had no fondness for "Yankees," which may explain his animosity.

Texas was among the first seven states to secede from the Union, following a vote on February 1, 1861, in which Texans voted 46,153 to 14,747 to leave the Union. During March 1861, when Governor Sam Houston refused to take the oath of loyalty to the Confederacy, he was deposed and replaced by Lieutenant Governor Edward Clark. Not wishing to bring civil conflict to Texas, Sam Houston rejected President Lincoln's offer of troops. On May 12-13, 1865, Union and Confederate forces fought at Palmito Ranch near the Rio Grande River. The Confederate forces won the battle; ironically, this was the final battle of the Civil War, taking place one month after Lee's surrender in Virginia.

The Union forces consisted of 250 men in the 62nd U.S. Colored Infantry Regiment and 50 men of the 2nd Texas Cavalry Regiment. The Confederate forces were aided by Mexican nationals from across the Rio Grande. Native Americans were reportedly also involved in the fighting.

When they were seated, they asked if there were any stray cattle in our herd. Ed said yes, then told them how he had tried to drive it off. Father had a big dog that would catch a cow or an ox and throw it, so they had him set the dog on the yearling and he caught it and held it until we drove our cattle over a ridge. He then turned it loose and headed for home, but as soon as it was loose, it came after our herd.

Then the owner released it, calling us all liars and thieves and everything he could think of. Ed put his hand on the man's shoulder pretty solid and told him he had to take that yearling out of our herd or he would take a gun and shoot it, as he did not intend to bother with it longer. He said he could drive it all alone, and Ed told him to get it out right away. They started out to where it was and chased it around among our cattle until Ed got mad and told him he could not run ours that way and if he did not stop, he would shoot it down. Then they lassoed it and tried to lead it, but could not do anything with it. Finally the other men that came with him got off their horses and whipped it along. They beat the poor thing unmercifully before they could get it to go at all.

After they got it started, one of the men came back and apologized for coming out there with this fellow, and said he had represented it to him that we had stolen the heifer and he wanted their help to get it back. He further said he did not blame Ed for getting mad. Ed told him it was all right as they had gotten it away, but if it came back he would shoot it, and if the owner said a word he would give him the same. It looked for a short time as if we were going to have a war right there. The man shook hands, got on his horse and rode off, and we saw no more of any of them, nor were we at all sorry.

After they were gone, we hitched up and started again on our way, for fear the yearling might get away and come back and make trouble, but we never heard from the party or the yearling again. We went on over the Divide and on our way met some people that were going to start to Arizona in a few days. So, Ed and I, together with Father and Mother went back to where we had left our things and gathered all together and struck out for Arizona; the worst move we ever made. Neither Mother nor I wanted to leave Colorado. We had sixteen cows and heifers and Pa had fifteen, but they must go somewhere. Ed really

wanted to go Montana, but none of the rest wanted that, as it was so cold there, so we all decided to get ready and go with the crew on their way to Arizona.

We had only a few days to get ready in, so Ed commenced going over his old letters and papers. Among them were some mining claims receipts that a friend of his took up and recorded, giving them to him, but he never thought enough of them to go see them; so when he came to them he said

These mining claim receipts might have been papers from Ed's association with Louis W. and Reuben Borton and the Borton and Boblett Mining Co. It is not known if Reuben Borton made his money on the mining venture, but he certainly was a successful man. Reuben built a mansion in Golden in 1859. Modest by modern standards, the L-shaped house was built completely of cut lumber, and, today, is the oldest cut-lumber building standing in Colorado.

Reuben was an attorney and established the first Masonic Temple in Golden. His wife, Leah, was a founding officer of the Ladies Samaritan Society in Golden that looked after victims of the Mountain Fever epidemic in 1860. Reuben took in tenant Diantha Ferris who opened her millinery shop, perhaps the first woman-owned business in Golden. Reuben sold the home to William A.H. Loveland and today the house is known as the Loveland House and is a protected historical site.

he was going to burn them as they were no good. I said, "I would not do that as they might be worth something." He answered, "I won't fool with them as they are of no account." He burned them, and if I remember right, the next day he got a letter to send his receipts, or come up there and look after his claims, for they were going to prove good. His receipts, of course, were gone, but the claims he could have proved up, but he was going to Arizona, so he never answered the letter. We heard afterwards they proved to be very rich and some one else got the good of them. We picked up and started for Arizona with all our stock. We could have made a nice fortune with our cows if we had stayed in Colorado, for butter was fifty cents a pound for years after we left there.

Chapter 6
New Mexico Territory
1864

*T*he first thing of note I can remember was a sand storm. The worst I think I ever saw. We had only traveled about one hundred miles, perhaps not that far. It was not long after dinner, we had hitched up and were travelling along when it came up behind us and would run the wagon on the oxen, when we were driving on level ground. They had to run or hold back all the time, and, as I have stated before, we were seated on a chest with our feet out over the end-gate of the wagon and lots of the time we could not see the oxen for the dust and sand.

We traveled that way for about two hours, when we came to a farm house and stopped there for the night. The poor cattle nearly gave out. Here we reached our crew. There were two families and several single men. There we hired a man to drive our loose cattle. The other families had cattle too. This was in March of 1864. We traveled rather slowly for we knew we had to cross the Raton Range and we had to give the cattle plenty of time, as the food was not as good as in the fall or winter.

When we got to the Sangre De Christo pass, we found two people that our folk knew by the name of Hathaway. They traveled with us when I was a girl the first time we crossed the plains to Colorado. They wanted us to stop there, but to me it was the loneliest place I thought I ever saw. We camped there over night, then started up the mountains.

We were all day getting to the top of the range and it was covered with snow and bitter cold. Besides, the poor cattle had nothing to eat. We gave them some flour stirred up with warm water. We had no water only as we melted the snow, and no wood save we hauled it, and the road being very steep, we could not haul very much. Everybody walked all the way to the summit. Next morning we got up, hitched and traveled down the mountain till we got out of the snow, before we got breakfast, and rested the stock for an hour or two, hitching again and on down the pass till night. By this time we had reached another climate. It was warm as summer; barley and grass were green and growing nice.

Not thinking there would be any danger of the cattle eating too much, we turned them loose, knowing they would never go very far away leaving good feed. The next morning, the stock was all right save my pet cow that we brought back when we last came to Colorado from Iowa. She had eaten too much and had burst her stomach. It seemed almost like leaving one of the family lying there. I cried, I thought so much of her. Pa gave her to me when she was a little calf and I used to boil hay and take that tea, thickening it with flour, and then feed it to her, so I made a pet of her. She would bawl after me as though she were my calf. She was the best cow we had.

We were traveling then on the head-waters of the Santa Fe River; we traveled down the river as far as Albuquerque, New Mexico. The first little town we came to, some of the girls and myself were traveling

The trail from Denver to Albuquerque was due south most of the way, turning in a westerly direction near the town of Pueblo. This was part of the old Santa Fe Trail. If Ed and Lois didn't wander off the trail, they would have covered about 450 miles.

Raton Pass was the most dangerous stretch of the Santa Fe Trail. Wagons had to cover 20 miles of difficult terrain, with an ever-present danger of tumbling off the road into a ravine or creek. Sometimes, an all-day struggle to climb the pass would result in only 600 yards of progress.

Richens Lacy "Uncle Dick" Wooten was considered one of Colorado's foremost mountain men. He was a trader, trapper, military scout, and hotel owner. An astute business man, he saw an opportunity to help the travelers on their journey and make a profit as well. In 1866, he built a passable road, cutting down trees, blasting and clearing rocks, and building bridges. Those who wished to use his road paid $1.50 per wagon and $.05 per head of livestock. Native Americans could use the road for free. Traders continued to use the Santa Fe Trail until 1880 when the railroad extended to Santa Fe.

ahead and one of the girls said, "Let us hunt a store, for I want to get some things." So I, being the oldest and married, was chosen to do the talking.

We saw a man coming toward us and I told the girls, "There comes an American. He can tell us where we can find a store." When he came up, I said, after bowing, "Mr. can you tell us where we can find a store?" He looked at us so queer and said, "No sabe." I did not know what that meant, but I supposed he meant he did not understand. I said to the girls, "I believe he is lying for he looks like a down east Yankee." He had light hair and blue eyes.

We were quite a distance ahead of our train, so I suggested we had better wait until the wagons came up with us; so we waited, and when we got to the town, there was no store at all. We told our men folk about this man and we all thought he was fooling us. We camped not far from the town and this same fellow came out to camp and bought a yoke of oxen and he had to bring an interpreter. Then we knew he did not understand us when we met him. We learned he was a Spaniard.

As we camped in different places, these Mexican women would bring eggs and give them to us and would not take pay. We thought them very nice people at first, but as we learned them we changed our opinions. They were very friendly to your face, but when your back was turned, they would steal you blind. The old women carry all the money. One time as we went to camp, two Mexican women stepped to me and, putting their hands on my head said, "Negro, Negro." I though they were laughing at me for being tanned so black, but I learned later to talk their language very fairly and then knew that it was my hair they were admiring, and it was very black.

One little town we came to had a Catholic Church and the old priest came out to our camp and talked a little. He could talk English, but I believe he was a Frenchman. He invited some of the men up to the church, so they went with him. Ed was one to go. When they had gone all through the church, the priest opened a chest and took out a demijohn of wine and told them it was Communion wine, and gave them all a drink saying it was "damn good wine." We all thought it was no wonder the people were so treacherous with such a man as a leader.

Lois and Ed were probably not fully aware of the volatile political situation in the Southwest. The Civil War actually reached into New Mexico Territory. Southern sympathizers in the territory seceded from the Union in 1861 and were in control until the Battle of Glorieta Pass on March 28, 1862. However, the Civil War was just the latest in a long line of conflicts dating back to 1680.

The earliest non-native settlers in this area were Catholic missionaries who arrived in the early 1600s. The Indian populations declined, due largely to diseases such as measles, chicken pox, diphtheria, and smallpox, introduced by settlers. As the Indian population shrank, Spanish settlements increased, leading to an Indian uprising on August 10, 1680. The Pueblo Indians had been subjected to religious intolerance, forced labor, and unreasonable levies on food and weaving. They killed many colonists and priests, driving the survivors down the Rio Grande and across into what is now present-day Juarez.

Twelve years later, Spain's newly appointed governor of New Mexico, Diego de Vargas, entered New Mexico with his army and regained control of Santa Fe and the province. Franciso Cuervo y Valdes became governor in 1704 and declared the formation of a new villa in 1706, named for Fernandez de la Cueva, Duque de Albuquerque. His first report read:

"I certify to his majesty: That I have founded a villa on the banks and in the valley of the River of the North in a place of good fields, waters, pastures, and timber, distant from this villa of Santa Fe about twenty-two leagues . . .naming it the Villa of Albuquerque . . . . There are now 35 families located there, comprising 252 persons, adults and children. The Church has been completed . . . the government buildings have been begun, and other houses of the settlers are finished with their corrals, irrigation ditches running, fields sowed – all without any expense to the Royal Treasury."

A savvy politician, he then wrote to de la Cueva asking for donations of gold and jewels for the church, assuming el Duque would feel honored and want to support a villa bearing his name.

Mexico refused to recognize Texas' annexation to the United States in 1845, considering it a rebel province. The Mexican-American War commenced in 1846 and lasted into 1848, ending with the signing of the Treaty of Guadalupe Hidalgo. On September 9, 1850, the U.S. created the Territory of New Mexico. It consisted of the present-day state of New Mexico, Arizona, and parts of southern California, southern Utah, and southern Nevada. In 1861, the northeastern portion of the Territory was attached to Colorado, and in 1863, the Territory was divided in half, and the western portion became Arizona.

Hostilities ended with the Mexicans but continued with the nomadic Indian tribes. The government built military posts throughout the area to protect settlers, miners, and transportation routes. These posts gained additional importance with the outbreak of the Civil War. The Confederate Army considered New Mexico critical to gaining access to the gold fields of California and Colorado, as well as the old trading trails.

The Confederate influence increased after President Lincoln's decision to withdraw Union troops from the area to fight Eastern campaigns. This left the settlers, there being only 2,500 non-Indians counted in the 1860 U.S. Census, unprotected against Indian attack. Mexicans were still in the majority in Arizona and constituted most of the mining force.

The federal government further isolated the settlers by commanding the Butterfield Overland Stage Line to move its route farther north through Nebraska and Utah. The Apaches and other tribes thought the closure of stage stations and forts meant they were winning their battle to drive out white settlers. Thus encouraged, they stepped up their attacks.

Most early settlers were from Texas and other southern states. Feeling abandoned by the federal government, they met in March 1861 and voted to separate the southern part of New Mexico Territory into the new Confederate Territory of Arizona. Colonel John R. Baylor issued "The Proclamation of the People of the Territory of Arizona" on August 1, 1861, establishing the Confederate Territory of Arizona. A Convention of the People of Arizona was held on August 28 and ratified Baylor's proclamation. The Confederate Territory became a reality when Confederate President Jefferson Davis issued his proclamation February 14, 1862. He then ordered the occupation of Arizona Territory and Colonel Baylor was named its Territorial Governor. Baylor was an excellent organizer but was also known for his hatred of Indians.

The situation Baylor faced was impossible. He had 650 men under command and they had to fight Union forces while trying to protect settlers from Apache raids and occasional raids by Mexican bandits. The Apaches proved to be a formidable enemy. In desperation, Baylor issue an order that Confederate commanders were to "use all means to persuade the Apaches or any tribe to come in for the purpose of making peace, and when you get them together kill all the grown Indians and take the children prisoners and sell them to defray the expense of killing the adult Indians. Buy whiskey and such other goods as may be necessary for the Indians and I will order vouchers given to cover the amount expended. Leave nothing undone to insure success, and have a sufficient number of men around to allow no Indian to escape."

Whether or not this action was ever taken is unknown, but upon learning of the order, Jefferson Davis deprived Baylor of his position in the Confederate Army and the governorship of Arizona. Ironically, Baylor's dismantling of the forts left the settlers at the mercy of the very Indians he pledged to destroy.

Baylor and Brigadier General Henry Sibley envisioned an invasion north to Denver, where they would control the gold fields, then on west to California, eventually adding southern California to the Confederacy. The Confederate forces occupied Tucson and were supported by the citizens as long as the Confederates kept the Apaches at bay and the stage line open. Union forces from California, about 2,000 men led by Colonel James Carleton, moved east to stop the Confederate incursion. The skirmish at Picacho Peak, 35 miles northwest of Tucson, involved just 22 men, resulted in the deaths of three men, and lasted a mere 1.5 hours, but it put an end to Confederate ambitions. Later several small skirmishes were fought but the Confederate Army did not have the money or men to expend on the territory.

Indians and the Reservations
The native peoples in New Mexico suffered under Spanish rule for 223 years that ended in 1821 when Mexico gained its independence. The Mexican government continued the effort to subdue the tribes, without success.

New Mexico became American territory in 1848 at the end of the Mexican-American War. While countries were fighting over the territory, Indian tribes were fighting amongst themselves. The U.S. government finally defeated the Indians and ordered them onto reservations that were often no better than prison camps. One of the worst episodes in U.S.-Indian relations was the infamous Long Walk of 1863. Kit Carson oversaw the relocation of 8,000 Navajos who were forced to walk more than 300 miles from the Four Corners area to the Bosque Redondo, on the Pecos River in eastern New Mexico. The Navajo were eventually given a 3.5-million-acre reservation in 1868, back in the Four Corners area that included parts of New Mexico, Arizona, Utah, and Colorado.

Operating a Hotel in Albuquerque, April 1864
We traveled down the Santa Fe River till we came to Albuquerque, and Pa's team gave out, also a team belonging to a man named Bay. We could not go on and leave Pa and Ma, so we stopped and laid over to rest our stock.

There was a hotel there and the two men who ran it had Mexican wives, and as they did not know anything about hotel keeping, these men got after us to take the place off their hands. We made up our minds we would try it. We had all the work we could do. There was a bar in the house and Ed said he did not want anything to do with it, so Mr. Bay said he would attend to that and the rest of us could look after the other part. We went to the hotel and went to work and had not been there long till we had all we could attend to.

It took Ed all the time to get in things to cook. There were no butcher shops and he had to get out and get sheep and kill five a day, together with what beef and pork we could get. Ed would dress the sheep and Pa would cut them up, scour knives and bring in wood, peal potatoes and like chores. Mother, Mrs. Bay and I did the cooking. We cooked five sheep each day with beef and pork in proportion. Mrs. Bay and I waited on tables. We could not get help except in the laundry.

For a long time, we had over a hundred and fifty for each meal, and four times a week, we had coach travel. Twice a week, it came at midnight and was always loaded full. We had to serve a hot midnight supper for from forty to fifty. These meals were one dollar, others fifty cents. Our vegetables were not very high and we could get all the eggs we wanted for five cents a dozen. We would have had a fortune if Mr. Bay had been an honest man.

We ran on for about three months and I needed a pair of shoes. So Ed went to get some money to get the shoes and there was none in the drawer; so he asked Mr. Bay for some and was told there was none. "Well," said Ed, "where is it?" Mr. Bay said, "You tell." Ed said, "I guess I can't." "Well, where is it?" Ed said, "It is in your pocket." At that, Mr. Bay hauled off and knocked him over. We had seen Mr. Bay take great rolls of bills to his room every day. He claimed it was expense money, but we never believed it. It was the money we had earned.

For two weeks we had a hundred soldiers and officers boarding with us. The officers wanted the men to enlist again as they were to be discharged. They were Mexicans, while the officers were white men. The custom was to put their pay under their plates and the officers settled their board, but nearly every one would put a dollar bill under their plates every time, so we had double pay for their board. We never knew anything about it till we would clear the table and we could not talk to them and explain so we could not tell them.

Now to return to where Ed was knocked down by Bay. A man that stopped with us was in the bar room and heard the quarrel and went in and stopped the fight. Bay was a stout Irishman, weighting over two hundred pounds, and he struck so quick Ed was not prepared. There was an old lounge sitting behind Ed and he was knocked onto that. Then Bay was on top and had it not been for the third party, a friend of ours, there is no telling what would have happened to Ed.

As soon as he got up he came in where we were and called me to our room. He put on his coat and put a revolver in his pocket and went back and talked to the rascal and tried to get him to say something so he could have an excuse to shoot him. Bay knew better than to do that. It was not long before the news had gotten round and some of the business men told Ed to shoot him down, but Ed had had time to think and he did not want to kill him. They offered to let Ed have money to buy him out. But just then another party came along on their way to Arizona, and they told Ed they would wait till we could gather up our things and get ready to go where we had started. So we settled with Bay, just common wages, and he paid us with the money we had earned and he had stolen, then we started for Prescott, Arizona.

Chapter 7
Arizona Territory
1864-1869

*W*hile traveling from Albuquerque to Prescott, a lady by the name of Simmons and I went out to pick some berries a little way from camp. She had been married before and had two children by the name of Charles and Isabelle Kerr. Simmons had three and the children quarreled and that made trouble, so she told me if she could find anyone that would take the children that had none and would care for them, she would give the children to them. I knew she meant us, for we had none, but I said nothing. When I got back to camp, I told Ed what she had said, and we talked it over. It would be an incumbrance to us and a source of trouble, so we said nothing.

On our way, we passed a little town and camped here. Two pink-eyed Mexicans came to the camp with their sticks they spun yarn on to make carpets and blankets with. That was the first time we had seen spinning done with a stick. We traveled on and the next thing of note was in crossing a stream, probably 50 yards wide and the water a foot deep. There were three wagons ahead of us and we saw a cloud coming up but thought nothing of it, for we often saw them.

The first wagon got through the stream all right, but as the others got about the middle of the stream the wagon bed floated off with a woman and two children in it. The rain was the worst I had ever seen. It was a cloud burst and the water poured into the stream like water over a mill dam, and it came down the stream four foot deep like a wall. Some of the men swam in and towed the wagon bed to shore on the side we were, and in an hour we could cross all right. Ed and I thought the force of the water would break in the wagons, it bent them so. The water roared so you could hear nothing else, and the bank was so high that we could not see what was going on either side. We could see the water coming but we did not know anyone was in trouble till we heard of it afterward. We had to camp and let the folk unload and dry their bedding, clothes and provisions. From this place on the road began to be pretty rough and we walked all we could.

One day we came to a canyon that did not look as though a team could get through, it was so steep and rocky. I can not see yet how we ever came through as we did. Such boulders in the road and everywhere. It was called Hell Canyon. We got through but had a rough time making it. I have often thought since, what a wonder the Indians did not attack us here. They could have killed us all and gotten our stock. All that hindered was they did not happen to be in the locality at the time, but before we got to Prescott, they slipped up one night and took two of our horses. One was Pa's and the other belonged to another man in the company. We were now nearing Prescott.

Housing the Territorial Legislators in a Tent, September 1864
We finally got through to the town and there were only a few small boarding houses. We set up camp and in the morning, a one-eyed man came to visit us. His name was Holaday. He said, "There are nine of

continued on page 54

In March 1862, the House of Representatives passed a bill to create the Arizona Territory using the north-south border of the 32nd meridian west from Washington, effectively removing the territory from Confederate hands. President Lincoln signed the bill officially recognizing Arizona Territory on February 24, 1863, with the first capitol to be Fort Whipple.

In 1864 the fort and capitol were moved south to Prescott, named for William Hickling Prescott, author of *History of the Conquest of Mexico*. Miners, merchants and government officials followed. When gold was discovered near Prescott, miners hatched a plot to remove the Tonto Apaches from the area. On February 23, 1864, King S. Woolsey enticed the Tonto Apaches to a conference at Bloody Tanks, Arizona, telling them he was a personal representative of President Abraham Lincoln. Once there, Woolsey fed the Indians strychnine-laced pinole, killing them and the chief, which led to retaliation raids by the Tonto Apaches.

Pioneers went Indian hunting, killing men, women and children. The Indians engaged in their own raids on isolated ranches and wagon trains. Indians also fought each other, the Maricopas and Gila Pimas against the Apache and Yavapais.

The U.S. War Department authorized Arizona Governor John Noble Goodwin to raise five companies of Arizona Volunteers to provide protection for the territory. By the fall of 1865, more than 350 men were under orders from nine officers. These were mostly Mexican nationals who had grown up fighting Apaches and Maricopas, just as their forefathers had. The rewards were few. Shoes and clothing were in short supply; the volunteers lived in hovels and were constantly on the move. Food usually consisted of beef jerky and parched cornmeal. However, they were well supplied with .54-caliber rifles and ammunition, as well as bows, arrows and war clubs. To make life more endurable, 16 women were allowed to join the camp. According to the Third Arizona Territorial Legislature, the volunteers inflicted "a greater punishment on the Apaches than all other troops in the territory." Traveling "barefoot and on half rations," they killed 150 to 173 Apaches and Yavapais while losing only 10 men in combat themselves. They were disbanded when the Civil War ended and federal troops arrived back in the territory.

The first Territorial Legislature convened in Prescott on September 26, 1864, in accordance with the proclamation of the Governor, and was organized by the election of Coles Bashford as President of the Council and W. Claude Jones as Speaker of the House. It lasted 40 days and the members were: W. Claude Jones, lawyer; John G. Capron, merchant; Danile H. Stickney, miner; Gregory P. Harte, surveyor; Henry D. Jackson, wheelwright; Jesus M. Elias, ranchero; Nathan B. Appel, merchant; Norman S. Higgins, mining engineer; Gilbert W. Hopkins, mining engineer; Luis G. Bouchet, carpenter; Thomas J. Bidwell, miner; Edward D. Tuttle, miner; William Walter, miner; John M. Boggs, miner; Jackson McCrackin, miner; James Garvin, physician; James S. Giles, miner; and George M. Holaday, hotel keeper.

In *History of Arizona*, Thomas Edwin Farish wrote:
"The First Legislature of the Territory was convened at Prescott September 26th, 1864, at the mention of which comes the reminiscences of the first political campaign, in the electing of the members of the first Legislature. Partisan feeling and strife hadn't then been nourished into life as a bridge over which the incapacitated might gently glide into office, but the man of the period was popularly chosen on account of his merits alone, which consisted not simply in book learning and local fealty, but of the then selfish requirements, to wit: The sufficient state of cleanliness, and the possession of garments of such purity as would be suitable and creditable to the high station he sought. One of the chosen candidates was possessed of an ample fund of the former qualifications, but was found largely wanting in the latter, and it was discovered that his opponents in other locations had woven his shortcomings into political capital against him. A public meeting was at once called, and as the result of the deliberations thereof, our candidate was taken to the creek, vigorously scrubbed,

gorgeously robed with articles donated for the occasion, put astride a mule, and sent forth to do battle. It is needless to say that he was elected by a large majority, served with distinction through the whole term, and became the idol of his constituency."

The location of the capitol of Arizona was made by the Governor, so it could be changed by the Legislature. This was attempted by amending House Bill No. 56, locating the capitol at Prescott, which was up for consideration in the House on October 24, when "Mr. Hopkins moved to amend by striking out the word 'Prescott,' and the words 'situated on the east bank of Granite Creek' and the words which follow thereafter, and which refer exclusively to the city of Prescott, in section 1, and insert instead 'La Paz,' and thereupon the yeas and nays were demanded, with the following results: Yeas – Appel, Capron, Elias, Harte, Higgins, Hopikins, Stickney and Mr. Speaker – 8. nays – Bouchet, Bidwell, Boggs, Garvin, Gills, Holady, McCrackin, Tuttle and Walter – 9. The amendment was lost."

The battle for the capitol of Arizona didn't end with this meeting. The capitol moved from Prescott, to Tucson, back to Prescott, and finally to its permanent site in Phoenix in 1889.

The early territorial legislatures were progressive in nature. Approximately 78 bills were considered, with most of them applying to the organization of the government itself, such as courts, judges, law enforcement officers, tax questions, and the formation of counties. Several other bills of interest were titled Education, the Divorce of Mary Catherine Mounce, the Mojave & Prescott Toll Road Company, Support of Poor Persons & Orphan Indian Children, Prohibition of Gambling, Appropriating Money for Public Schools, Provide for Payment of Expenses of Indian Campaign, and Incorporate Arizona Historical Society.

The issues they dealt with sound familiar 150 years later. House Joint Resolution 8 was to provide books for the Territorial Library. Resolution 12 appointed a translator and interpreter "who shall act as a Commissioner to publish the Laws required to be published in the Spanish Language." The Legislature was meeting for the first time and already asking for a raise.

House Memorials were as follows:
• Asking an Increase per diem for Members of the Legislative Assembly, and an Increase of the Salaries of the Territorial Officers.
• Asking that the Tract of Land in the Bend of the Colorado River opposite Fort Yuma be attached to the Territory of Arizona.
• Asking an Appropriation of $150,000 for placing Indians of the Colorado on a Reservation.
• Asking an Appropriation of $150,000 for the Improvement of the Navigation of the Colorado River.
• Council Memorial 1 requested an "Appropriation of $250,000 in aid of the War against the Apaches."

The legislators banned all forms of slavery and supported education, roads, and railroads. However, the 1865 Howell Code, Arizona's original set of laws, did contain some laws based on prevailing prejudices of the time, such as: "no black or mulatto, or Indian, Mongolian, or Asiatic, shall be permitted to give evidence in favor of or against any white person." This law was overturned by the Stewart Bill of 1870.

The Southern delegates probably stayed at the Juniper House. It was the first hotel, opened July 4, 1864. The menu was based on an ample supply of venison. Breakfast consisted of fried venison and chili with bread and coffee with milk. Lunch offerings were: roast venison and chili; chili baked beans; chili on tortillas; tea and coffee with milk. Supper was chili, from 4 o'clock on. The hotel derived its name from the tree under which the cooking and eating was done. The men appreciated eating in the shade.

By 1867 Prescott had a population of 400 to 500 citizens. There were no banks, free schools, or churches, but, as usual in a frontier town, saloons were the first busiunesses to open. The first saloon was opened under large pine trees on Goose Flat. It was built of cloth and timber with us that want a place to board, can not you board us?" Ed said, "There is a hotel here, can not you board there?" "Yes," he said, "but we are members of the legislature and we are from the North and the Southern delegates are all there and a fight is on for the capitol, and we want board where we can talk things over by ourselves."

Ed told them we could board them if we could get anything to cook. "Oh," he said, "there is plenty here, and we can eat off tin plates under a pine tree."

We went to work and set our wagon boxes down on the ground and put a ridge pole up between them, sewed the wagon sheets together and then put the wagon boxes just as far apart as we could and had the sheets up high enough to turn the rain. Then we sewed sheets in the gable ends and that made a dining room. We fixed a place outside to cook and the next day, we started a boarding house in a tent under a big pine tree, with nine of the first legislators that ever met in Arizona.

They won their fight and the capitol remained in Prescott. After it was all over, they came to us and wanted us to get a supper for the entire number. They said they could get the dining room of the hotel, together with their dishes. They would furnish the waiters and clean everything up after it was over and they would furnish everything, giving us $40 to do the cooking. We did the cooking and when they came to pay us the next day, they would not take anything that was left, so we got nearer $60 dollars than the $40 for our work. They went away well pleased.

We stopped here under the pine tree for a time; this was the time of the rebellion [Civil War]. We were close to the hotel and the people that kept it traveled with us from Colorado to Albuquerque where we had to stop because Pa's team had given out. They were seceders and we were union folk, but we were as good friends as could be expected under the conditions.

One evening, one of the daughters, a young lady, was over at our tent, and we heard a little noise, and she jumped up and said, "Here they come." She flew for home as fast as she could run.

We wondered what she meant, but we suspicioned there was something going on we were not aware of. We did not sleep very sound that night and the next day we found that the Southerners were intending to come and massacre all the Northerners of the place, but one of their outfit got drunk and told. Then the Northerners got together and armed themselves, standing guard for a long time.

A Ranch in the Verde River Valley, 1865

We concluded we did not care to stay in our tent much longer and as there was a saw mill about a mile from the main town, and they wanted someone to cook for them, Mother and I went and cooked for them. Ed worked at the mill and Pa took care of the stock, keeping them close by. One day, he let them get a little too far and the Indians got a fine yoke of oxen. Pa thought they had just strayed off a little way and he would find them the next morning. Next day, Ed took his gun and went out that way and soon found their tracts and some Indian tracks too. He came home and told Pa not to let the cattle out of sight of the house; he did not and we lost no more that winter.

We stayed at the mill until spring, when there was a crowd going down the Rio Verde River to take

For Lois and most of the people moving west during the Civil War, the war was something they read about in the papers, often weeks after the particular battles occurred. If the Bobletts hadn't been in Arizona so soon after it had been part of the Confederacy, the war might not have affected them at all, other than the lack of federal soldiers for protection. Women living in the rural areas of the eastern part of the country in the 1800s expected hard work and deprivation if the crop wasn't good that year, but the war added a new level of anxiety to their lives.

Ellen Jane Bland Flick was a typical woman living on a small farm carved out of the woods on a rocky slope of mountainside. She had eight children, some old enough finally to be a real help on the place, when war was declared. Her husband, William Madison Flick, owed a gambling debt to a neighboring landowner. Hoping to pay off the debt, 42-year old Madison sold his services to a local man to go to fight in place of the man's son. Madison fought for the Confederacy, going AWOL twice, to help Ellen get in the crops that she and the children had managed to plant and care for by themselves. He was captured in 1865 and interred in a prison camp. By the time he was exchanged for a Union prisoner, he had developed pneumonia and died without ever reaching home.

Ellen Jane hadn't recovered from Madison's death when the landowner claimed the farm stating that Madison had died without fully paying his gambling debt. Ellen Jane couldn't read or write, but she took the man to court and won. This was almost unheard of at the time, but sympathy for widows was high at the end of the war and the judge ruled in her favor. Women who kept the families and homes together during the war realized their potential and began demanding more recognition and the ability to continue to make their own decisions. Widows like Ellen Jane had no choice but to fight to keep what little they had left.

Although Lois and the other settlers were far removed from that war, they had to be constantly on guard to protect themselves and their property from Indians.

❧　❧

The Bobletts joined a party headed by James M. Swetnam, a physician from Phoenix. In early January 1865, eight men set out to find a location for a farming colony in the Verde River valley. They were James M. Swetnam, William L. Osborn, Clayton M. Ralston, Henry D. Morse, Jake Ramstein, Thomas Ruff, Ed Boblett, James Parrish, and James Robinson. Thomas Edwin Farish detailed their experiences in the 1899 book, *History of Arizona*. The party understood they could come into contact with the Apache Indians, but they were well armed, young and brave, and felt themselves equal to the task they had undertaken.

"The men were all on foot, taking along a single horse on which was packed their blankets, cooking utensils, and provisions for ten days."

After three days travel, they were 50 miles almost due east of Prescott. They set out to explore the Verde River Valley, sighting Indian tracks and dead campfires. They finally decided to locate on the 'V'-shaped point between the Verde and Clear Fork on the north side of the latter. This site offered access to the river for irrigation purposes, a good position for a "fort" for defense from Indians, and a large amount of cut stone – the remains of an ancient edifice.

The party then returned to Prescott to gather supplies. Some of the residents tried to persuade them to abandon the enterprise, "insisting that the whole things was impracticable; that it was impossible for a party even of three times the number to go into a region so far from assistance, and surrounded with such Indians as the Apaches, and succeed in holding possession of the valley." They were not expected to survive 60 days.

Plows and ditching implements were purchased. Barley and wheat seed cost $20 per cwt. Corn cost $22 per cwt. They had to travel 18 miles to get it and pack it to Prescott on donkeys over an almost impassable trail. Finally, in early February, all was in readiness. The party, numbering 19, loaded supplies loaded into six wagons drawn by oxen and set out for the colony.

Theirs was the first crossing of Grief Hill by a wagon and by August 1865, a steady stream of freighters and settlers were attempting the trail. Company K, 1st New Mexico Cavalry, learned how difficult the trail was when their wagon tipped over within 100 yards of descending into the valley.

Lois worried about an Indian attack while crossing into the valley, but records show only two genuine attacks. An army private was killed in December 1866, and a train departing from Fort Whipple was attacked by a band of 100 to 200 Indians in May 1869. One guard died, and the Indians escaped with the train and its goods.

The *Arizona Miner* of February 1870, called the road "an infernal breakneck pitch known as Grief Hill." The road was used until 1870 when a new route opened through Copper Canyon.

up land, so Ed went down and located a piece for himself and one for Father. So we gathered our things and started. There were three families of us and some single men, fifteen in all. It was only fifty miles and we thought we could make it in a week anyway.

It was early spring and the ground was soft and we would mire every short distance. A person would almost get mired. One day I remember I was walking and there were a good many flat rocks and I thought how I would keep out of the mud for awhile, but when I stepped on them, they would go right down out of sight and sometimes slip out from under your feet, so one had to be careful or else get a tumble in the mud.

We had an awful time till we got to the summit, then we had a long hill to the river bottom. A man by the name of Eliot had a heavier load than any of the rest and, of course, mired oftener, and he said, "Well, if I mire down going down hill and have to be pulled out, I'm going back."

We finally reached the top of the Divide and we had now been over two weeks. Some days, we could have gone back and brought firebrands to start our camp fire at night from where we had camped the night before. Sure enough, as we were going down the mountain, poor Mr. Eliot mired down and it took about two hours to get him out. I asked him if he were going back and he said, "No, I could not get back." We finally decided to call the mountain "Grief Hill" for we had such a hard trip over it.

We were not long getting down again and pitched camp. We raised our wagon tongue and made our bed down on the ground that night and stretched a fly tent over it. In the night a rain came up and we were so tired we did not waken up till the first thing we knew, we were nearly covered in water.

We had been accustomed to sleeping in our wagon. Ed made a double box for it about six inches wider than the other and we had slept in it all the way from Colorado, but on this trip he thought he would leave it off and make our load that much lighter. We crawled out and made a big fire to dry by, but not without reflecting that we might attract the Indians and thereby invite trouble. However, we did not, so we were not troubled. The Indians could easily have made trouble for us when going down Grief Hill, had they been in that locality, as there was brush and rocks on either side all along. I have often wondered how we got through and they did not find us.

We got to our stopping place at last all right and the black crammer grass was nearly two feet high. We did not think the cattle would eat such looking grass, we had never seen it before. It sheds its leaves in the fall but the stalk remains green and, as it is very sweet, the cattle like it and get fat on it.

Our location was a lovely place, being a little elevation above the surrounding country. There was an old ruin here, and it seemed to be that of an old stone building about forty feet square, with a six foot wall on the extreme outside, with several inside walls. The men took the inside walls and patched the outside wall, building stone enclosures for the cattle with a cabin at each corner and one on each side. Then we took rocks and built fireplaces and hauled wood.

We had to pack water from the river over a quarter a mile away, so the men set to work to dig a well. They found plenty of water, but we could not drink it. We tried to cook with it, and took some beans and cooked them till noon, but they would rattle on our plates as though they had never been cooked at all. We put them back and cooked them all day, but they were just the same. The men thought we would have to have a ditch to irrigate with so they went to look at a stream nearby to see if they could bring the water on a level with our cabins. Some said it could not be done, but Ed said it could be done very easily. They went at it and in a few days they had plenty of water for all their claims and it came close by the cabin.

Meanwhile, Mother and I dug up a patch of ground and planted some peas. The men laughed at us because it was so early, but we watched it and kept it clean of weeds and on the eleventh of May, we had our first mess of green peas. We then wished we had put in more. Ed and Pa put in fifteen acres of barley and corn. This was in the spring of 1865. Our corn grew fine and we had a nice patch of sorghum, melons, pumpkins and squashes in abundance.

Indians Attack, Summer 1865
One day I was looking down across the valley and I saw something black, and as I looked, I could see three black objects. Then I said to some of the men, "Is that crows or Indian's heads?" One of the party had a field glass, so he went and got it and then we could plainly see it was Indians.

Pa was taking care of the cattle, so we told him to keep them close. He did, but one day near the middle

Thomas Edwin Farish interviewed Dr. Swetnam for his *History of Arizona*, written in 1916. Swetnam described the building of the "fort":

"The first work was to build a place to secure the cattle and provide for their own defense in case of an attack from the Apaches. The next morning before the sun was up they began work. The stone of the old ruin was used to make an enclosure 60 feet long and 40 feet wide. The walls were built to a height of seven or eight feet, being four feet thick on the bottom and two feet thick at the top. The stone enclosure compete, they built a cabin on each corner.

"These cabins were built of poles, notched at the ends, and made a very substantial habitation. The floors were leveled, wet, and pounded so as to make it hard and smooth. The cracks between the logs were chinked and plastered with mud. There was one door and one window to each cabin, and those were closed with strong shutters. There were loopholes looking out from the exposed sides and end of each cabin. The [roof] was made by using poles round or split for a foundation, covering this with grass, and then piling dirt to a depth of fifteen to eighteen inches on top of that."

Swetnam described challenges the party faced in bringing water to their fields. First, the men selected a site for a dam on Clear Fork about a mile and a half from the fort. Ralston made a plumb bob and tried to survey the land for an irrigation canal. The men set up a division of labor; two would stand guard over the animals and the fort and the others would dig. The plan was to have a ditch that was three feet wide at the top and 15 inches deep.

Work was interrupted by the need to return to Prescott for supplies. They found no game in the valley except two or three geese and as many ducks. On March 20, a party of five set out with one wagon and two yoke of oxen.

The party returned in six days, bringing with them Aretas and Lydia Whitcomb, Charles Yates, and John Culbertson. They also brought more stock: 33 head of cattle belonging to John Osborn and 10 or 12 head belonging to the Whitcombs, bringing the number of cattle on the ranch to between 55 and 60.

Culbertson took a look at the ditch and informed the men that it wouldn't work. They tested the flow and found Culbertson was right. They had to start over.

At the same time, the settlers began the hard work of clearing the land. They worked so diligently that by May 10 more than 200 acres had been planted in barley, wheat, corn potatoes, beans, melons, and garden stuff. The Indians were scouting around but had not bothered them, and they became careless about closely guarding the cattle.

of June, seven of our cows together with six of Father's and two heifers were gone. That was a great loss to us for butter was two dollars a pound and beef fifty a pound. Pa came back and gave the alarm and the men went out to see if they could find where they had driven them to. After that, the cattle were driven in the corral where they were safe.

Another day, he had them near the river and was herding them towards the house, as it was getting near noon. Ed had been down in the field at work and it was a very warm day, so he came up to the house to get a drink. We used to put the water in a stone jar wrapped in wet blankets to keep it cool. These were set out in the sun and wind but the evaporation kept the water cool and nice. Ed came in for water, and as it was near noon, laid down to rest till dinner. He had not been lying there very long when we heard several gunshots.

We all knew Pa had been attacked. He was not three hundred yards from camp. We had three big dogs with us and they went with all speed for Father, getting between the cattle and the Indians, starting the cattle on the run for home. Ed jumped up and said, "Father has been killed."

There was now and then a bunch of sage brush to hide Pa and the

Indians. Ed's gun happened to be empty. They did not have Winchesters those days, but muzzle loaders and he thought he never was so long getting his gun loaded. I guess the time seemed longer than it really was.

The rest of the men all ran to Pa's assistance and saved the cattle. I was watching the Indians and the men and I saw a man about Pa's size and he had a white shirt on like Pa's, so I said to Ma, "Oh, Pa is all right, I can see him driving the cows home." In a few moments I saw Pa coming to the house and I knew he was wounded, so I started down the hill to meet him. He was shot through the hip; he thought he had been hit twice. He had a Sharp pistol on a belt. On the small of his

back, one bullet hit a square piece of steel and fell in his scabbard, another hit a little thing he had to measure powder with when loading. There were 15 shots fired at him, besides a cloud of arrows.

> The Apaches weren't the only tribe waging war on settlers. A number of tribes called the southwest their home. The Pai were a grouping of three tribes that used irrigation to grow crops on rancherias and traveled across wide areas following wild plant harvests. The Pai considered the Yavapai enemies.
>
> Hostilities involving Pai tribes in Arizona almost broke out in April 1861, when drunken white settlers murdered a Pai leader. In retaliation, Pais severed transportation routes between Prescott and the Colorado River posts. Freighter W.H. Hardy was able to bring calm to the area and reopen the toll road between Prescott and Hardyville. Unfortunately, his peace lasted only nine months. Chief Wauba Yuma of the Yavapai was murdered while presenting a copy of Hardy's treaty to a group of freighters. What became known as the Hualapai War spread across northwestern Arizona.
>
> The Pais attacked freighters and stoned miners to death. Cavalry detachments counter-attacked, burning rancherias, wikiups, and cornfields, taking women and children captive. The Mohave Indians sometimes joined the cavalry, avenging old grudges against the Pai. Between 1867 and 1868, 68 Pai rancherias were destroyed and 175 Pais killed, a quarter of the tribe. Epidemics of whooping cough and dysentery further decimated the tribe. Within a year of the end of the Hualapai War, 50 of the surviving Pai had joined the cavalry to fight against the Yavapai.

I helped him to the house and then the men came with the cattle. Ed and others of the party got him to bed and dressed his wounds. They had just finished when the Indians jumped some of our men that were tramping barley. Their claims were about three quarters of a mile from our camp and they had gone over there to harvest their crops. There were three men, one was tramping barley with a yoke of oxen and the other two were hauling the barley in to be threshed. The Indians jumped the man that was tramping. He saw them creeping up on him and stooped to pick up his gun, and they shot him in the hip almost exactly where they hit Father.

They ran the oxen off into the brush and killed them. Mr. Boblett said to the rest of the men at camp, "Boys, we must go over and help those fellows." So, Ed and three other men took their guns, muzzle loaders, and went over. When they saw them coming, the Indians gave way. They went to the men and put the wounded man into the wagon and what little stuff they had left, for the Indians had gotten nearly everything they had taken over there.

Then they started for home. They had a strip of brush to go through at first. When they got through the brush, Ed said, "They can go the rest of the way safe enough; let's slip back and see if we cannot get a

Living at the Verde River Valley ranch was not elaborate. It was coffee, bacon, beans, and bread for breakfast; beans, coffee, bread and bacon for dinner, and bread, coffee, bacon and beans for supper.

At Prescott flour was $30 per cwt., in greenbacks; bacon $0.50 a lb. But when new vegetables were ready, the settlers fared better, and when sweet corn and green beans came, followed by potatoes and melons, they lived like kings.

The first crop of barley wasn't choice, and included an occasional scorpion or rattlesnake, but once cleaned it sold at Prescott for $17 per hundred.

The Apaches continued to raid crops, especially sweet corn. Swetnam and James were guarding the field one dark night when they heard the snap of corn ears being picked. They crept through the field, trying to time their footfalls with the snapping of the corn. Suddenly, a large object appeared dimly before them. One of the men fired his gun as an arrow flew through the air between their heads. Everyone hit the ground, and all became still, except for the rustling of corn stalks in the wind. As the sky lightened, the men realized that they were alone and that what they had killed was a blanket full of corn that one of the Apaches must have been carrying on his back. The blanket was kept by Swetnam as a trophy for a long time.

The soldiers were unable to protect the settlers. An attack in October left Sanford and Culbertson wounded. The party sold up.

"The government made arrangements to take all the corn and grain which the settlers wished to sell, paying for the corn, without its being shelled, thirteen dollars per hundred. This was some compensation, but when it is remembered that during the season the Indians had destroyed or carried away barley and corn to the amount of nearly $2,000, driven off horses to the value of $500, and cattle to the value of over $6,000, for none of which the settlers have ever received any reimbursement, the profits were not large, considering the labor, anxiety and privations, not to mention the sufferings of the men who established and maintained the first settlement in the valley of the Verde."

They retuned to Prescott, but at least they survived.

shot at them." They went as far as safety would permit, then sat down behind some big weeds and watched. Shortly they saw an Indian coming out of the brush where they had killed the oxen and they kept coming until there were nine of them.

The first one was a large fellow. Ed said, "Now that there are only four of us, two will shoot and two will reserve their shots," fearful we may run out of ammunition. This was agreed to and they questioned as to who should shoot first. It was agreed that Ed and another fellow were the best shots, so should shoot first. Ed said he wanted to shoot the first one, so the other fellow took the next and so on. There were also a lot of Indians out in the field burning bunches of barley and, at the crack of the gun, they ran for cover.

Our men lay still and soon they heard splashing in the river and they waited further until they could not hear any sound, then going out where they shot at the Indians coming out of the brush, they found two bows and arrows and the boy's coffee pot full of the entrails of the oxen they had killed. Also a pair of moccasin soles they had cut out of the hide. There was blood everywhere, but as they had killed the beef here, they could not tell accurately how much damage they had done.

Ed said he noticed the Indian he had shot had something black hanging on his arm. Ed picked up the bows and two arrows and coffee pot and brought them home. We kept them for a time, when one day we came across a fellow who was hunting specimens and curios for the government museum at Washington, so Ed let him have them. I suppose they are there to this day. Father and Jake Ramstein, the other man that was wounded, got along all right.

After a long time, the news of our attack went up to Prescott and the Government Post sent some soldiers down for our protection. Pa could not herd the horses as he was yet confined to his bed, so the soldiers told them that was all right, they would herd their stock with ours. We told them that was all right and we would pay them for their trouble. They replied they did not want pay. The looked after our stock and we felt pretty safe.

One day on or about the 31st of July 1865, the Indians came again. Our men had their riding horses picketed right by them and the rest of the herd was loose. They jumped on their horses and rode for camp as hard as they could, the loose horses following, getting away from the Indians, but the cattle were stolen by the Indians, leaving us nothing except a few chickens we had raised. The raiders drove the cattle up on a table mountain and some soldiers and citizens slipped around to head them off and get the cattle, but they could not although they exchanged shots

> The Indians got away with 19 head of cattle, worth at the time $3,000 to $4,000. A horse wounded in the fight recovered, but in less than two weeks the horses on the ranch, in spite of all vigilance, became property of the Apaches.

with the Indians. They said they killed one Indian and one of the citizens came back with an arrow stuck in him under his arm. The soldiers were afraid to take it out; fearful he might bleed to death before they could get him home.

We remained there until we got done harvesting and, as the soldiers were going after more provisions, we gathered up our stuff and they took us, together with Father and Mother, back to Prescott. Pa's black mare was taken at Balls Springs, near San Francisco Mountain. Ma and Pa went back to the mill to cook for the men while Ed and I rented a house preparing to keep boarders.

Children Join the Boblett Family in Prescott, Winter 1865
Before the Indians took our cattle, several of the men with Ed and myself, took two yoke of oxen and went up to Prescott, a distance of about fifty miles for provisions. Before going up, we had come and called the place Grief Hill, we learned of an easier road, following a ravine. We cut brush as we went and as the going was hard, we all walked. I was always a great admirer of flowers, so I gathered till I could not carry any more, so when we stopped to rest the team, I sorted my bouquet, taking only one bunch of a kind. After that, I would only pick something I had not yet gathered, and when we got to the top of the Divide, I had all I could carry on my arm. I never saw such a variety anywhere, also beautiful flowering shrubs that I had never seen before or since.

When we reached the top of the Divide, we all got in and rode till we came to a creek and here we camped for the night. There had been a hail storm and we shoveled nearly a foot deep before we were able to make our beds on the ground. This must have been in the latter part of May. My poor flowers were chilled, so I had to throw them away. In the morning, we started and got through, putting up at the hotel that we camped near when boarding the nine legislators.

Here we found the two children that I have referred to before, whose mother said she would give them away if she could find someone who had no children. I asked how the children came to be here and Mrs. Osborn, the landlady, told me their mother had died and so they had the children. When they got supper for the family, we sat down with them to eat. There was plenty of room for all, but these two poor orphans had to wait till we were done and take what was left. It hurt terribly to see that.

We stayed at Prescott for a day or two with another family by the name of Ehle. They had a large family of their own. I told Mrs. Ehle what I saw and she said we ought to take them, but when we thought of the Indians and that we might lose everything and possibly get killed, we felt we did not want any children to look after. As soon as we moved back there, these officers came to us and told us they had taken the children from these people. It seemed they had promised the mother they would not separate them, but one of their own girls got married and they gave the little girl, two and a half years old, to her for a servant girl, making her wash all the dishes.

One day, they had meat for dinner and the poor little girl went to wash the platter and, it being so heavy, fell, breaking the dish. The woman whipped her so she carried the marks for two weeks, so the officers took both the children to Ehle's and hired them to take care of them till they could make other arrangements. They came to us asking us to take them and we consented.

Flour was fifty dollars a barrel and bacon seventy-five cents a pound, so also was sugar, coffee, tea and any kind of dried fruits. Butter was two dollars a pound, eggs two dollars a dozen, calico was fifty cents a yard. Any kind of dress (cheap) goods one dollar and fifty cents a yard, so we thought it was quite an undertaking. But many a dress for the little girl was given us by the soldiers.

The first 13 settlers in the Prescott area arrived October 1863. The following month a party composed of 24 men arrived from Santa Fe, followed by a second group of miners. Among the settlers who arrived in 1864 were Joseph Ehle and family, Daniel Stevens and his wife and four children, T.M. Alexander, his wife and six children, John Simmons and wife and three children, and J.P. Osborn, his wife and seven children. These were the families that Lois and Ed traveled with from Albuquerque. The first child born in Prescott was Molly Simmons on January 9, 1865. Perhaps Mrs. Simmons died in childbirth; she certainly was dead by that fall. She was probably the wife of Thomas Simmons, son of John Simmons.

Was Isabelle Kerr really forced to work as a dishwasher at such a young age? A search of later census records helps establish her age. According to the 1870 U.S. Census for Washington Territory, Seattle, Isabelle Kerr was living with Lois and Ed Boblett, along with her brother, Charles Kerr. Isabelle was eight years old and Charles was 10 years old. In the 1880 U.S. Census for Washington Territory, Spokane Falls, Isabelle was 19 years old, married to W.D. Farris, and the mother of a two-month-old son, Wm. E. That means Isabelle was born in 1861 or 1862. Isabelle noted on the 1880 census that she was born in Missouri, but she left blank the spaces that told where her parents were born. She and her family were living next door to Lois and Ed.

Lois never learned the children's background, but research by family genealogist, Lois McNaught, found that their father was Thomas Kerr, who was born in Kentucky and died in the Civil War. Catherine was born in Illinois and married Thomas in Missouri, where both of the children were born. Whatever happened to Mr. Simmons and his children is not known.

By the end of 1864, there were still only 28 women living in Prescott. Some of the women had large families of their own, so there were few opportunities for orphaned children. Life was indeed hard for orphans in the 1860s.

One day a soldier took Charley, the boy, to a store and gave him a suit of clothes, hat, shoes and socks. That helped us out materially. Charley was four years old, while Isabelle Jane was two and a half years when we took them. Their surname was Kerr and they came from Missouri; we never knew whether they had any living relatives or not.

We rented a small house and went to keeping boarders for a living. The Masons used to come to us to get me to prepare their lodge suppers, and once I got a wedding supper. Another time they came to me to get a supper for a dance. One man living with a Mexican woman was not invited to the dance. He supposed we were responsible for the invitations and was very angry, threatening to shoot Ed. But as it happened, Ed was out and a fellow who used to help in the dining room was there when this fellow came, using abusive language, so he collared him and put him out. He went home, got a revolver, and swore he would kill Mr. Boblett, or Ed as I always called my husband. That day there was a funeral and Ed attended it, and as they were marching out to the grave, a friend of ours told Ed of the incident and gave him a revolver to defend himself. Ed kept out of his way till he sobered and then he was not so quarrelsome.

We did not live in this house much longer as it was too small, so we moved to a larger place. There was a saloon and bowling alley adjoining it, but no door was to be open between. One day, two men got in a fight, and one was beating the other over the head with an iron pin and the other, in trying to get away, burst down the door and came into our part of the house with blood streaming from his head. I can not remember their names, but others got them out of the house and parted them. Everything went fine for a time until one evening they commenced shooting in the saloon and some of the shots came in our part, into the living room, and all of the yelling and smashing of windows I never heard before or since.

The children and I were very much frightened, so Ed took us to a neighbors till the row was over. A lot of soldiers had come up from the post, taking offence at Mr. Holaday and the saloon-keeper, and were bent on making mischief. Of course, they did not intend to do us any damage but when they got drunk, they did not know what they were doing, so began throwing cordwood at our dining room window until some of the more sober ones took them away. One rather large stick was thrown on one of the tables that all set and broke several dishes. Ed took his gun and went in the room and possibly have shot

George W. Holaday wore many hats in the early days of Prescott. He was a member of the Legislature, temporary Speaker of the House, hotel keeper, business agent, deputy postmaster, and Judge.

Several mentions in an early newspaper, the *Arizona Miner*, tie into Lois's story and one gives us the date of the saloon brawl.

"January 24, 1866 – Holaday has left his little room on Granite street and taken the bar at the Montezuma. We learn that in addition to the fine stock of liquors he recently received from California, he has bought the stock of Campbell, who is going inside. Holaday undoubtedly has the genuine article and Shanks, his barkeeper, knows how to deal it out."

"February 14, 1866 – There was a lively row at the Montezuma on Sunday evening, the 4th inst. Several shots were fired, one man was wounded in the wrist, and the furniture was badly smashed. The belligerents were soldiers, most of them very drunk. Holaday has abandoned the establishment and gone to California."

Holaday didn't stay away for long though, as reported on August 22, 1866.

"Judge G.M. Holaday arrived in Prescott, from California, on the 9th inst., after an absence of some six months in San Francisco."

An advertisement for the Pine Tree Saloon, printed in the *Arizona Miner* on September 12, 1866, told of Holaday's new enterprise:

"This noted stand situated on Montezuma Street, third door from the southwest corner of the plaza, where the choicest of LIQUORS, WINES AND CIGARS can be had, purchased from Campbell's new and selected stock, fresh from San Francisco. NEW CIDAR AND LAGER BEER, constantly on hand. Customers promptly waited upon and kindly received, for the ready cash. G.M. Holaday." Holaday added a bakery connected to his saloon in October 1866 and pledged he will "always keep on hand fresh pies, cakes and bread, and will get up a lunch at any hour of the night."

someone, had not the more sober ones realized the import of the situation. However, they kept it up in the saloon until they had broken everything Mr. Holaday had, even to the chairs, pouring out all his liquor. Finally, when they had accomplished their job, they left and we were glad to enjoy the quiet again.

The Tollgate on Mohave Road, 1866

We stayed there until the next spring, when a man came to us and wanted us to go out forty miles from Prescott to keep a tollgate on the Mohave Road. There was lots of travel on that road, so we thought it would be a good place. We got good wages for keeping the gate and all we could make off the travel. This was in the spring of 1866. We made up our minds we would go, and there was a man with his wife and little boy who wanted to go with us. They thought they could take a ranch close by us and we would be company, one family for the other. Their name was Steinbrook.

Mr. Steinbrook had a mule team and a wagon. We went out with the government train as there was one going for supplies. When we got there, we found out there had been a lot of Indians there the night before and wounded the man's dog, got his horse and burned his hay. He was terribly frightened and I did not blame him, for there had been a lot of them around the house. The man stayed with us until there

was a train going into town, then he gave us his double-barreled shotgun and said he would never go anyplace where he would need it and as I could shoot pretty good, he thought it might come in handy. As we were going out, the man in charge of the train told Ed they had lost a mule there at the foot of Juniper Mountain, where we were to stop, and if he could find it, he could have it. Ed took his gun and walked out and soon found him and this made us three mules.

One time, Ed and Steinbrook sat down to play cards, as that seemed all there was to do to

Figure 8: Freight Wagons on Montezuma Street, Prescott, circa 1880. The wagons had to go through the toll road to reach Prescott. Call #FT107P, ID 2038, Sharlot Hall Museum and Archives, Prescott, AZ.

pass the time away, and as they sat down, Mr. Steinbrook made the remark that if the Indians got his mules while he was playing cards, he would never play any more. They played three games and went out to see it the mules were feeding, and sure enough, they were gone. They followed along until they saw Indian tracks, then they came back home. We heard nothing more of this until one day a mule train came out from Prescott going after provisions, and in the train was one of Mr. Steinbrooks's mules. He asked them where they got the mule and they said he was running around at a place called Williamson Valley, some twenty miles away, with a long larriette around his neck. The men told the story of the Indians running off with the three mules about a month before and that the mule belonged to Steinbrook. The train gave him back to us and then we had a mule once more. This time, Mr. Steinbrook kept him picketed near the house.

At another time, a man came along on a horse going to Prescott. We knew there were Indians all around so we urged him to stay; his name was Brooks. We had but little provisions, but there was lots of game, but it was not safe for one man to go hunting alone, and it was not safe for the women to be alone.

Lois and her family arrived at Tollgate in the middle of the Haulapai War, dependent on a military presence that stretched more than 150 miles. Camp Tollgate was about 40 miles from Prescott. It was later renamed Camp Hualapai. The Indian threat brought greater military presence into the valley. A military encampment was set up at Beale's Springs in 1866. August 23, 1867, a second post was established at Camp Willow Grove (also known as Camp Willow Springs), about 76 miles northeast of Fort Mohave. Willow Grove was located between Tollgate and Beale's Springs. This section of the toll road passed through mountainous terrain covered with juniper and pine.

According to Dan W. Messersmith in his *Camp Beale's Springs, A Short History*, soldiers led a hard life and keeping them in the service was a challenge. The cavalry was simply outnumbered and had too much land to protect. Captain S.B.M. Young, the commanding officer at Fort Mohave, details the beginning of Beale's Springs military post:

"... I established a small Post Consisting of One Sergt. one Corpl and Six men of 'K' Co. 8th Cavalry and One Corpl and Three men of 'E' Company 14th Inf. at Beal Springs on the 27th day of March 1867 with instructions to patroll the road from that point to Fort Rock Constantly with the mounted force, and the Infantry to guard Supplies. Also to furnish an escort for the Mail between those two points. The Cavalry however deserted on the 12th inst. and I have now at the Post One Corpl and Three men (mounted) and the same of Infantry whose duty is merely to hold the Post at present until my Company of Cavalry (which is now detached on escort duty with Dr. McCorniick Col. Reese & General Rusling, and with Lieut. Stevenson pursuing deserters on the trail toward the Mormon Settlements[)], returns it is my intention when a sufficient number of men withdraw the Post already Established at Beal's Springs and scout the Country North and south of the Prescott road wherever and whenever and Indian sign may be see."

By 1868, approximately 90 men were stationed at the Willow Grove Camp. Seven men were assigned to the Beale's Springs outpost and 10 men escorted the mail. The camp consisted of two log buildings and nine pyramidal tents built on stockades. By 1869, there were 156 men stationed at the camp. On September 30 of that year, the camp was dismantled and moved to Tollgate, thus the name Camp Hualapia. After the military pulled out, the small town that had grown up there became known as Juniper, but soon became another one of the ghost towns that dot Arizona's landscape.

Mr. Brooks decided to stay until a train came along. He and Mr. Steinbrook went out hunting but got

Captain William H. Hardy arrived at Fort Mohave (10 miles from present day Bullhead City, Arizona) January 20, 1864, with a little money and a store of merchandise. He became an associate of the Mohave and Prescott Toll Road Co. headed by Rufus E. Farrington, who was granted the franchise to build that road by the first Arizona legislature.

Hardy established a post office and ferry crossing at Hardyville and a stage line and mail route to Prescott. He bought out Farrington and T. Alexander in 1866. The road spanned 165 miles from Prescott to the Colorado River. The rates were established by the Legislature:

"Each wagon and two horses 1 1/2 cents per mile and each additional animal 3/4 cent per mile; one horse and vehicle 3/4 cent per mile; pack animals 1/2 cent per mile; horned cattle, horses and mules and other in droves 1/2 of 1 cent per mile; sheep, goat, or hog 1/8 of 1 cent per mile."

Building the road was the easy part; securing safe delivery of goods and passengers was more difficult. Every freight or mail run was a potential target for raiding bands of Indians.

By 1866, wagon master Virgil Earp and his 15-year-old brother, Wyatt, were regulars on the road, hauling goods between southern California and Prescott. Later, Virgil worked in Prescott at the saw mill. Moving away for a time, he returned in 1877. In October, he was deputized along with some other men by Sheriff Ed Bowers who was organizing a manhunt. Two men had ridden into town and were shooting up saloons and other resorts. The duo road out of town and set up camp at the Brooks Ranch, then sent word into town that "if any of the officers wanted them to come and get them." When the posse arrived, the men started shooting and Sheriff Bower's horse was hit. Virgil, armed with his Henry rifle, crept up along the creek, spied one of the cowboys crouched beneath an oak tree, and shot him. Virgil was appointed Deputy U.S. Marshall in 1879, shortly before moving to Tombstone with his brother, Wyatt.

Throughout the 1850s, the Hualapai had extracted their own "tolls" from settlers and traders by running off or killing livestock or demanding sacks of flour and sugar. In May 1865, a drunken man killed Anasa, a Hualapai leader, near Willow Grove. The March 1866 killing of Ed Clower, as described by Lois, at the Willows fanned the flames. Retribution killings spread across the countryside. In December, Yavapai Rangers attacked a Hualapai camp and killed 23 men, women and children. That same month, the military established a post at Beale's Springs (near present-day Kingman, Arizona) to escort the mail.

nothing. This was in March of 1866. The next day, Mr. Brooks and Ed went out. Before they went, Mr. Steinbrook told Mr. Brooks to bring his horse close by so we could watch it if the Indians came. He said he would take no chances, he rather the Indians get him than have the horse go hungry.

Along about ten o'clock, our three dogs began to bark. We stepped to the door thinking a train was coming our way, but no train was in sight. We looked at Mr. Steinbrook's mule and I never saw an animal show such fright and hatred as it did.

We knew the Indians were there so we went and brought the mule right up to the door and several times the dogs would bark fiercely, indicating that the Indians were not very far away from us. The mule would paw and snort and look, but the brush was very thick within twenty feet of the house. I took my shotgun, Mr. Steinbrook his rifle, and his wife a revolver, and we went out and around the house to let them know we were ready to fight.

Finally we hear them yell, slapping their hands on their mouths, over where Mr. Brooks had tied his horse and then we knew his horse was gone. Soon we heard them again away up the canyon and the dogs and the mule quit their restlessness, and we knew the Indians had gone for that time. I really hoped they had shown themselves so we could get a shot at them, but they did not.

Along towards night Ed and Brooks came home. They struck the Indian trail on their return and Ed said he never was so frightened in all his life. He said there must have been a hundred at least, and he expected we had either been killed or dragged off prisoners. I know he was very pale when he arrived; he broke down and cried for joy to find we were still alive and safe. They had killed a big brown bear and a small deer, but the bear was too large. Next morning, we took the mule and brought in half the bear and the next morning the rest of it. Ed sold the hide.

The train came along shortly and we sent forty pounds of bear meat to Father's and sold forty pounds to the men with the train and still we got thirteen gallons of the finest lard I ever saw out of the remainder, and had all the meat we could use.

We had a caller who knew we had venison, but was not aware we also had bear meat. He came after dark and went before daylight on account of the Indians. As he was eating breakfast, he said, "Well, Boblett, I do admire your venison, it is the finest I think I ever tasted." Ed laughed and told him his mistake. The meat was very choice as the bear had fattened on juniper berries. The juniper berry is about the size of a cherry and very sweet. I have gathered lots of them. We had to crush them, pouring boiling water on them and let stand for a day, then strain, and we had a very fine vinegar. When it first begins to work, it makes a fine drink.

We finally moved down where we could see around a little better and where we could make a little garden. We had to wait for someone to come with a team to haul our stuff down, as it was about three miles to the place where we wanted to go, and we had to camp out until we got our cabin built. We made our house mostly of poles as there was nothing else nearby and we dare not go far. We also put poles on top for a roof, with brush and grass thrown over them for covering. On top, we covered it with a foot of dirt. We took the door out of the other cabin and then we thought we were all right. We made portholes, two on each side of the house so we could peek out to look for Indians. We kept them stopped up only when we thought Indians were around, especially after dark.

Many a night we were up nearly all night, being on the watch. We never lit a light so they could see us and we could always tell by the way the dogs acted and barked, whether they were barking at Indians or some wild animal. We all lived in the one house for a time, till another cabin could be built. Mr. Steinbrook and family moved out but close enough so we could mutually protect each other. We all lived this way for two or three months. We entertained Mr. Governor McCormick, the first governor, in this house with a dirt roof and a dirt floor. We often entertained officers and their wives.

One time I remember we were out of provisions. We knew a train loaded with government supplies was due, but just when it would get in we could not tell, so we had to pinch ourselves pretty hard until its arrival. Before it came, we had eaten the last thing we had, that being a little rice boiled with a little salt for our breakfast. About one o'clock the teams came in sight. We had decided that if we could not get supplies we would go to Prescott.

The first territorial governor was John N. Goodwin, who was appointed by President Lincoln. When Goodwin was elected to Congress in 1865, he appointed Richard C. McCormick as acting governor. Ben C. Truman wrote an article in the *New York Times* June 1, 1890, reminiscing about a trip he took through Arizona in 1867. He described Governor McCormick as "a very exemplary man, and yet immensely popular with the frontiersmen of Arizona, who, although they would frown upon almost any human being who dared to decline a cocktail a dozen times before breakfast, sent McCormick to Congress three times, and fairly worshiped him for his energy and perseverance in behalf of the then new civil government and for his sterling and unimpeachable good character." McCormick later served as Assistant Treasurer of the United States.

Another article printed in the *New York Times*, February 2, 1868 read:
"INDIAN OUTRAGES IN ARIZONA – ARRIVAL OF GOV. MCCORMICK-
         "San Francisco, Saturday, Feb. 1 – Late advices from Arizona state that the Indians had made a descent on Bale Springs Station and Camp Williams, shot and carried off all the stock. A mail carrier and a military escort of four men belonging to the Railroad Survey party were lost in the wilderness seven days, and came near starving. Gov. McCormick, and other civil officers of the Territory, arrived at Tuscan on the 17th of December. The citizens escorted them into the town, and gave a grand supper in their honor."

We had plenty of money to buy with when we got there. This was in the fall and it was raining, sleeting and very cold. There was a large family, with two teams loaded, one to sell in Prescott. Ed came in and said, "Lois, we can get anything we want now," and told me there was a woman and a lot of children along, so I went out and asked them in out of the storm. After they had gotten warm, I said to the lady, I think their name was Hart, "If I had anything to cook I would ask you all to stay and I would get you a warm supper, but we ate the last we had for breakfast." "Oh no," she said, "We have plenty in our wagons, we only wanted to get warm." Well, they got warm and went back to their wagons.

Ed wanted to buy some provisions from the man but they were afraid he was not offering as much as they were worth in town and they would not let us have an ounce of anything. Ed told him just what the prices were the last time we got our supplies and offered if they raised to make the difference good, but they would not sell. Ed told me he would try the wagon master and see what he could do, and go out and demand some of the supplies. I begged him not to do that for we would not starve before we got to town, but the wagon boss let us have a sack of corn meal, some bacon, sugar and coffee, so we were all right for a time.

When the train got into town, the boss went to the man that was to send us our provisions and told him of our situation. He sent provisions and everything went quietly for a time. Then another train came along and told us that a man by the name Ed Clower at the next station had been killed by the Indians and burned in the house. There were two other men there in partnership at this place, a Mr. Monehan had gone out to lay in their winter supplies, while the other fellow [Mr. Hadley] was out hunting deer. Mr. Hadley had followed a drove all day trying to get a shot at them, thinking they would soon lay down and he could then creep up on them and get one, going home by moonlight as it was to be a full moon that night. However, there was a total eclipse and he could not get home, nor did he get any deer meat, so he had to camp until morning, going home only to find his partner killed and burned and the place covered with Indian tracks. Mr. Hadley started to meet the other partner, I believe he was two or three days without food before they met. Then he turned back with the train and came to our place on their way to Prescott.

We were very much alarmed for our safety, so Ed proposed they stop with us, and they did.

It was now coming spring again, 1867. We put in a garden and there was plenty of rain and we raised a pretty fair garden and six or eight bushels of potatoes, as nice I believe as ever I saw. We were offered fifteen dollars a bushel for them but we did not take it, as we wanted to keep them for seed the next spring. The next spring was very dry and we did not raise a potato as big as a walnut!

Was there really a total eclipse of the moon on the night Ed Clower died? A total eclipse of the moon did occur on the night of March 30, 1866. On April 25, 1866, the *Miner* reported the death of Edward Clower:

"The story goes that Clower had lost his horses and been engaged for a day or two in hunting for them, assisted by a Hualapai Indian. On the night in question, the night of the eclipse of the moon, when Clower returned to sleep in the cabin, the Indian was permitted to sleep there also, and it is suspected that he first murdered Clower and then started the fire. This suspicion is strengthened by the evidence that all the arms and provisions had been removed from the cabin and no traces of the Indian being found. Two men encamped near the cabin thinking Indians had gathered in numbers, were afraid to venture there until daylight, and they started next day for Hardyville. After a day or two, they met with Mr. Milton Hadley of Prescott, whom they met at Cottonwoods, and who had been living with Mr. Clower and was returning from a hunting excursion . . ."

Clower's death lead directly to the murder of Hualapai chief Wauba Yuba and the outbreak of the Indian warfare that plagued the territory for years.

We often had people come to put up for the night, so the men built another cabin across the road from ours for extra sleeping quarters. We had the mail carriers into town and out twice a week. The mail was carried on mules, so we had the carriers to board. We built a stockade for the safety of the animals with a cabin in one corner. One day, there came a train going to town, and one of the fellows had a hundred and ten gallons of grape brandy which he hoped to dispose of. There had been a good many barrels taken in and one party coming back that had taken some, met these people at our house and said he might as well ship it back as he could not sell it. The man got at Ed and Hadley, but they said "No, they would not sell liquor." But Monehan said he would sell it over there in their cabin and it would be no trouble to us. Finally, they consented and Monehan fixed up a bar and went to selling brandy. He did not sell long till he took a notion to leave and go to town, so he and Steinbrook went. Ed and Hadley had the liquor to sell out. The mail carriers and their escorts took possession of Steinbrook's cabin.

One day when the mail carrier came along, he had a great big soldier with him. They said he was a prize fighter, and I guess he was. He also had two or three others as a guard for the mail. For some reason he left the two at our place, this great big fellow and a smaller man. They were drinking some, especially the big fellow and he carried with him a great big dirk knife. They always got their meals at our house and this big man came in to get his supper and he flourished this awful knife until I think I was more afraid of him than I would have been of an Indian, but he did not harm any of us. The next day, they did not get up till the mail carrier came and the big fellow got up and gave the other a kick in the face and told him to get up. He did and went over to where they were saddling the fresh mail animals and asked for a gun, but no one paid any attention to him. He went back to the other cabin, got his own gun and the first thing we knew, we heard the shot of a gun, looking up to see that the small man had shot the big fellow and he was coming after him with his big knife.

The children were playing at the door and they came running in terribly frightened and said, "Ma, come quick, there is a fight out here." I looked and saw the small man hitting the big fellow over the head with the breech of his gun to keep the big man from stabbing him, at the same time backing up to where they were saddling the mule. They had gotten about half way when the big man began to reel and Ed jumped and caught him and laid him down. I never heard such vile language as this fellow used when he came to after fainting. They took him back into the cabin and I closed my doors and windows to shut out the cursing, but it seemed I could hear him curse with every breath. This continued until about six o'clock when he quieted down. He asked for pen and paper to make his will, but before they could get it for him, he was gone.

What an ending! How many times I was tempted to knock in the heads of these barrels and let out the miserable stuff on the ground, but I knew it was not Ed's or Hadley's fault. Our money was in it and we wanted to get it out, but we never got a new supply and when this was all gone, we were all glad. That was the first and only time my husband sold liquor.

Josiah Comes to Prescott, 1866; The Whitcombs Arrive Spring 1867
My brother and his family came to Prescott in the fall of 1866. About this time, we sold our place to Mr. Hadley, and took one joining on the upper side, building a better house and stockade. We made this of cedar posts twelve inches in diameter and set them four feet in the ground. By this time, it was a pretty good fort. There was lots of travel on the road and it became necessary for the government to send soldiers out to our place to protect the mail carriers and their horses, for the Indians were getting worse.

Father and Mother came out to live with us. I think it was in the spring of 1867, and the next fall Hadley was killed. We built a cabin across the road for the soldiers, and Ed built a pole corral to turn the cattle or horses in to get water. We had a ditch from a spring to the house and then led into the corral so the cattle and horses could get a drink without being exposed to the Indians. One night the stockade was full of horses. Mr. Hadley, after he bought us out, went away, being gone all winter, coming back with a wagon and two span of horses. He stopped at our place, intending to stay until he could get his stockade rebuilt. The Indians had tried to burn it down while he was at our place.

Ed had put the oxen in the corral and the Indians saw they were out there, so in the night an Indian came up from the bank of a dry branch of the river, so that the dogs could not scent him, because the wind was blowing the wrong way for the dogs. He got to one corner of the corral and got one pole down, when our big dog discovered him and chased him back across a piece of plowed ground. The next morning, we saw where the Indian had gone across the plowed ground at about fifteen feet at a jump, with this big dog at his heels. We had to laugh as we saw him in our imagination trying to get away.

Milton Hadley is Killed by Indians, 1867
After breakfast, Mr. Hadley said he guessed he would go down and see if the Indians had done him any more damage while he was gone. He had gotten him a rifle like the Winchester, but I have forgotten

In *History of Arizona*, Thomas Edwin Farish documents April 18, 1869 as the date of death for Milton S. Hadley at the hands of the Indians.

Lois's brother, Josiah Whitcomb, decided to join Lois and Ed in Arizona in 1866. He wrote to the family back home in Iowa and described his trip to Arizona and included news of his wife and new son.

"Plumber Creek, Col.
July the 22, 1866
Dear Brothers and Sisters, Affectionate Friends,

"I promised you in my last that I would give you the particulars in this. As I have already given them up to the time the baby was born. We will commence there. We started when the baby was two weeks old, Eliza was quite smart. It rained every day and twice on Sunday and the cars past each way every day, got to Shins Ferry was two days getting over, got in a good train of emigrants. Drove to Kearny through mud and ruff roads as bad as I ever saw here. We was obliged to organise, elect a captain and he was commissioned and had to report at every military post we past. We past Ofalons Bluff, there was a few Indians there.

"There had been a large band of them crost the road an hour or two ahead of us, probably five hundred or a thousand. Told some of their friends to be on their guard in twenty days. They were towards the Republican, we saw no more till we got to big sandy ridge. One day below Beaver Creek, thee we saw a few at a distance apparantly secreting themselves from us and watching. The hills was full of trains all day, the Indians was seen by different parties frequently all day. We fell in with a mule train all camped together a few miles above. The appearance of the Indians gave some uneasiness. We started in the morning at three o'clock. The Indians was seen in our camp ground about daylight by another train. Probably, they intended to stampeed our stalk at daylight or take us by surprise, if so they failed.

"It is thought there will be more trouble on the Platte this year than has been before. The ranch men are all fortified and preparing for war. The treaty with them at Laramie has been a falier. They was on their return from the place of treaty or counsil when they past us. They came out boldly and talked with the whites as the past and told them plainly that they had fought the whites for two years and they were good for ten years

more. They say they have never failed when they have made an attempt. It is too true we saw the remains of ranches and the remains of trains all the way acrost. They have had the Indians at Laramie for a long time trying to treet with them. The Indians proposed to treet as follows - if the whites would give up the smokey hill route they would not trouble the Platte route. Neither whites nor Indians would yealde. The Indians left in anger and I fear the consequence. They appear very bold and daring.

"We go on the Plumb Creek two weeks ago yesterday, I espect to stay here about another week. The mules are getting in very good order again. I will go to see Enos this week. We are stopping with Mr. Goodwin on the head of Plumb Creek.

"Edward, left your Goodwin note with L.M. Sprague, Denver, Colorado, care of H.L. Tityer. Mr. Goodwin told that he would be ready to pay it in a few days when I first got here but he has been disappointed in the sale of his place, now says he will be able to pay it the first of the winter. Wants you to write two or three weeks before hand if you go to Arizona this fall and he will get it for you some way. He is getting very well off.

"We are getting very well rested. We have got about 600 miles to go yet. Once about four weeks ago we thought the baby was dead. It did not breathe nor there was no pulse. Everyone thought it was gone. We started to make a coffin but it revived again and by the help of God it is alive and well and grows firmly and has got a name, Clarence. We have looked in the offices in different places along and have been disappointed for we have not heard from you since we left there. There is no game here on any account. No room for compliments, Josiah Whitcomb"

Josiah wrote a second letter to Iowa with news of Lois and the country. He was obviously becoming more worried about the Indian situation.

"Prescott, Arizona November 25, 1866
Brothers and Sister, Affectionate Friends

"With pleasure I take my pen to let you know that we are yet alive and well. We got here the 14 November. I would have written before but I had the misfortune to get my finger mashed so that I could not. We are at the mill where Father has been all the time. Ed lives at the Tollgate 45 miles from here. I have not yet seen Ed. Lois came here today.

"We have had a dreadful time a getting here on account of the wet weather and the Indians. It rained all most all of the time after we got to Colorado till we got to Los Pinos. The Indians have been troublesom all the way and I was obliged to travel alone or nearly so all through Colorado and New Mexico. I was in Colorado near two months waiting for company and to recruit but we had to go alone to Los Pinos. Here I waited for a government Expedition to return to California that went this way and we slipped threw with them. There was about 115 men strong. We find the Indians more troublesom in Arizona than any other place. I do not like the country as well as I thought I would. I am not sorry I came for I can make money here. The mines are good but the Indians are very ------ awfull troublesum, and I am afraid they will be for years. News coms in every day of men and even trains being taken in by them.

"I think there is a very little encouragemint for men to come here now to settle on farms. I see nothing that I like first-rate except the mines, that is the quarts, they are very ritch indeed. There is money here, miners get 75 to 100 dollars a month and board, and they call it dull times now. Father has laid up a good little pile. I do not know what I will follow yet for I have not looked around any yet. Father has 600 feet on one quarts lead that is very ritch. If we could get quarts crushed I would go to getting them out but there is but a few mills and they crush their own quarts. There lead here 4 to 6 feet wide that you could see the gold in allmost every piece. Mr. Courtice got a fair looking piece the other day that weighed one pound. We beat it up in a mortar and washed it out and got eight dollars from it, and there was lots as good as that. Water is scarce toward the placer mines. I have kept a regular list of the distances from Colorado here. The distance from Denver here is about 1,000 miles and a bad road. I will send you the distances from place to place as soon as I can copy with a full discription of the country.
This from your affectionate,
Brother Josiah Whitcomb"

the name, and that morning he took his gun and dog, for he had brought a dog, and started down to his ranch. The wind was blowing very hard down the valley towards his place. He had been gone two or three hours when his dog came back to the wagon and crawled in. We recognized the dog as soon as he came back and that he had been shot in the neck, the gun being so close to him that he was powder burned.

Ed went over and saw the dog and said, "Hadley is killed."

Two of the soldiers and Ed took their guns and started out to look for him. They did not dare go the road, so they went on the high tableland through the cedar and brush about thee hundred yards from our house and close to the road. Ed said, "Boys, let us go out where we can see the road here." They did and there lay Mr. Hadley in the road, dead and stripped of everything he had but a pair of canvas shoes.

They came back and made a coffin out of some lumber we had and buried him where they found him. I believe this was in the fall of 1867 instead of 1866. The wind was blowing down the valley or we would have heard the shots.

There were soldiers sent out several times to chase the Indians away but they would come back every few weeks so we had to be on our guard all the time.

One day Ed and I thought we would take a little walk and gather some juniper berries, so we went up in the hills not far from the house, when we struck a fresh bear track, and we thought we would try and get him. We had two of our dogs with us, one was a white dog and the other was a hunting dog. This hunting dog was good to track deer or antelope, but did not care to track a bear. We could follow the bear pretty well ourselves, and before we knew it, we were some miles from home. We came up on top of a ridge and was looking around to see if we could see the bear when Ed laid his eyes on an Indian going towards our house.

Pointing his finger, he said, "Look!" Our big white dog stood on a point in plain sight, and he understood what Ed meant when he said for me to look and he too saw the Indian. We spoke to him and told him not to bark and he did not, but he would not come down from that point. We looked a little, afterward, and we could see three more, so we squatted down and let them pass on. We were in good gunshot. We only had a muzzle loader and we were afraid they might crowd us. They had not seen us so we sat still till they passed on over the ridge. Then we took off down a ravine that led us out about a mile from home farther down the valley. When we started, I was so weak Ed had to pretty near carry me, but I did not get far till my strength came back and I could travel with him. I think, however, no one ever went over that ground any faster than we did. I never wanted to go out for a walk after that, not while we lived there. When I think back to those days, I get nervous.

We had bought a span of horses and Ed and my brother took the horses and their guns to go out to get some game, and as they were riding down the ravine, they rode within 50 yards of nine Indians. The Indians did not see them till they rode back about fifty yards when my brother's horse struck a rock and they heard it and jumped. Ed was watching them and as soon as he saw they had discovered them he shot at them and they ran up into the hills.

Ed said to Josiah, "Come, now is our chance. We must dash down through where they were sitting and on out to the open ground before they see there are only two of us or they will get close enough to reach us with their arrows." They did this and when they got through the narrow place on to the open ground, they stopped and the Indians shot at them, the bullets falling close to their feet. They returned the shots and came home.

Father put in a big crop of corn and Josiah concluded he would put in a crop too at our place, then go to his family. The corn, being on new ground, did not have to be hoed much because there were not many weeds. Then he would come back in the fall and harvest. In the spring, a man by the name of Nick Thede came out with two yoke of oxen and he and Ed put in a big crop of corn. This was in 1866. Once Ed, Nick and I went to Prescott forty miles away and drove across an Indian trail. There must have been one or two hundred of them and their tracks looked as fresh as ours. It seemed as though I could feel the hair raise on my head, but we got through all right.

When we came back, we had a big dog with us which we had gotten in town. While in town, we stopped at Pa's place at night as it was only one half mile from the main streets. When we went down to do our trading, I did a lot of calling and I noticed a big black dog everywhere I went, but never thought he was following me. It happened it was lodge night and Ed wanted to stay and go to lodge and he asked me if I was afraid to go out to Pa's alone. I told him no, as I would go early. I stayed a little later than I intended for it was growing dusk. I heard that Pa's neighbors had been up town a few days before and going home about this time in the evening, ran out four Indians from the brush close to the road. I felt rather queer about it, but I struck out as fast as I could walk and as I got close to this place where the dog had chased the Indians, I heard a sound like something running in the road.

I felt my hair raise and my heart began to thump and I looked around expecting to see an Indian ready to grab me, when to my surprise, it was the big black dog that I had seen so many times during the day. I nearly fainted at first, but I soon came to myself and said, "Why, doggie, did you come along to keep the Indians away from me?" The dog seemed very much pleased because I spoke to him and came up to me and put up his paw for me to take and make friends with him. He went on with me to the house and would let no one come near the house unless I called him off. When Ed came from lodge, I had to get up and go to the door before he could get in. We supposed the dog belonged to somebody, so Ed inquired of everyone if they knew to whom he belonged, but no one seemed to know about him, other than that they had seen him about town for a few days.

We were going home in a few days and did not want to take a dog that belonged to someone else, so we did not feed him for three days, thinking he would leave, but he did not. If we went to a neighbor's, he went too, and would stay at the door till I left. When I got in the wagon to return home, he took his place under the wagon and went with us. After we saw we could not get rid of him, we fed him, for he was too faithful an animal to go hungry.

We had to camp one night on the way home on a large prairie valley called Williamson Valley, about half-way between Prescott and where we lived, called Walnut Creek. We camped here, getting our suppers and then made our bed some distance from the fire, tying the oxen near where we slept. Mr. Thede made his bed so he had to pass near by to where we lay to get to his oxen in the morning. All night long the dog lay close to me, and when Mr. Thede went to pass our bed in the morning, the dog stopped him. This provoked Mr. Thede and he drew his revolver and was going to shoot the dog, but Ed grabbed his rifle and dared him to shoot a dog that would guard me like that. Mr. Thede stopped and said, "Yes, I was too hasty, pardon me." I said, "That is all right," and the dog came and laid down again, and the man loosened the oxen. I think if he had been an Indian, the dog would have torn him to pieces. Ed and Josiah had this dog out with them hunting when they ran on to the Indians in the ravine and had to run the horses down through where the Indians were when Ed first saw them.

It was in the spring of 1868 that my brother Josiah and Father put in the crop. Ed and Nick Thede raised a good crop and sold it at nine cents a pound. The Indians would come in at night and gather lots of it. We could hear them but did not dare to go after them. We had a Mexican working for us gathering corn.

One day, the Indians crept up to him and shot him; however, he managed to get to the house and we all thought he would die. The Mexican said he would bloat up about midnight and die before morning but he did not. He told the men not to send for the doctor as he would not live until the doctor could get there. This went on for three days and then we sent a soldier to the government post for a doctor. The doctor came with an ambulance and took him to the post and he got well, never the less. Ed said it would have killed a white man.

In the fall of 1868, if I remember correctly, my brother came out to our place with two span of horses and a wagon to gather his and Pa's crop of corn. We all picked the ears off, leaving the stalks in the field. They got it all gathered and hauled to the house and piled up in a pile between our house and the stockade, and Ed and Mr. Thede got ours all hauled. Then we had nothing to do but husk the corn, which took several weeks. The ground was very dry and there was no dew there and no rain at that time of the year and we were afraid of the Indians attempting to come between our house and the soldiers in the stockade. One day there came along a company of a hundred soldiers and officers going to Fort Whipple, close to Prescott. So my brother, Josiah, and Ed and another man by the name of King thought it would be a good time to go to Prescott.

So Josiah hitched up his teams and loaded his wagons with corn and hay till the bed was full. As it was his team, of course he drove. There was a camping place twelve miles from Prescott and they kept liquor there. The soldiers and Officers were drinking

Williamson Valley sat at the base of Granite Mountain. Located in the valley was the American Ranch, the stage stop for all traffic going to or from Hardyville and Ehrenberg. J.H. Lee owned property just north of Prescott and wasn't interested in purchasing more land. He changed his mind after meeting with Dan Conner over coffee at "Uncle Ed's place." Ed Boblett had the first restaurant in the plaza, built of pine saplings and roofed with burlap. It contained a fireplace and was furnished with tables and benches that Boblett made from pine logs. Kit Carson was also said to have been entertained there by the Bobletts for several days in 1868.

Conner was tired of the hardship and Indian problems and wanted to go to California, but needed a gun and ammunition for the trip. He talked Lee into riding the 10 miles out to the ranch. At first sight, Lee knew it was the place for him. Conner made Lee an offer, "I'll tell you what, I'll trade this place to you for your revolver." Lee agreed, but refused to turn the gun over until they had returned safely to town.

Lee built a small house on the ranch with one special feature, a tunnel accessed through a hole in the floor. His foresight paid off when torches were fired at the roof one night, setting the house ablaze. He simply entered the tunnel and escaped unharmed. By 1867, Lee had built a thriving business on the ranch. He had a two-story home that would accommodate paying guests, an open dining room, and a farm that provided enough food to supply Fort Whipple's needs as well as his own. Indians remained a problem and guards were posted around the ranch, and the men carried their weapons to the fields. In 1877, a new route to Ehrenberg opened and the ranch's glory days were over.

Williamson Valley entered into history with the legend of Mrs. Stephens. She and one old man were credited with holding off 50 attacking Apaches for six hours until a group of passing cowboys came to their rescue. One of the rescuers carried a message to her husband in Prescott,

"Dear Lewis: Apaches come. I am almost out of buckshot. Please send me some more. Your loving wife."

Mrs. Stephens' husband was a member of the legislature and away from home at the time. There are several versions of the story, with the number of Indians ranging from 50 to 20, but with the basic facts of the attack all agree. The particulars in the letter differ also with two other versions:

"A little more shot, Mr. Stephens," and "Lewis, the Indians are here; send me plenty of powder and lead. Don't neglect your duties by coming home, for I am master of the situation and can hold the house."

some and when it came time to hitch up, they seemed to make no move, so Josiah said, "Let us hitch up and go on, probably they will stay here all night and I am anxious to get home."

He had been at our place for a month and when he left home, his little boy had been real sick but was better. He had not had any word from his family so they agreed to go on. There was a discharged soldier who said he would go with them. He went on horseback and the others rode in the wagon, making four men in all and they thought they would be safe. They hitched up and started, the soldiers seeing them pull out, hitched up and followed after. Ed and Josiah got within four miles of Prescott where his family lived when they came to where the Indians had killed a man only a few weeks before.

Josiah is Killed by Indians, 1868

They were talking about this when Josiah said, "I have often wondered it was not me, when I hear of men being killed." Mr. King said he had often thought the same thing. Ed later remarked he never said a word, but it was not five minutes after this until Josiah was killed and Mr. King wounded. They would all have been killed had it not been for the dog I spoke of coming to me. As soon as the gun cracked, the dog jumped in the brush among the Indians and began snapping first one and another so they could not shoot, till Ed had time to shoot in return and grab Josiah by his belt as he was falling, also grabbing the lines, whipping the horses into a run.

The Indians ran after them for a quarter of a mile, then they would have come out on open ground. Ed never stopped to look around but kept whipping the horses to keep them on the run. King said he believed they would cut them off yet. Ed asked him if he had no shots but he said yes, but he could not hold up his gun as he had been shot. Ed asked him if he had a revolver. He had one and Ed began shooting at them and they stopped. It looked as though the Indians thought they had no more shot as they got Ed's gun. After shooting, Ed threw his gun on the wagon when he grabbed Josiah and the lines, for he knew Josiah was killed as he heard the breath go out of him.

It was only a short distance to a cabin where they stopped and let the team rest. In a few moments, the soldiers came on the run. They had heard the shooting and knew there was trouble and came as quickly as they could. They said the road was covered with arrows, this too with gun shots that had been fired. It was a hard thing to take Josiah home a corpse, but it had to be done. Ed tried to get a government ambulance and an escort to go out after us, but they would not take a chance, so we never knew anything about his death till after Ed came back, and all this taking place only forty miles away.

Then Ed came home with the same team and only two men with him over the same road. We had all been planning while Josiah was with us to get away from here and to somewhere from the Indians, as they were getting very bad. They were so bad Ed did not try to hunt anymore.

The morning before Josiah started to town, we were all talking and he said, "Mother, I wish we were all ready to start this morning, how glad I'd be." I never can forget the look as he said it and the evening before, we were husking corn and he looked up and said, "I wonder what will happen to me this time. I never see the moon over my left shoulder without some bad luck coming to me."

He seemed to know something terrible was just ahead for him. I can never forget how the dogs howled all night after he was killed. In my sleep that night, I was startled by someone trying to lay a corpse on my bed. I told it to Father and Mother in the morning and said I felt as though there was something wrong with Ed or Josiah. They said that surely could not be for there were over a hundred men that went with them. I told them, I can not help that, there certainly is trouble.

When I saw Ed coming with Josiah's team and he not there, I went out to meet him knowing just what happened, almost as well as though I had been told. Ed did not tell me until Pa and Ma had gone to the house to get ready for his coming. Ed then told me and suggested I tell them by degrees for he knew it

Josiah's death was described in an editorial printed in the *Miner* on October 31, 1868.

"Sunday last, about four o'clock in the afternoon, Josiah Whitcomb, William King, and Boblett were coming to Prescott from their ranches at the Toll Gate, and when near the Burnt Ranch about four miles from Prescott, fire was opened upon them from both sides of the road. Whitcomb was shot dead and King, while in the act of firing at the savages received a severe bullet wound in the left leg. Boblett, who rode on the seat alongside of Whitcomb, escaped without a scratch. A discharged soldier who rode behind the wagon also escaped. Upon being shot, Whitcomb, who was driving, dropped the reins, and would have fallen out of the wagon had Boblett not taken hold of him. Boblett then got hold of the reins and drove out of the trap as fast as possible. When the attack was made upon the party, a large body of new recruits were coming on behind them close enough to hear the firing, but not near enought to render assistance. Mr. Lee, of the American ranch, informed us that the ground in the vicinity of the place where the attack was made was literally covered with arrows. Mr. Lee was with the volunteers coming into Prescott.

"Mr. Whitcomb was buried in this place on Monday, resting in the Masonic burial ground. He leaves a wife and three small children, and an aged father and mother, all of whom reside in this vicinity."

Figure 9: Josiah Whitcomb, circa 1865. Photo courtesy of Marlayne Boblett.

Figure 10: Josiah Whitcomb's Tombstone. Josiah Whitcomb, Born: Lisbon, Grafton, New Hampshire 07 Sep 1832 Died: Burnt Ranch, near Prescott, Yavapai, Arizona Territory 25 Oct 1868, Buried: Masonic cemetery. Plot: AM/D060 Spouse: Eliza (Miller) Whitcomb, Parents: Aretas & Lydia (Priest) Whitcomb Occupation: rancher, Remarks: Civil War Vet. Co B 1st DAK Cav; (m) Sept. 16, 1855, Auburn, Ia; killed by Indians about 4 miles from Prescott while traveling from his ranch at the Tollgate. Photo courtesy of Judy Wight Branson, Prescott, AZ.

would be a terrible blow to them. Oh, how I hated to tell them, but when I went to the house, they too saw it in my face and Pa said, "Lois, Josiah is dead, I know it, I can see it in your face." I had to tell him, "Yes, he is buried." Pa then fainted and we got him on the bed and brought him to, only to see him a raving maniac for three days and nights. We had to watch him day and night. We would have gotten out immediately but we did not have enough money to go with, everything was so high, it costing so much to live, so we made up our minds we would have to stay until we could sell out, so we did.

The Bobletts Sell Their Arizona Ranch, 1869

Early in the spring of 1869, a lot of soldiers were sent out to build a fort on Mr. Hadley's place, just below ours. We then felt pretty safe. One day the officer sent a squad of men up the road in the canyon to get timber. About noon, we heard someone yelling at the top of his voice and we ran to the door to see one of the soldiers coming on a horse as fast as he could, yelling, "Indians!" and rode on past down to the post. Soon there was a squad of soldiers going back at a very fast gait. The Indians had surrounded the 18 soldiers and were shooting at them; the officer in charge ordered one to go for help and another volunteered to go with him. The one that was ordered to go for help was just a little ahead and as he came up to them, he was killed and his horse shot also. They were about eight or ten miles from camp, four miles from them were some citizens cutting clapboards. They saw the horse coming riderless and soon the other soldier came whose horse had been shot and taking the horse to him, he told them what had happened.

When the recruits came up to where they were, they followed them for several miles and one of them got sight of one Indian behind a tree. One went on either side of the tree and when the Indian stuck his head out, one of the men shot him. That was all they got of the Indians. The Indians had cut off the poor fellow's head that was killed and took it up on the side of the mountain out of reach of the soldiers' guns, but to where they could still see them. Sticking his head on a pole, they planted it in the ground and danced until the recruits go near enough to hear them yelling. The soldiers brought the body down and buried it headless. I did not go to the burial but Ed did and he said it was a terrible sight. We stayed there until the fall of 1869. The Indians did not bother anymore and we raised a big crop of corn and again sold it for nine cents a pound.

We also sold our ranch.

There were no schools or churches in Arizona when we went there and for several years afterwards. When we became responsible for Charles and Bell, I was very anxious for them to have a better chance than I ever had, so I wondered how I would manage it as I had left all my school books on the Rio Verde where we lost all our cattle. We took no papers and I thought of some little pie plates we had. They were tin and had the alphabet stamped on them, so I began teaching them their letters and when they started a Sunday School in Prescott, they sent me papers and I taught them to read and spell from these.

There were no other children to play with and as they were afraid to go out and play much, they gave good attention to their studies and made good progress. One day, they went out to the wagon close by to play and Bell had her doll with her. Some way, she dropped it on a rock, as they were plentiful, and broke it all to pieces. They both screamed and we thought the Indians were after them. Mr. Boblett grabbed his gun and I followed him expecting to see them being dragged away by the Indians. When we found out what the noise was about, we sat down and laughed and cried together.

Four sets of land records exist for Ed Boblett. On September 21, 1867, T. Snediker and E.A. Boblett sold their lot in Prescott to A. Henderson and W.P. Kelly for $600. The lot is described as being "Lot number one in block number thirteen, having fifty feet frontage on Granite Street, together with the building situated thereon, now occupied by said parties of the second part as a store. Together with all and singular the tenements …and appurtenances there unto belonging." Duly recorded in Book Three of Deeds Records Yavapai County, Arizona, Folios 764, 765, 766.

Ed and Nicholas Thede purchased 168 acres of land along Walnut Creek and adjoining the ranch of King and McCarthy, for the sum of $200. Recorded and filed on the 27th of January, 1868, in Book Three of Deeds Records of Yavapai County Arizona, Folios 861.4-862.

The next sale is recorded on August 28, 1869. E.A. Boblett and Aretas Whitcomb sold the property consisting of 168 acres on Walnut Creek for $300. The land is bounded on the East by the claim of Milton Hadley, deceased, and on the West by the claim of T.M. Alexander. It is recorded in Book Three of Deed Records Yavapai County, Arizona, Folios 1212, 1213.

The final land record is dated August 31, 1869. Ed Boblett sold to L.D. Kerokis and F. Manning, one half undivided interest in 160 acres of land on Walnut Creek and formerly owned by Ed and Nicholas Thede, bounded on the East by A. Steinbrook and on the west by Taylor and Walker. The sale price was $100 and is recorded in Book Three of Deeds Yavapai County, Arizona, Folios 1210, 1211.

Lois does not mention Mr. Steinbrook again, so perhaps he remained at the Tollgate station. His name does appear in a letter written in 1932 by William G. Shook, aged 92, who was reminiscing about the wild times around Walnut Creek and Camp Tollgate, but he doesn't give any dates:

"There was a herd law in those days, people had to herd or take care of their stock, or pay damages. A man named Thrasher owned a place on the northeast side of the creek and Andy Stenbrook had a place joining on the west. Thrashers horses got out of the corril and destroyed some of Stenbrook crop and Steinbrook corralled them for damages. Thrasher tracked them up and found them correled, and what transferred no one will ever know. A Dutchman working for Thrasher went to hunt Thrasher and found him in the correll. Steinbrook lay with two sixshuter bullets in him and. . . and Thrasher with an army model gunball through his bust."

Chapter 8
California
1869

*A*fter we sold our ranch, we went to Prescott and sold off and gave away our things and hired our passage with a government train to California. We started on the 8th of November 1869. I felt as though it could not be possible that we would get through without being attacked by the Indians, but we saw none save peacable ones along the journey. I remember we encountered a fearful sandstorm. We had to cook out on an open fire; we had two men besides Pa and Ed and, Oh, my! how everything was full of grit, but they all knew how the grit came and also how we could not keep it out. We had quite a desert to cross but I do not recall how long it took us to cross it. How glad we all felt when we got out to where people lived, then we knew we were safe from the Indians.

The first place we came to was a farm and there were several girls there from ten to eighteen years old; they were called the "wild girls" because they would always run and hide when anyone came. There I saw my first green figs. I do not remember how long we were getting to Wilmington where we took the steamer for San Francisco, but I remember getting to a wine ranch called Coco Mungo Ranch. I believe there were 360 acres in grapes and they made wine from these.

Lois's and Ed's party passed through Rancho Cucamonga at a turbulent time. The Rancho's history began on March 3, 1839, when the new governor of Mexico granted 13,000 acres of land around the area called Cucamonga to dedicated soldier, smuggler and politician, Tubercio Tapia, for services rendered. Tapia built a fortified house, raised great herds of cattle, and started a winery, all with Indian labor. The name Cucamonga comes from a Tongva place name, meaning either "sandy place" or "place of the villages where the waters come out." The area was removed from Mexico's sphere when it was annexed in 1848. California became a state in 1850.

The prosperous estate was purchased in 1858 from Tapia's daughter by John Rains and his wife, Maria Merced Williams de Rains. They paid $16,500 for the ranch. Rains began expanding the vineyards Tapia had planted and imported bricklayers from Ohio to construct the family home at the cost of $18,000. The landmark home was completed in 1860. It was a modern marvel. Its flat roof was waterproofed by tar from brea pits in Orange County. An open flume carried water from springs through the kitchen, into the patio, and under the house to the orchard, thereby cooling the structure. The home had an entry hall, parlor, three bedrooms, dining room, kitchen, a padre's room, and two guest rooms.

The couple moved with their three children into the house in 1861. On November 12, 1862, John and Maria Merced signed a mortgage for $16,000 on the house and a hotel. Five days later, John drove off in a wagon toward Los Angeles. En route, he was lassoed, shot, and dragged into the bushes near San Dimas. His body laid there for 11 days. He was 33 years old.

Robert Carlisle, John's brother-in-law, accused one Ramon Carrillo of the murder. Carrillo was tried and acquitted. On March 14, 1864, Carlisle obtained power of attorney which resulted in long and bitter legal battles. In May of that year, Ramon Carrillo was shot from ambush. Again the murder was never solved. In a twist, Maria Merced married Jose Carrillo, a relative of Ramon. In July 1865 Carlisle died from a gunshot wound suffered in a duel at the Bella Union Hotel. The argument was about Maria Merced's property. Maria Merced and Jose continued to live in Cucamonga,

They had a big vat and they had a lot of Indians and Mexicans tramping the grapes in the vat. The vat was alongside a well-traveled road and, as there was no fence there, the Indians being barefooted when taking a notion would jump out of the vat, run across the road and then back into the vat with whatever accumulation they had gotten while out of the vat. Previously to this, I had a notion wine was pretty good, but after what I saw, I never wanted any more.

They told us to go out into the vineyard and get all the grapes we wanted and we did. Ed was a little ahead of us and he picked a bunch and commenced to eat. As we came to him, he said, "Don't pick any more for I have picked a bunch and it is more than we all can eat." There were six of us and we were fruit hungry, however, we had all we could eat for two or three days. I believe the bunch would have filled a half bushel measure. I never saw anything like it. The whole vineyard was a sight to us. They didn't let the vines run, but pruned them off about five feet high, tree-like in shape.

Wilmington, California, and the Pacific Ocean, 1869
We finally went on to Wilmington and stayed all night. This was the first time any of us had see the ocean. We had seen many things

having four children of their own to add to her five Rains children. Her daughter, Fannie, who was born after Rains' death, married Henry T. Gage in 1880; Gage became governor of California in 1889.

When Lois visited, the Rancho's affairs were in disarray and it went into foreclosure and was finally sold in 1870. People continued to stream into the area via the Mojave wagon trail, the Butterfield Stage line and eventually the Union Pacific Railroad. The influx of people combined with fights over water rights brought an end to the Rancho days.

Wilmington, California, played an important part in the Civil War and was an early, busy port on the Pacific Coast. It began as the town of New San Pedro in 1858. Phineas Banning built a wharf at the foot of Canal Street and the town grew up around it. This was one of the first towns established in Los Angeles County after California became a state.

The Civil War brought prosperity to New San Pedro. A telegraph line was routed through the city of Los Angeles to the rest of the county to maintain communications for the Army. It had taken 10 days for the news of Fort Sumter's surrender to reach California, via a combination of telegraph and Pony Express. The U.S. Army spent $1 million to build the Drum Barracks, Quartermaster's Headquarters, and Depot near Banning's Landing. The buildings were fabricated on the East Coast and shipped around the Horn. This important post supplied horses, mules, camels, arms and equipment for soldiers at 215 army forts and outposts in the territories of Arizona and New Mexico.

The California Volunteers fought in Arizona and New Mexico against the Confederate forces and the Indians. They were responsible for holding California for the Union and keeping gold flowing into Washington, D.C. The soldiers and supplies that traveled through Lois's and Ed's Tollgate came from this depot.

When General Carleton readied his men to march from Drum Barracks into action, he gave them orders that included the supplies they were to carry: Each was to wear the "uniform hat without trimmings," a blouse, trousers, stockings, woolen shirt, drawers, a "cravat in lieu of the leather stock," and a good sheath knife. His knapsack was to contain a greatcoat, blanket, forage cap, woolen shirt, pair of drawers, pair of stockings, towel, two handkerchiefs, a fine and a course comb, sewing kit, a piece of soap, a toothbrush, one fork, spoon and plate, a tin cup and a canteen."

His instructions for the proper care of the troop's horses were equally precise:

now on our trip that was new to us. We had seen cactus 30 or more feet high, pepper trees 40 feet and the lemon trees which we had never seen before. But to us, the ocean was the grandest sight.

The next morning, there was a fearful wind and the waves were very high. The ocean steamers did not come into the wharf but stopped outside some three miles. The wind calmed down so there were no white caps about the time we had to go out to the steamer.

We went on a ferry boat and then climbed aboard the steamer just as the bell rang for dinner. I said all the time I knew I would not get sick, but when the bell rang for dinner, we were all hungry and went to the table with the others. I gave my order for what I wanted as the steamer started but never saw it as I went to my stateroom and got into bed and stayed there for three days and nights, never tasting a mouthful of anything, not even water. Just as we were getting into San Francisco, the stewardess came to my stateroom and asked me if I had eaten anything. I told her, "No, the very thought of eating made me sick." She said I would have to eat something or they would have to carry me off the boat. Finally, I told her to bring me a cup of tea with no sugar in it and she did, together with a nice slice of toast. As soon as I took a little of the tea, I got all right and then ate the toast.

Ed did not get sick at all. He would come down and tell me the sights he saw and wanted me to get up and go on the deck and see too, but I could not move and I felt as though I would be glad if the boat would go down so I could get out of my misery, I felt so sick. Ed came down one time and said I just must get out and see the coal-oil on the water as we were passing an oil spring and it was the most beautiful sight he had ever witnessed, so he dragged me out of bed, but he was glad to put me back again, for I was as limp as a rag, I could not even raise my hand to my head.

Well, after getting the tea and toast, I got up and washed and dressed and combed my hair and was ready to go ashore. I might have gotten out to see what was to be seen, but nearly all the passengers were sick and the stewardess was kept busy. Those terrible big swells together with the smell of fresh paint, as the boat had been recently painted, was more than I could stand. For several years after that, I could not stand the smell of fresh paint without getting sick.

Chapter 9
Washington Territory
1869-1879

We had to pay just the same for the children on the boat as for ourselves; I think it was $35 apiece. We had to pay the same at the hotel in San Francisco, $3.60 a day each and we had to stay there a week before we could get passage to Seattle, as that was the place we all had talked about too, before my brother was killed. There was a steamer only once a month and it had sailed out the day before we had gotten to Frisco. There was a sailboat called the *Jebnie Pitts* and the captain's name was White, whose boat was to sail in a week. We took passage on it along with seven other families. We all went below where our baggage would be handy. There were a lot of trunks and boxes down there and the captain had the sailors put them on each side of the boat and nail cleats in front of them to make them secure. We used them for seats. They rigged a long table in one end of the boat and our bunks in the other end. The cook would bring our meals down to us and pile it there and everyone helped himself. Of course, in a number like that, you could expect to find some who were inconsiderate of others and often times the one who practiced manners went without.

There was a tremendous safe down there too. We sailed along nicely for a few days, when the sea became a dead calm. There was not enough wind to fill a sail for nearly two weeks. The captain said we had drifted nearly to China. Of course, we could see nothing but water. Finally, we struck a light breeze and they set sails for the Straits. When we got near enough to land again, there were sea gulls, whales and sharks aplenty and the wind died again. We had to stay there and be patient. I do not remember how long this continued, but I know we got awfully tired of boat life.

One day Ed said to the captain, "I have often heard of a storm at sea and I would like to see one." The captain said, "Well, I think you will get your wish before we get to Cape Flattery." He could see it coming and he had the sailors down lashing the big safe. They had it lashed so tight I thought it would never move, but they tied it over and over again and we wondered why they were doing so. We asked the captain and he said, "There is a storm coming and if that safe should break loose, nothing could save the boat, but if I can make that secure, we will be safe in a short time."

By this time, we had gotten so near Cape Flattery we could see the lighthouse. I began to hope we would get in before the storm would get to us, but it was an idle hope, for it was not long before we knew we were in a gale. The first high wind tore the main-sail in two and burst all the cleats that were nailed to keep the trunks in place. We had our big dog with us and the poor fellow had to run and jump and climb to keep out of the way of the trunks. Some of them were very large and, being on casters, would go across the deck like a train of cars. Finally, Ed came down to see how things were and he got hold of the dog and pulled him back to our bunks. He was so tired he lay down and did not stir until morning.

Sometimes the waves would strike the boat and one would think the boat had struck a rock. It creaked

Cape Flattery is the farthest northwest point of the contiguous United States and is situated where the Strait of Juan de Fuca empties into the Pacific Ocean. The lighthouse sits on Tatoosh Island.

Nothing involved with the Cape Flattery Lighthouse was simple. Captain James Cook named the place Cape Flattery in March of 1778. An opening along the coast had fooled Captain Cook into thinking he had found a harbor or passage. His notebook reads,

"In this very latitude geographers have place the pretended Strait of Juan de Fuca. But nothing of that kind presented itself to our view, nor is it probable that any such thing every existed." Captain Cook also noted the terrain of "beetling cliffs, ragged reefs, and huge masses of rock cut by the waves abound on every side."

When Lieutenant Trowbridge arrived in 1855 to make tidal observations in the vicinity of the Straits of Juan de Fuca, he found the natives hostile. They attempted to sell poisoned provisions to the ship's procurer and tried to gain possession of the schooner to stop the survey.

Early surveys concluded that the point deserved a lighthouse to protect shipping. The 12-mile-wide Strait of Juan de Fuca is the entryway to the usually calm waters of Puget Sound. The weather in the Strait is a different story. Often dense fog, strong currents, and treacherous tides make for hazardous conditions. Disabled or unwary ships can be carried as far north as Vancouver Island by the strong currents and rip-tides.

Gales blowing in from the Pacific can bring winds above 100 miles per hour. The lighthouse is situated on the highest point of the island, 90 yards from its western point, 25 yards from the cliffs, and 97 feet above the sea, and stands 65 feet tall. Storms frequently drive spray high enough above the cliffs to coat the windows with salt.

The U.S. set aside $39,000 to build the lighthouse, with $30,000 of that sum to purchase the island from the Makah tribe in 1855. The construction crew's reception on the island was less than welcoming. An 1853 smallpox epidemic had killed several hundred members of the tribe and the "Bostons" were blamed. The Indians continued to use the island for their summer fishing and whaling. Tensions remained so high the crew constructed a blockhouse for protection and posted around the clock guards. Fortunately, the only casualties were some lost tools and supplies. The lighthouse went into operation on December 28, 1857, with a light that could be seen 20 miles out at sea.

Eventually, the Indians worked for the lighthouse keepers, transporting people, supplies and mail to the island. The Makah were not only extremely skilled mariners in their canoes, they were also fearless. One Makah, who went by the name of Old Doctor, lost three dugouts on the rocks while trying to deliver supplies. Supposedly, a piano and a cow were delivered by the Makah. The going rate was $1 per trip in calm weather and doubled in stormy weather. The island is named for a Makah Chief.

Life on such an isolated site was difficult and lonely and tempers sometimes flared. One of the first keepers, Francis James, became enraged at an assistant and splashed hot coffee in his face. This called for a duel! The two men met in the yard and took three shots at each other before declaring it a draw and shaking hands. Another assistant keeper had wisely removed the bullets from the shells.

Figure 11: The Lighthouse at Tatoosh Island with Cape Flattery and the Entrance to the Strait of Juan de Fuca (seen in the right center). *Pacific Coast. Coast Pilot of California, Oregon, and Washington Territory*, by George Davidson, 1869, p 179.

and cracked as though it were being broken up into kindling wood. The Captain came down several times to see how the safe was. We were being driven back to sea and, for three or four days, went back as fast as the wind could carry us. I went up on deck once to see how it looked. I was not a bit sick this time.

When I got to where I could see, it looked like huge snow-capped mountains. There was another vessel loaded with lumber on its way to Frisco. They were so close it seemed as though we might talk with the other crew and then we would go out of sight, one or the other, so we could not even see their masts, so heavy was the sea. The other vessel was heavily loaded between decks and we had a deck load of lumber, too, but it was all swept away in the storm, together with the railing.

The third evening, the wind calmed down and the Captain turned for the Cape again and we were not long getting there. My, how good the timber looked to me! I sat out all the time looking at it. We had been on the water for so long even the rocks had an inviting appearance. We were just three weeks coming from Frisco, landing at Yesler Wharf at Seattle. This was some time in the latter part of October or the first of November and everything was as green as at spring time. Ed and Pa rented a house and we moved into it.

Seattle – Roses in Winter, January 1870
The house was close to old Dr. Maynard's. He was an old settler and had lots of roses and several fruit trees and, on the fifteenth of January 1870, he picked his winter apples. Up to this time there had been no frost. There were some raspberries in bloom in the south window in our house and this bloom brought berries that got ripe, the children picking and eating them. There was some corn just coming in silk and the ears filled out nicely. There were some tomato vines as green as mid-summer, but they had no fruit on them.

On the morning of January 16, there had fallen about a half inch of snow and the Doctor's roses of different colors sticking up through the snow presented a very striking appearance. We had supposed we were coming to a very cold climate, it being so far north, but we were happily surprised.

That winter, Ed and a man by the name of Richards worked out all winter in their shirt sleeves. We had very little rain, the snow going quite as quickly as it came and it was not long before the roses were fresh and green.

> Lois didn't explain the relationship, but the Richards who traveled from Prescott to Seattle with them were, in fact, Richard Richards and his wife, Eliza, Josiah Whitcomb's widow. The Richards were married prior to leaving Prescott.

On the morning of March 4, 1870, there was about eight or ten inches of snow. It turned cold and the ponds froze so the boys skated for a week. We had about ten bushels of potatoes just outside the door in a dry goods box with some boards for a covering, but we lost only about a peck.

Ed and Mr. Richards bought some lots on the hill back of Yesler orchard and put up a two-story house, dividing it in the middle above and below so it would accomodate our two families. We were living there at the time of the cold snap. This was in the spring of 1870. Ed and Mr. Richards hunted about to take up a piece of land. They went up on what was called the Cedar River to see what they could find there and, as they were walking along, Ed picked up a chunk of coal and showed it to Dick, as we called Mr.

continued on page 88

Upon their arrival in Seattle, Lois and Ed met two of the most interesting pioneers in Washington Territory, Henry Yesler and David "Doc" Maynard.

Henry Yesler was born out of wedlock in Maryland in 1810 and receiving little attention from either parent, he was on his own from an early age. He didn't let a lack of formal education interfere with his ability to make a dollar. He worked as an apprentice, learning carpentry and millwork skills, then spent the next 20 years learning sawmill operations.

He married Sarah Burgert in Ohio and became the father of a son, but money, or the lack of it, was a continual problem. Finally, leaving her and his creditors behind, he headed for California and the gold fields. Like most prospectors, he quickly decided he would have to find another way to make a living. He was employed at a saw mill in Portland, Oregon, when he decided to build a saw mill in the Puget Sound area with his partner, John Stroble.

When he sailed into the harbor in 1852, he saw the trees running down to the shore and knew this was where he wanted to build the first steam-powered mill in the area. Yesler built his wharf to load the lumber onto ships headed to California. He also built a cook house that became the venue for traveling road shows, concerts and Seattle's first professional play, Harriet Beecher Stowe's "Uncle Tom's Cabin."

He became Seattle's first millionaire, but not without help from a silent partner. John E. McLain put up $30,000, at 8% interest, to get Yesler's mill up and running. Being more interested in making money than spending it, Yesler put off repaying the loan until McLain hauled him into court in the 1860s. Yesler was ordered to pay the remaining $18,000 due on the loan.

The saw mill wasn't his main source of income; he made most of his money in real estate. He bragged that the cook house alone brought him $60 a month in rentals. He was trusted by the Indians, whom he employed in his mill, and as an Indian agent visited their camps to propose peace terms, most of which were accepted. Of course, it was to his benefit to keep the peace because he didn't want to lose good workers. During the troubles of 1856, he was given advance warning of planned Indian raids on Seattle. He was one of the few who defended the Chinese immigrants when the Chinese were forcibly expelled during the labor riots in February 1886. Still, he took care of his money and was often in court suing someone or being sued. He preferred not to pay his bills until absolutely necessary.

Henry and Sarah Yesler were unusual people for their times. They believed in astrology and spiritualism, perhaps because of the loss of their son. When Sarah finally joined Henry in Seattle, she left their 12-year-old son with family in Ohio, planning to bring him out when she was settled. The boy fell ill and died in 1859. Another son had died young.

Sarah was in for a surprise when she arrived in town. She discovered that Henry had fathered a daughter, Julia Benson Intermela, by a Native American mistress. The girl was then three years old. Sarah eventually took Julia into her home. Sarah calmly took her place in society and became a leader in charitable and civic projects, including the first public library. She was also a strong proponent of women suffrage and "free love," having a passionate relationship with at least one woman. Even so, she and Henry had a strong, loving marriage.

After Sarah died, Henry went into a decline. The year he turned 80, he surprised the town by marrying a cousin, 24-year-old Minnie Gagle. After his death two years later, rumors persisted that his widow and doctor had destroyed his will and perhaps even hastened his death. Considering how fond Yesler was of "taking it to court," it seems appropriate that the battle for his estate ended up in the courts and lasted 10 years.

Old Doc Maynard was another fascinating character in those early days in Seattle. Money back home had been hard to come by, and his wife was tired of doing without. David "Doc" Maynard sold whatever he could, gave the money to his wife, Lydia, and headed West, broke and alone. He hired onto a wagon train and hoped to make his fortune in the California gold fields. He found more than he expected on the trip.

Seattle historian, James R. Warren, quotes Maynard's June 7, 1850, journal entry from the westward trek:

"Find plenty of doctoring to do. Stopped at noon to attend persons sick with cholera. One was dead before I got there, and two died before the next morning. They paid me $8.75.

"Deceased were named Israel Broshears and William Broshears and Mrs. Morton, the last being mother of the bereaved widow of Israel Broshears. We are 85 miles west of Fort Kearney (Neb.)"

Israel's widow was left in dire straits. Catherine Broshears was ill and unable to drive her wagon or care for her oxen. Since the train had to keep moving, Doc rode his horse back and forth to her wagon, helping as much as he could. He decided the best thing to do was to see her to her brother's home in Tumwater, near Olympia, Washington Territory.

Her brother, Mike Simmons, led a group of seven families to Budd Inlet in 1845 after being ordered not to by the British. They were the first Americans to settle north of the Columbia River. One man in the party was George W. Bush, the first African-American man to settle in the Territory and for whom Bush Prairie is named.

Simmons proceeded to build a flour mill and saw mill. He was on his way to making his fortune in this new thriving community. Lee Terry, John Low, and Arthur Denny visited and decided that they could do what Mike had done and headed north to found their own town near the tiny village of Duwamps that had been settled by three families, including the Mapels.

Simmons might have had plenty of money, but Doc was still destitute when he arrived in Tumwater. Needing money to continue on to California, he split 400 cords of wood and accompanied it to San Francisco. Once in California, however, he decided he missed the Widow Broshears.

The idea of a grocery store in Olympia appealed to him, so he used his proceeds from the sale of the wood to purchase merchandise and headed back to Olympia. Unfortunately, he had no head for business, being too generous with credit and too low with his prices. He also developed a reputation as a man who liked his drink. When he was under the influence, he gave away his merchandise. The other merchants invited him to leave town, which he did, at the urgings of his good friend, Chief Seattle (or Sealth). They traveled by canoe to the village of Duwamps.

The new plan was to fish for salmon, salt it down, and ship it to California. He soon shipped 1,000 kegs of salted salmon to San Francisco, but as usual, his luck didn't hold and most of the fish spoiled. Apparently, too little salt was used in the process. Trying to recoup his losses, he turned to shipping pilings and shingles to San Francisco. When Yesler opened his mill, Maynard provided the first logs.

Maynard took time to get permission from the authorities to divorce his first wife so he could marry Catherine. Maynard declared,

"It was good, after the weeks on the trail, to relax in a house with windproof walls, to listen to rain on the cedar shakes . . . to eat white bread and fresh vegetables [and] to talk to Catherine Broshears, who was beautiful or even to her sister-in-law Elizabeth Simmons, who was not."

Through his friendship with Chief Seattle, Maynard became a friend of the natives, who called him their medicine man. He was able to persuade the local Indians to remain neutral during the uprisings in 1862. Governor Stevens appointed him Indian Agent.

Always a doctor at heart, Doc opened a hospital with his wife serving as nurse. Theirs was happy marriage, even surviving his first wife's unexpected arrival. Lydia wasn't aware that a divorce had been granted. Without any fuss, she moved into the Maynard home and remained there until the courts decided which one of the women was his legal wife. In the meantime, Maynard would be seen walking along the streets with a wife on each arm.

Doc was a romantic. When a couple came to him pleading to be married, he discovered that the bride was only 13. He was so impressed by their determination to wed, though, that he devised a plan. He wrote the number "18" on two pieces of paper and had the girl put them in the bottom of her shoes. He then escorted them to the Reverend Daniel Bagley and swore that the girl was "over 18." The marriage proved to be a long, happy one.

Nothing ever worked out perfectly for Doc. He was pleased when the courts decided that Catherine was his true wife, but since he had taken half of his land claims in Lydia's name, he now had no claim to them and the government took them back. This turned him into a pauper again.

It was Doc Maynard who suggested the name of the town should be changed from Duwamps to Seattle in honor of his friend. Fearing that the use of his name would bring unrest to his spirit, Chief Seattle wasn't pleased with the suggestion, but the name was adopted by the citizens.

Richards, and told him, "Now we must hunt that out." They did and located it but they fooled along with it all summer only to get discouraged as they could not get help to promote it, neither was the land surveyed. They then decided to hunt for a place where they could make a home when they met a man by the name of McCalester making brick; he asked them what they were going to do with their [coal] mines.

There was indeed a John S. McCallister in Seattle in 1870, whose occupation was listed as a brickmaker with a net worth of $400. He was listed as a brickmaker in the 1880 census and as a farmer in the 1889 Washington census. By 1879 half of Washington's coal production was from King County mines in the Cedar River drainage. Seattle had become the major West Coast coal port.

They said they were going to throw it up, so he asked them to give it to him. They did and in less than two years he leased it for ninety-nine years for forty thousand dollars.

We had gotten a letter from my sister and her husband living in Dakota and we told them of the roses being in full bloom in the middle of January. They said they were coming to where the roses bloomed in winter. We picked some and sent them and, at that time, their potatoes were frozen solid in their cellar. Father and Mother had gone up the Duwamish River on Mr. Sam Mapel's place. They were only about three miles from Seattle. Ed, Richards and a man by the name of Stanley went to work to build a boat to hunt with. They had heard of land up near the British line [Canadian Border] that was level and as there were no boats making the trip, they had to build one.

When my sister and her husband, Amos Dexter, came, they went out to Pa's as Amos was no carpenter and he could not help with the boat. When they came, Ed and I went down to the wharf to meet them. The boat came alongside of the wharf and they threw a rope on the dock and a man fastened it. Then the boat started off. I thought they would pull down the wharf. They called for someone to cut the rope and a man rushed up to do so when the cable broke, striking him in the leg and breaking it in two places. This all happened within ten feet of where I was standing. Finally, they landed after fooling around for an hour or two. We were certainly glad to see each other after the five years we spent in Arizona, going through what we did and coming here and finding it so pleasant.

I had planted potatoes in my yard and, on the Fourth of July, I had new potatoes as large as my fist. They were the Peach Bloom variety. No wonder we were in love with this country.

The men finished their boat and went down to the British line and there they found what they wanted. Dexter wanted to buy Government land and there was a tract of land that he could buy at the Government price and good land, too, but it was three miles from where Ed wanted to take up a homestead. So, they each took a claim and came back to Seattle. Ed and Richards sold our house and lots and we all joined together. Dexter, Richards and Ed chartered a steamer called the *John Libby*. There was no wharf to land on at the east side of Semiahmoo, so they landed us on the spit, as we had several cows and the deep water came pretty close to shore. They had to push the cows overboard and they had to swim to shore. We got down in a small boat and were taken ashore that way. When we got our stuff all ashore, there was an old house that we all went into till we could get our own places located and were ready to go into them.

It was beautiful weather and Mrs. Richards, my sister and I went for a walk and we picked a big bouquet of wild roses and wild strawberries in October. We thought surely we were in a new world. There was an old board shanty on the east side of the bay, so as soon as we could, we moved across, but we all had to work together, for we all put up log houses. We lived together until Dexter and Richards got their cabins up and moved, for we all had to use the one boat that Ed and Mr. Richards made when they first came down to look at the country. Afterwards, we also moved.

Blaine, Washington, 1870
Shortly after this, a Mr. William Smith, a man who came with us from Arizona and another man by the name of Crampton, came with an Indian canoe and located what is now the original town site of Blaine. Crampton did not seem to like it here very well. Soon after, another family came by the name of Hoisington and they moved in with us in the shanty and everybody worked together till we all got cabins and moved. I was very much pleased to have another family on our side of the bay and they were real nice people, too.

The next spring in February 1871, my father and mother and the Kingsleys came and settled where their son Byron now lives. Upsons came at the same time. A man by the name of Clark had come down with a schooner peddling dry goods several times and finally located on the spit and started a grocery and dry goods store. We were glad as we had been going to Whatcom, as it was then called but later changed to Bellingham, some twenty-five miles away. We had gone several times, as this was our nearest post office and store. I well remember having to lay on the beach three days, it was so rough, a hard wind was blowing, before we could take the boat. I believed it was in '71 that the Hughes family and Dave Miller came.

From this on I cannot remember, for they came pretty fast for a time. In 1871, a Methodist minister by the name of Mr. N.J. Luark was sent here to preach and he organized the first church. Not long after that, I joined the church. Soon after, my husband and two children joined and quite a number more.

There was a splendid feeling among the people. About this time, the Cains came and bought out Mr. Crampton. Mr. Smith made his home with us and he used to hunt a good deal for the meat that we required for the table use.

continued on page 93

The town of Blaine would grow up around the Bobletts, but they couldn't have imagined that when they stepped ashore. The first settler in the area was a man named Shaw, who came in 1857 with his Indian wife, built a house, and started building a wharf. Soon, about 100 U.S. soldiers arrived with orders to work on the U.S.-Canadian boundary lines. Shaw made a fatal mistake. He thought he could make money selling liquor to the rough soldiers. Looking for more liquor one day, the soldiers went to Shaw's house and, finding Shaw was away from home, assaulted his wife. Incensed, Shaw grabbed his gun and headed to the camp to find justice. He shot at the first soldier he saw, Sergeant Langley, wounding him in the hand. Langley shot and killed Shaw before he could reload.

This wasn't the last incident involving the soldiers. One was shot while trying to desert and one was drowned. Campbell Creek was named after another soldier who deserted, then was captured by the Indians. He eventually died when he was thrown from his horse while intoxicated. Two men died when a tree fell across their tent, although 16 others escaped injury. The men were buried in a spot nearby.

Smuggling seems to have been the main industry in the area. American soldiers smuggled liquor into Canada, and the British supplied beef and other commodities. The king of the smugglers was Judge Bramford, superintendent of the Hudson Bay Company's farm on the Fraser. He killed most of the company's cattle, storing 400 barrels of the beef sunk in the mouth of Campbell Creek. He was also accused of swindling the Bank of British Columbia out of $10,000 before disappearing.

For a short time in 1858, the Fraser River had its own mining excitement. The Indians had a well-traveled trail from the mouth of Campbell Creek up to the upper Fraser country. White miners improved the trail by building bridges and clearing logs. Named Langley Trail, it was the route hundreds of miners took to Semiahmoo Bay where they hired Indians to take them in canoes further up the sound or to Victoria.

A Mr. Hall settled on Hall's Prairie in early 1858. Joe Little tried to jump his claim, but Hall would have none of that. He attacked Little with his gun and broke his arm. Little fled and rumor had it that some years later he went to prison for killing his wife.

The soldiers remained in the area through 1859. From 1857 to 1861, astronomers on both sides of the border used star readings to plot the 49th parallel. In 1859, the Americans cut the first 10 miles, the Canadian the next 10, and so on until the border was marked. The line was cleared 30 feet in width through the woods, and iron posts were set every 200 feet, mile, or two miles depending on ground conditions. The posts bore the legend: "Treaty of Washington, June 15th, 1849." After the boundary was marked, the soldiers moved away and quiet descended upon the land. There was no commerce and ships no longer dropped anchor in the harbor.

The first permanent settlers were the Bobletts, Dexters, Whitcombs, James Brookins, J. and L. Chestnut, D.S. Miller, Z. Jones, H. Stoltenberg, J.F. Tarte, J. McBee. The Bobletts arrived on the *J.B. Libby*, the first steamer to run into the harbor. There were no roads; all communication between neighbors was by skiffs or on foot over trails among the logs and brush. It would take a man all day to travel 10 miles through the woods. Several hundred Indians lived on the Campbell River reserve. Their long house was used for potlatches and feasts, and the settlers often joined in the celebrations. Within 30 years, the number of Indians had dwindled to 40 or 50.

For the next 10 years, Semiahmoo was the headquarters for business, the people traveling in boats for their mail and provisions. Blaine was platted in 1884 and received a post office in 1885. Ed became a real-estate investor, going into business with Frank Robertson as builders. Ed took a prominent role in the new town. He was elected to the town council, school board, and board of trustees to take charge of the public cemetery.

While Lois and her family lived in Blaine, other family members either visited them or moved to be near them. Ed and Lois's sisters eventually moved to the Blaine area. Michael Rosbrugh, Ed's brother-in-law, arrived.

The Free Methodists held camp meetings at their home. In September 1888, the U.S. Survey Steamer *Fuca* invited several citizens on a cruise across the bay to Port Roberts. Lois was one of the women who enjoyed the cruise, while Ed was busy surveying the streams east of Blaine, hoping to find enough clean water to furnish the city.

Ed and Lois donated lots in March 1889 for the building of a new Episcopal Church. One section of town became known as Boblett's addition. An editorial in the *Blaine Journal* warned that

"Blaine should take warning from Whatcom and Sehome. Those places are losing population which might stop and settle there just because there are no houses for them to move into. Not less than 50 families today are living in tents around Bellingham Bay, and as many more are existing in shanties built of shakes or small logs. We hope to see a number of small houses for rent put up at once in Blaine, so we can take care of the increase of population which is sure to come in."

Local newspapers recorded the daily life of the people in the new towns all over the country, and were often among the first businesses in town. Life in a small town was seldom boring, as a search through the *Blaine Journal* shows. News about the Otto family from Wisconsin appeared in the June 27, 1889, issue. While the family was passing through Montana on the train,

"two of their children, the older a boy of nine and the other some younger got off the cars to pick flowers. When the train started the children ran to catch it, and the older one succeeded, but the younger only caught hold of the car to be thrown down and cut very badly in two places, and knocked senseless. The train had left the unfortunate little fellow 90 miles behind before the family found out about the accident, and then they could get no word about him by telegraph. The little fellow lay beside the track a long time before he was found, but at last a cowboy came along and lifting the child's limp form to his saddle took him carefully to the farm of a rich cattle man. A doctor was sent for 20 miles away and everything done to make the wounded comfortable. The family came on to Seattle and rented rooms, while the father went back for the lost one. He found the child doing nicely and the cattle man wanted to adopt him as his own child, but little Julius could not be spared by his parents, and so came on to Seattle. When the fire came the Otto family was among the sufferers, losing everything they had in the house but the clothing they wore and some goods at the docks; among other things lost were several chests of valuable tools with which Mr. Otto worked at his trade. Then they came on to Blaine, and are now living about three miles east of here on the township line road, while Mr. Otto gets a large slashing burned off his place just over the line in British Columbia. They have had a pretty warm reception to Washington territory, but we hope fortune will smile so favorable on them hereafter that they will not be sorry they came."

Also printed in the *Blaine Journal* in March 1889 was this story of love thwarted:

"Last Thursday night there arrived in Blaine from the south a middle aged man accompanied by a handsome girl of 18 summers. They came in a buggy, and seemed in haste to get across the boundary line, which they did, leaving their buggy there and taking the stage the next morning for Westminster. Next day Deputy Sheriff Brown from Whatcom came along looking for H.W. Hart and Nellie Gallagher of Bellingham Bay who he said had eloped together. The couple registered at the hotel as uncle and niece, and Hart said he was going over to Westminster to place the young lady in the sister's academy there. However, they were arrested there and held until Hart's wife and Miss Gallagher's parents arrived, the first of this week, when they made some sort of an agreement by which the girl returned home with her parents and Mrs. Hart brought back her husband. Hart is a Whatcom saloonkeeper, and Nellie Gallagher has been acting as house-keeper for him while his wife was away on a visit east. The parties passed through Blaine on their way home on Tuesday, taking the steamer *Brick*."

Although Indians and wars were no longer a threat, life still held its share of challenges and dangers as an article in August, 1886 showed:

"On Tuesday evening last Miss Laura Lindsay, of Hillsdale, placed a lamp on a shelf in her room, and while reclining on her bed studying, the lamp exploded, the force of the explosion going upward and tearing ahole through the ceiling and roof of the house. The young lady was stunned by the shock, but as nothing caught fire no serious damage was done."

A September 1889 article pointed out the dangers faced by early construction workers:

"Charles Anderson, a native of Scotland, 65 years of age, was killed on the Bellingham Bay Water Co.'s right of way Wednesday. In excavating to lay pipe a blast of sandstone rock was made, and Anderson, who was at work a quarter of a mile away was struck in the forehead by a piece of rock. Money and securities to the amount of $120 were found on his person. He is supposed to have been a single man. Dr. Bragg did not think an inquest necessary as the death was clearly accidental. He was killed and buried within three hours."

Disaster struck a local coal mine in 1895:

"An explosion from supposed fire damp occurred at the Blue Canyon coal mine near Whatcom at 3 o'clock last Monday. Twenty-four men were employed in the mine and all but one perished. This in point of fatality is one of the largest accidents which has ever befallen our county. The list of dead include the superintendent, D.Y. Jones, and the following miners; James Kirby, Andrew Anderson, James McAndrew, Charles Silverson, Mike Leilski. The unmarried ones are: John Williams, William Lyster, E.P. Chase, Alexander Anderson, George Roberts, Benjamin Morgan, Charles Ramberg, Lon Latka, Thomas Conlin, Ike Johnson, Martin Blunn, William Evans."

Gun accidents, drowning, death and injury in the saw mills and lumber camps, or on the roads from horse and buggy accidents were commonplace.

"Last Saturday [July 1891] two wagons loaded with a happy party started to go around the bay to visit the Dexter homestead. Among the company were Mrs. E.A. Boblett and her mother, the aged Mrs. Whitcomb, who were sitting together on a high spring seat in the back of one of the wagons. At a rough spot in the road the seat was overturned and the two ladies were thrown backward from the wagon to the ground with terrific force, stunning them and injuring them so badly that they were unable to ride home in the wagon and were brought across in a boat. At her extreme old age it is feared that Mrs. Whitcomb may not survive the terrible shock she received." Mrs. Whitcomb survived the accident and lived to celebrate her 95th birthday.

Life could be particularly difficult for single women with children to tend, as illustrated in these articles from the *Blaine Journal*, February 1889:

"Mrs. Mahala Evans, in trying to split a fir knot with a dull ax one day last week severely wrenched her back, so that she will be confined to her bed for several weeks. This will be very unfortunate, as Mrs. Evans has to depend on her own labor to support her little family."

Two articles told of Lucy Stanley's problems:

"Mrs. Lucy Stanley is in distress caused by a hurt hand, little Dick is disabled, and Dee is sick from a cold. No one in the house is able to do any work except nine year old Allan, and he has a hard time as cook."

"Yesterday Mrs. Stanley met with a distressing accident, which may prove to be a dangerous one. She, with her little boy it seems were working together, when by some means the boy brought the axe, with which he was working, down full force on the back of the hand, laying the bones bare and we believe shattering them considerably. This is a very unfortunate accident to Mrs. Stanley, as she is depending on her own labor to get her spring work done."

Some independent women preferred to make their own way. Since the Homestead Acts didn't discriminate between men and women, many women took advantage of the Act and moved to the West, although most of them chose land close to settlements and few were as adventurous as Mary E. Dye. Her story appeared in the *Reveille* on November 18, 1891:

"One of the most remarkable women in the county visited New Whatcom, yesterday. Her name is Mary E. Dye. She is a widow with one son, a lad of 14 years. Four years ago she settled on the South Fork of the Nooksack, and a twig have never been cut by a white man within five miles of her ranch. Her household goods were brought to her from Nooksack Crossing in an Indian canoe. She got a log shanty up and went to work. For six months she saw only one woman, and that was a squaw. She has now several acres cleared, a garden which is the pride of the South Fork, fruit trees started, and this year with only her son to help her she has made 157 rods of good wagon road, chopping down trees, hauling them away and grubbing. She wields an ax in a very certain and reliable way. She has pigs, cows, chickens, and her dinners are celebrated all along the river. Last fall she gave a Thanksgiving dinner to the government surveyors which pleased them mightily, and all that she set before them that was not raised on the ranch was coffee, sugar, pepper and salt. Boulder Creek empties into the Nooksack at her place, and at any time in the year, save July and August, in ten minutes time she will have a salmon or trout ready for the pan. Salmon weighing 20 pounds have been caught in the creek. Trout can be caught, from the big salmon variety to the little brook trout."

One day, he went down to the beach and saw some fine ducks and he crept up to them and shot four, all there was. When he went to pick them, he saw he had killed somebody's tame ducks. He brought them home and asked Ed what he should do about it. Ed told him to take them to the owner and tell him about it and offer to pay for whatever damage he had done. He did and the man just laughed; he had a pretty hard name and Smith was afraid he would be mad, but he saw it was a mistake and he would not take any pay, though he did not want to lose the ducks.

Another time, this same Mr. Hemphill's dogs were coming in with a deer and Smith grabbed his gun, and some way, we never knew how, he shot off the gun in the house over Mr. Boblett's head. We were all very much disturbed; Smith was as pale as death and so was Ed, as it just missed his head. Smith did not want any deer meat, so he did not go with the hunting party. This was in the winter of '70 and '71. Finally, Smith went to British Columbia to work in a logging camp.

If I remember correctly, we tore down our house in '72 and moved it out to the front early in the spring. Ed was a carpenter so Mr. Kingsley got Ed to build his house. It was built of lumber. Then Dexter wanted a lumber addition to his cabin, so the children and I worked in the garden and did as much clearing as we could while Mr. Boblett was working for others.

Our first Fourth of July celebration was held in an evergreen grove at our house. Mr. Stewart's two oldest boys, William and Edward, climbed the tallest tree in the grove and fastened the Stars and Stripes high enough that it

A mention of the house "bee" appeared in the *Blaine Journal*, February, 1898 in Catherine Kingsley's obituary.

"In Memory of Mrs. Catherine Kingsley, Who Departed This Life Feb. 19th, 1898.

"Our venerable fellow townsmen Edward A. Boblett and Mrs. Boblett, had preceded in Kingsleys in their settlement here. Our inimitable Uncle Billy Patterson had found a home in those parts at that time. Alexander Hemphill lived on the Runge place then. Hemphill, long since deceased, was a man of herculean strength, that was put to use at time in an old fashioned 'bee' gotten up for the purpose of removing the building now occupied by Ed. Boblett from a place near the present residence of Alex. Vreatt to its present location. There were no teams in the country and the logs that formed the building had to be carried by main [sic] strength. It required the strength of at least two men to carry one log in all trips that were made except when Hemphill done his 'turn.' He scorned the necessity of assistance and good naturedly place a log on his back and walked off with it."

floated fine and we all enjoyed the occasion. They all went home, some on foot and other in boats, and that night we had one of the worst thunder storms I ever witnessed in this section.

Mr. Smith had taken a claim adjoining ours on the east and while over in British Columbia, he ran across a man by the name of John Wagner, an old friend of his, and a few days before Christmas, Smith and Wagner came over carrying a big piece of beef on their backs from New Westminster, a distance of 18 miles and also brought raisins for a plum pudding. They said, "Now we want everybody invited here for Christmas." They went around and invited all of the folk around the bay and we celebrated Christmas of 1873. We had a fine time, all were comparatively young, healthy and happy. I remember the night before, there fell about six inches of snow and those that liked snow-balling enjoyed the sport to the full, before the snow all disappeared the next day.

In the fall of 1873, Ed and Mr. Richards went down to Tacoma after putting in their crops, leaving Mrs. Richards and her children to tend their garden, while the children and I attended to ours. For nine years we lived here, without experiencing much change except as the settlers cleared their land and made improvements, but this was slow work as we had very little money and the men had to go away to work through the summer to live through the winter. Of course, there was no such thing as style in those days. We used to busy ourselves many times when the tide was out, digging clams. It was an old saying, that when the tide was out, the butcher shops were open.

One year, Ed and Charley, our boy, were going to Mud Bay, British Columbia, to work, helping to build a corduroy road across the flats; the contractor wanted a cook so I hired out to go over and cook for the crew. There were twenty-five men and I cooked nearly all summer and got my $45 a month. I felt quite rich when we got through and came home. We all worked that summer. Ed helped to lay out the first road from Blaine to Bellingham, a distance of twenty-seven miles, then he helped to clear nine miles of it. We used to walk to Whatcom occasionally after they got the road brushed out.

After we all got a chance to work one summer, we got ahead a little, so Ed could stay home for a time and we all worked at clearing and fencing and got quite a farm cleared, together with some fruit trees and berries planted. Then Ed and Charles used to make shingles by hand, and many a bunch of shingles have I packed for the market. They were the same as money to the early settlers. I have known people to make shingles and carry them two miles to get them to the Bay, then load them in a skiff and take them to the Spit as it is called, where they could be loaded on a steamer.

We used to raise potatoes and carry them also because there were no teamsters to haul our merchandise. In the spring of '71 or '72, Mr. Wagner and Mr. Smith had several sacks of potatoes left over, more than they wanted. This was before there was a store on the Spit. As they were going to the logging camps to work, they wanted a little money, so they carried their potatoes to the Kingsley's place where we kept our boat to be handy for all, this was in April, expecting to take them to Whatcom the next day in the skiff. That night it tuned cold and froze every one of them and they had carried them on their backs two miles. That summer, the Clark brothers started a store so we did not have to pull a boat to Whatcom to sell potatoes or get groceries. The first fair in this county (Whatcom) was at Whatcom.

We had some of the largest cabbages I ever saw, so we thought we would take four of the largest heads to the fair. We pulled them and they seemed about the same size all over the patch. We intended to take them to the fair as we had pulled them, but when we came to get into the boat, there was not enough room because of our bedding and eatables. We had to take plenty as we could not tell how long we would be on the trip because of the storms. We had to cut the stalks off and then there was hardly room for us to get in, but we did, and pulled out and when we got to the other side of Birch Bay, we had to go ashore and wait several hours for the wind to go down. Finally, we got to the fair and old Mr. Bennett, the man who promoted the fair, weighed our cabbages and they weighed forty-three pounds each. He asked why we did not leave them as we pulled them; we told him the circumstances and that it was impossible. He said he would like to see them as they were for they were the finest cabbages he had ever seen. We had one rutabaga that year that weighed thirty pounds, but we did not take it because we did not have the room.

The United States Centennial – A 100-Year Celebration
The year of 1876 we had a grand Fourth of July celebration on the Spit; that was the Centennial year. Everybody turned out from everywhere, even from British Columbia. We had our celebrations on the Spit after the first one because it was a dry grassy place and there were a few large fir trees there and the gravel beach made it an ideal picnic ground and people could land there when they could not get ashore elsewhere. We used to have lovely times because of the fellow-feeling we had for one another in those days.

I remember one time Laura Lindsey, Jasper Lindsey's daughter, took diphtheria. They lived about four miles from us and Lizzie Cain and I walked up to their place. We pulled off our shoes and stockings and waded Dakota Creek, then put them on again and walked on to California Creek, thinking we could catch a ride across it, as the banks of the creek were very muddy. When we got there, we waited for a boat to come along, but none came along, so we pulled off our shoes and stockings again and waded the creek and went on up to Lindsey's. We sat up all night and came back the way we went. The girl got better soon so we did not have to repeat the trip. We thought nothing of walking three or four miles to an evening meeting and back again after a hard days work at that.

One morning I was awakened by hearing someone on the Bay calling for help. I knew it was blowing pretty hard and I raised up and I could hear them plainly. I called Ed and he just laughed at me and told me to lie down and then I heard them again, so I told Ed to get up and he would know there was someone in trouble. He got up and said, "Yes, there is someone in trouble." We dressed as quickly as possible, Ed being ready before I was and ran down to the Bay at Dave Miller's. He had heard the call for help and had gone out after them and was bringing them in. They had gone out to take care of old Aunty Ellwood on the Spit. She was very sick and her nephew, James Ellwood and a man whom I do not now remember, were capsized and were hanging on to the boat. Ed came up to the house and told me and I got ready and went over and took care of her for two weeks, when she got better and I returned home.

During the early days, there were very few deaths here, some of them were sick when they came. Among them was Mr. C. Kingsley, Byron's father, and two sisters. We were always there when there was sickness. Mr. Kingsley was our first class leader in the Methodist Church, and he was a good one too, but

Nearly every issue of the *Blaine Journal* contained the story of a child or young mother dying, either from childbirth, consumption, or the current epidemic. Doctors did their best, but there were no hospitals or miracle drugs. Smallpox, scarlet fever, meningitis, mumps, and tuberculosis took the lives of a number of the citizens. The neighbors became nurses and entered the homes of the stricken to help in any way they could, even at the risk of contracting the disease themselves.

"Mrs. Hannah Van Luven died at the Walworths's Monday evening October 22d, 1888, of the dread disease small-pox. She was nearly 35 years old at the time of her death, having been born in Ontario, Canada, December 31st, 1853. She was the daughter of Mr. and Mrs. Henry D. West, and was married to Schuyler Van Luven about 15 years ago, and now leaves him and four young children to mourn her loss.

"One of the nurses from the Walworth settlement told the *Columbian* that 'Mrs. Van Luven died on the 13th day of her illness of confluent smallpox, and her death was considered a happy relief, as both her eyes would have fallen out had she lived. She was buried at 10:30 the next morning in a rude coffin furnished by friendly hands. A funeral service was held in the house by Mr. Alex. Anderson, who performed the last rites over the body of Mrs. Van Luven and the two unfortunates who had died before. The two children were very low at this time, and their recovery seemed almost hopeless. But skillful treatment had its effect and both recovered, although the right eye of the youngest child fell out. Even after convalescence the poor children suffered terribly from abscesses which broke out all over their bodies. The little girl's face had to be lanced ten times in different places, and also many times on other parts of the body.' When they first arrived at the Walworth's on September 30th, they found several of the patients delirious, and Mrs. Chas. Walworth especially so. They were compelled to tie her feet and hands and put her in a straight jacket, and then it required two men to hold her at times. She died at 8:30 that same night. After the disease had subsided everything was thoroughly disinfected and eight pounds of sulphur was used in fumigating the house, which was tightly closed during the process. The clothing was burned."

There is something sad about the death of these young mothers. There is something inexpressibly sad about Mrs. Van Luven's death after convalescence had begun, after her weeks of faithful toil among the sick.

Children were victims of many epidemics that swept through the community, such as scarlet fever in March, 1890:

"Little Mabel Ray Harvey, daughter of Mr. and Mrs. John Harvey, died on Sunday morning, March 23d, 1890, at 9 a. m., of scarlet fever. She was three years, eight months and 11 days old at the time of her death."

the poor man had consumption and so did their baby.

In the winter of 1875-76, Mr. Boblett's parents sent money to him so he could go to them for a visit. I well remember it was the coldest winter we had experienced here; the thermometer registered 12 degrees below zero for six weeks, with eighteen inches of snow on the ground. If there had been good roads and horses, we could have had plenty of sleigh riding that year.

We had a preacher that winter by the name of Dennison. He commenced revival meetings in Kingsley's house, as it was the most suitable and nearest the Bay. People came from all directions to attend the meetings. Finally, they thought it might be more central for some if they held the meetings near California Creek, so they transferred them to Mr. William Steward's place. They had a large house, yet it was filled every night. These meetings continued until every one that attended them claimed conversion, save one, and he became a convert soon afterward. I attended them with the two children, but it was quite a walk after doing the milking. Finally, Charley said, "You and Bell stay up there and I will attend the cows and come up with the other boys." We stayed then until the meetings closed and it was the best revival I ever had the privilege of attending.

That spring was certainly an ideal spring. We had no frost after the first of March. Charley and I attended the crops and about the middle of June, the children and I went over to visit my father, mother, sister and brother-in-law. They had lots of red raspberries going to waste and they wanted us to stay and pick them the next day. Charley said he would go home and do the milking and Bell and I would stay. Mr. Dexter was to bring us home the next evening.

When Charley got home, he found that Dave Miller's oxen had torn down our fence and all the cattle of the neighborhood were in our garden. We had a strong rail fence and all heavy and we thought that it was cattle proof, but some way it was torn down. When I got home and saw the condition of the garden, I sat down and cried until I was sick over the affair. To think we had worked so hard with prospects only to have it destroyed by cattle made us feel pretty bad. However, there came a big rain and I could hardly believe it, yet the cabbage I thought were all gone commenced to grow again and head up and in the fall you could scarcely believe there had been any incursion of cattle in our garden. This served to teach me never to cry over anything, especially when I could not help it.

This next fall, Ed went out hunting one day and he came on some deer tracks over across the British line. There were no laws then to prohibit hunting as there were no settlers nearer than Mud Bay, some seven miles distance. Ed followed the deer for some miles and he found a prairie with lots of grass. He came home and told the neighbors and they all turned out and cut a trail to it so they could drive the cattle over there to grass. They did very well until spring. Nobody told us we had to feed them hay in winter and we had lived so long where stock would not eat the best of hay, so we neglected putting in a crop. As I said, the cattle got along very well until spring when the slough grass began to grow. We lost four of our cows. One poor cow got mired and Ed found her and he said he never could see how he did it but he lifted her out of the mud and got her to solid ground, but she could not stand. He stayed with her all night and kept a fire near her to keep her warm and rubbed her, but he could not get her to stand. Finally, he pulled a lot of grass for her and came home. Charley and I used to go over and carry chop feed to her every other day and pull grass for her. We did this for two weeks and one time one of the neighbors went over with

---

If the reader had never met Charles Gott, he would have become emotionally involved by the final article in which Charles appears. The Gott family had moved to Blaine from Iowa just that April. Lizzie Gott was the daughter of Michael Rosbrugh and the niece of Ed Boblett.

"Last Saturday Dr. Reeves found it necessary to amputate the third finger on the right hand of young Charles Gott, in order to check the sway of blood poisoning which had already destroyed a portion of the finger. The condition of the young man is still critical, but the physician has hopes he will ultimately recover." (Friday, May 3, 1895)

"Charley Gott is still quite low, but Dr. Reeves thinks there is a slight improvement in his critical condition." (Friday, May 17, 1895)

"Died May 20th, 1895, in this city, Charles Hinton, son of D.R. and Lizzie Gott, aged 18 years, 8 months and 23 days. In this demise, the second since the last issue of the *Journal*, we record the death of a young man who was known to us all. Quiet, unassuming, honest and industrious are some of the characteristics of young Gott. Charles was the eldest of the sons and was born in Guthrie county, Iowa on Aug. 27th, 1875. The funeral services were held at the Methodist church on Tuesday afternoon last, and was made the occasion for a most affecting discourse by the pastor, Rev. J.W. White, and an example portrayed to the younger portion of the large congregation, which cannot help but bring forth good fruit. The family and relations have sympathy from the entire community in their sad bereavement."

Ed and got her on her feet, but she could not stand and Ed had to shoot her.

One day as we were going over, we were close to the place where Mr. Boblett found one of the cows drowned in a creek. We had the same dog that ran the Indians across the field in Arizona with us; I always felt safe when he was along. Charley was a boy fourteen or fifteen and he had an old musket-loader with him. All at once, the dog jumped into the brush and began to bark loudly. We could see the brush shaking but could not see what it was. Charley said if anything came out, he would shoot, but I said no, for I knew it was something big by the noise it made in getting away. It did not come near us and I was glad.

We stood still until the dog had driven it some distance, then I said let us go and see what it was. I felt sure it was a bear by the noise. However, when we got there, we found that it was a mountain lion. We went on and fed our cows and came back and told some of our neighbors who were trappers and they went right out and baited him and soon had him in the trap. He was seven feet from the tip of his nose to the tip of his tail. The next year, all the neighbors went over on the prairie and put up hay, then we had hay the next winter for the cattle and they did very much better. The following year, they concluded they would make a road over the prairie so they could get the hay home. It soon got noised about that there was a road in there and settlers took up the land and that ended the haying for this settlement.

About this time, there was a young man living in Mud Bay who came over very often to visit our young folk; I have forgotten his name. He was working at a logging camp and with another man was falling timber. They were working together and, in falling a tree, he was unfortunate enough not to jump in time to a place of safety and was crushed by the falling tree. They brought him to Blaine and held his funeral at our house.

A Short Time in Westminster, British Columbia, 1879
In 1879, in the early spring, Ed and Charley were going over to work in a logging camp at Mud Bay. I said, "I will go too, if I get a chance to cook." I did and worked there until fall, then we moved to New Westminster, British Columbia. Charley never lived at home after he started in the logging camp, and has followed logging ever since. He would come home occasionally, but always went back to camp. He has been a boss in the camps for years and now has a farm near Gettysburg, Washington, where he and his family have lived for some time.

Belle Marries, November 2, 1878
Belle married a man by the name of William Ferris soon after we moved to New Westminster. They lived there for a time, then moved on a farm along Frazier River. They sold the farm and came to Spokane where we were for a time located, but they did not like it there very well, so went back to Victoria, British Columbia, where they now live. I visited them once since Mr. Boblett died and I stayed a week.

I did all I could to help them get the beginning of an education. One day, I was working with them when a man came along and saw how I was trying, and he gave me an Arithmatic book. I never had studied one but went to work and as I learned, I taught it to the children, so they were not so backward, considering the little opportunity they had been given.

Spokane Falls – Don't Meddle with a Strange Horse, 1880

We lived in New Westminster until August 1880 then we started for Spokane. We took a steamer for Victoria, then to Tacoma, there we took the train for Kalama. This being my first train ride, it was a novel to me. There we took a boat up the river as to Portland and from there we went to Walla Walla, part of the way by boat and then by train again. There we stayed for three days before we could get our belongings hauled to a stopping place. Some thirty or forty miles from Spokane, we got a man who was hauling lime, going to the government post, and that was as near as he would take us to Spokane. We stopped there thinking we would have little trouble getting a team to take us through, but there was no team to be had as it was harvesting time.

When we got to Walla Walla, we saw such sights of grain, two sacks deep and as high as a man could stack it along the railroad track for hundreds of yards and on either side of the track, waiting to be loaded on the cars. We thought possibly we would locate there, but the next day when we took a walk over the town and went out along the road where they were hauling wheat, the dust was so thick we could not see the teams, but knew they were on the road because we could hear the wagons. There was no wind at all and all we could see was a cloud of dust.

The road was as smooth as a floor to look at but it was full of chuckholes and, as the teams passed over them, the dust was so thick one could not see them. We walked in all, I think about three miles; I had on a new black dress, but when we got back to the hotel you could never have told what color it was. The dust had gotten into the goods so that I could not get it out until I ripped up the dress and washed, making it over again. We concluded we did not want anymore of their alkali dust so we went as far as we could get with the first team available. We were two weeks getting to the place where this teamster left us. He had a heavy load and drove slowly.

When we found we could not get a team for further travel, we decided to walk to Medical Lake, some eighteen miles. We stored our belongings at a farmhouse with a widow as proprietor and told her our intentions to walk to the lake. She looked at me in astonishment and asked me if I realized how far the walk was. I told her I did and had often walked that far, climbing higher hills at the time, many a time. She said she did not think a woman could walk like that. We started at about half-past one and we reached there before dark, getting supper and lodging. We met the teamster on our way and as he had asked us to come to his place before locating, we stayed at his place for a day. I believe his name was Harris.

This Mr. Harris had brought in some horses from the range, and another fellow wanted Mr. Harris to take him out to look at some land, so he did, leaving the two horses tied in the barn. One had a colt on the prairie and the other horse, getting loose, was kicking the mare fearfully. Ed and I went to the barn and Ed caught the loose horse, but he seemed determined to fight the mare, so I went in and untied her, not knowing she had a colt on the range. I led her out thinking I would tie her outside while Ed was caring for the other animal, but she gave a jump knocking me down and getting the halter rope around my hand, dragged me for fifty yards over the rocks. Finally I made a desperate pull and got hold of the rope with my other hand, getting to my feet and held her till Ed came to my relief. The flesh was all torn off my knuckles and the flesh was separated on my thumb to the bone where the rope had been around it. This taught me a lesson I never will forget, not to meddle with a strange horse.

Spokane Falls, August 1880

The next day we went on to Spokane; there were only twelve buildings there at the time counting barns and all. It did not look very promising to us.

Not a days work could Ed get at anything and we only had a few dollars left after paying a week's board. There were quite a number of men there and, as the lady of the house had lots to do, she asked me to help her. My hands were pretty sore yet, but I was glad to get a place to work and earn something so we could have our board and room, Ed paying one dollar a week in excess of what I earned. There was a saw and grist mill there and finally Ed got a job carrying lumber, so we were now both working. The woman told me if her boarders increased in numbers, she would increase my wage. I guess she forgot her promise as she never increased my wage, while her boarders increased from six to over thirty.

Lois might well have been disappointed when she arrived in Spokane Falls. The 1880 population was only 350, and Spokane Falls and Cheney were engaged in a fight for the county seat. After an election proclaimed Spokane the winner, Cheney residents claimed the election had been rigged. Some of the citizens stole into Spokane Falls in the dead of night, kidnapped the election official and his records, and declared Cheney the new county seat. The city's name went through several changes. Prior to 1883, it was Spokan Falls, an "e" was then added making it Spokane Falls, until the "Falls" was dropped from the name in 1891.

With the arrival of the Northern Pacific Railway, Spokane's population increased rapidly, and by 1886 it had enough votes to win the county seat back from Cheney. The Coeur d'Alene mining boom brought additional prosperity to Spokane so that by 1890 the population was almost 20,000. To break the monopoly held by the Northern Pacific, Spokane gave away free land to bring the Great Northern Railroad Company through town. Just as fires had leveled Seattle and Rathdrum, a devastating fire swept through Spokane in 1889, leaving 32 blocks in ruins. From then on, brick was the building material of choice.

There was a hotel there and the owner saw Ed and told him he would give me $45 a month, so I left the boarding house and went to the hotel. The boarders at the hotel increased until we had over eighty. Ed too began to get better work. He was a carpenter and there began to be some building. This was in the spring of 1881. We soon had enough to get an outfit to begin keeping boarders ourselves, so I told the hotel proprietor I was going to leave. He did not want me to but it was too hard work, so we rented a small house and opened our own boarding house. I soon had all the boarders I could handle while Ed kept at building.

Mr. and Mrs. Ferris (our daughter Belle) came to Spokane that spring and while we were at work, we heard some yelling and I guess I turned pale. Belle said, "Ma, what does that mean? That sounds like an Indian war whoop." She had heard them when we lived in Arizona and although she was only a little girl at the time, she had never forgotten it. I did not want her to get excited, so I went to the door but I was so frightened I could hardly walk. I saw an Indian on horseback coming down the street as fast as his horse could carry him and giving a war whoop at every jump. I told her it was only a drunken Indian but I knew he could not be very drunk the way he could ride.

There was a man with his family camping some little distance from town and some Indians came along pretty drunk and one was determined to ride over his little children. The man led his horse around them three or four times, and the father finally got mad, drew his revolver and hit the Indian over the head with it, cracking the Indian's skull. This was the occasion of the war whoop as the Indians were pretty mad and had it not been for an old Indian by the name of Curley Jim, we would have had battle with them. Jim came to town and begged the white man to wait and not act too hasty, then he went to the Indians, said they should not fight, if they did they would all be killed. He got their guns away from them until they cooled down a little. A doctor went out and fixed up the Indian's head and he got well, so that ended their wanting to fight. This also ended our Indian troubles.

Lois Receives a Smallpox Vaccination, 1881
In the second year of our stay at Spokane, smallpox got pretty bad there. I had a doctor boarding with me by the name of Morgan and I told him if I thought the vaccine would take, I would be vaccinated. He said, "I will guarantee it will take if I vaccinate you." I said, "It has been tried on me three times with little if any results." He said, "Let me try." He did and what a time I had. I could not sit up to have my bed made for a week. The old doctor would come in and laugh at me until I felt if I could only get up, I certainly would whip him, but when I got up, I forgot about the teasing for I felt if there was anything in being vaccinated, I certainly would not take the disease. It took me a long time to get to my former condition.

Chapter 10
Idaho Territory
1881-1884

*I*n the fall, Ed was going out in the Coeur d'Alene region with some other men with a team prospecting. The doctor told Ed to get some good red flannel for underwear for me, sell out our restaurant and take me to the mountains. Ed came home with the flannel and told me he was going to sell the restaurant and take me along with him, as the doctor had instructed him to do so. I felt myself the change would do me good so I sent for Belle, as she was yet in Spokane, to come over and help me get ready. She came but tried to persuade me not to go. She said, "Now Ma, you will just go away off there up in the mountains to die alone." I told her I was going to get well and if I stayed there, I would surely die, for I could not keep anything on my stomach. She would help me get ready and then she would break down and cry, but I would laugh her out of it and told her I would soon come home well. This was in the fall of 1882; we were gone about three months.

The first night, I tried to get supper but I could not. I ate a little but I could not hold it in my stomach. I felt like giving up the trip and possibly would have if there had been any way for me to get back without making the others go back with me. The next morning, I ate a very good breakfast which I retained. In fact, I did not lose any more meals after this. We were three days getting to our camp, and several places I got out and walked up the steeper hills. We got to our camp just in time to get our tents up and supper before dark.

The next morning I felt quite like myself and when breakfast was over, they began to plan prospecting. I did not want to stay alone, so I said, "Are you going to let me go with you?" Ed said, "Yes, if you can stand it." I said I would try it if they were willing. I went and we tramped around all day walking twenty miles or more. We were within two miles of camp when I felt I could not go further, and I said, "Ed, will there be any danger if I sit here on this log and let you go into camp?" I knew they were hungry for we did not take a very big lunch with us. Ed said, "Why no, there is not any danger, but if you want to rest I will stay with you."

So we sat down and as soon as the other men got away, I threw myself down on the grass and cried, I was so tired. Ed scolded me for not stopping before, but I thought I could take it. I had gone as far as my strength would permit before I gave up and I thought I never would get into camp. When we got there, the men had supper ready, so all I did was to eat my supper and lie down. I was afraid I would be used up so I could not go as far as the men wanted to go.

We prospected until we were tired and finding nothing, moved on. We sank a shaft trying to get to the gravel bed we thought lay under the clay. An old California miner with us told us he thought such a bed existed and that it might have gold in it. I do not remember how far we sunk the shaft, but it was as far as we had conveniences to work with. We decided to move on as there was no water on the mountain and where we were camped some eight inches of snow fell and it was pretty cold. We decided to come down in the valley by a stream and put up a log cabin. This we did and it was more comfortable, however, we found no gold.

Winter in Spokane Falls, 1881
We rented a house above the falls about a mile and wintered there. In the spring, the water was very high. We had gotten another family to move in one part of the house so we would not be alone, as it was quite some distance from town, but not far from a ferry.

I was sick in bed and Ed and the other men were working in town, when one day we heard someone calling for help down by the river. I was real sick and the other woman said, "Shall I go and see what the trouble is about?" I told her to go. I could still hear the cry for help. Finally I crawled out of bed, got my clothes on and went out of doors. I knew someone was in the river above the falls and like would perish. I tried to go down to the river but could not, I was so weak. After a time, the woman returned and told me an Indian man, his squaw and a baby strapped to a board, were crossing the river and had capsized and all were threatened with drowning. They got the squaw out and the Indian was going down for the last time when assistance came to him and he was rescued, but the poor little baby was never found. The Indians hunted for a week but could not find it.

The Move to Pend Orielle Lake, Spring 1882
Not long after this, we moved to Steamboat Landing on Pend Orielle Lake. Ed was working on a steamboat there, getting it ready to launch. They finished it and

> There is no record of the water flow over the falls at the time Lois lived near them, but Spokane Falls is one of the largest waterfalls by volume in Washington State. The falls had a drop of 75 feet and an average width of 400 feet. The average volume of water was 6,732 cubic feet per second. The maximum recorded volume was measured on May 31, 1894 at 49,000 cubic feet per second. The falls were dammed shortly after Spokane was founded to provide power and irrigation water. Even today unwary swimmers are taken by the falls.

got it into the water and we rode on it when it made its trial trip. I do not remember the name they gave it. Then Ed went to work on another, a much larger and nicer one, and when it was finished and launched, we again rode on it while it was making its trial trip. I tried to get some of the other women to go aboard, but they were all afraid, so I was the only woman aboard during the trial trip.

There was a saw mill here to make lumber for boats and necessary buildings. We got a room at the back of the store, a small place, as I intended not to keep boarders, since there was a cook house here and I did not think it would pay. However, it was not long before they began to come to us begging for me to board them, so I did. This did not last long as they got through with the work there and moved down the Lake to the place where the Great Northern Rail Road was to pass through.

One time while at Steamboat Landing, we went to Spokane on a little business and we had to go several miles to get to the car line where they were running a construction train to Spokane and we had to wait a couple of hours for the train to come. While waiting, we thought we would walk down the track a little distance and while doing so, a man came running through the bush. We did not know what to think; we thought possible he was crazy. But when he got to us, he said, "Have you got a gun?" We told him no. Ed then said, "What is the matter?" "Why," he said, "there is a big bear right up here on the track and he

Pen d'Orielle City (old spelling) appeared in 1864-65 and was the precursor to Steamboat Landing located in Buttonhook Bay at the south end of Lake Pend Oreille. It was founded by Zenas Moody and consisted of five houses, a hotel, a bar and pool hall, and a grocery store. Pen d'Orielle City was an overnight stop for miners and freight merchants using the Lake Pend Oreille-Clark Fork River route to the northeastern gold mines.

Captain Moody built a steamboat, the *Mary Moody* (named after his wife), and launched it on Lake Pend Oreille in 1866. This steamer carried mail, transported miners headed to the Wild Horse Trail and Mine in British Columbia, or to the Last Chance Gold Mines of Helena, Montana. The steamer held 55 passengers, 85 mules, and 10,000 pounds of freight at the rate of $.13 a pound. The *Mary Moody* was scrapped in 1876.

Figure 12: Steamboat Landing, Amelia Bay, Pend Orielle Lake, 1883. The steamer *Henry Villard* is in the background. Haynes Foundation Collection H-1117, Montana Historical Society.

The next large steamers to ply the waters were the *Henry Villard* and the *Katie Hallett*. These might have been the boats Ed worked on. By mid-1881, Northern Pacific railroad gangs were completing sections of track from Spokane Falls to North Lake Pend Oreille, and by 1882, grading crews were working along the Clark Fork River. The workforce consisted of nearly 4,000 men, including 2,600 Chinese laborers. Boom towns filled with saloons and restaurants and flop-houses proliferated overnight along the route.

Hope, established in 1882, was one of those boom towns. Until 1900 it was the main city on the lake. It was named after Dr. Hope, a veterinarian who worked for the railroad. He held an important post; the railroad couldn't have been built without the use of animals.

The boom towns in Idaho were supported by the convergence of mining fever and construction of the railroad. Life changed drastically when construction ended at about the same time miners abandoned the Coeur d'Alene fields to search for gold elsewhere.

The public's imagination was so captured by the tales of gold that East Coast newspapers sent reporters into the gold fields. One reporter traveled through the Coeur d'Alene Mountains in 1884 and described the downturn in fortunes. His report was printed in the *New York Times*, July 28, 1884:

"Since I last wrote, the business situation has become worse by half. All towns along the line of the railroad are lying dormant. Prices of goods have fallen greatly, and many persons are selling at cost to save themselves from loss. Let no one who reads what I have written be fooled into coming here to start business of any kind. There is no trade for him, and there will be no room for him if business should become brisk tomorrow, with the hundreds now watching for a chance to step in. Many people are going out of the country, few are coming in. Things are indeed in a bad way for many, and hundreds would be glad to get out if they could do so without loss . . . The claims are thoroughly taken up, there is still no employment, stocks of goods are unsalable because of competition and the scarcity of money, and a large portion of the community is hanging on by the eyelids waiting for something to turn up. But claims can be bought cheap in many instances, and capitol would not run amiss to come here."

The Ellsport that Lois wrote about later in her memoir has had three names. A saw mill was built there to provide wood products for the railroad and local construction. It would have been a perfect location for a boarding house. Although it was known as Amelia Bay at one time, it is called Ellisport Bay today.

Another short-lived town in the area was Seneacquoteen. In the late 1800s, it rivaled Hope in size. Railroad land was sold to settlers for as little as $2.60 an acre. Elmina Markham discovered that cheap land did not necessarily bring close neighbors. She and her husband, with their seven children, settled in Seneacquoteen in 1883 where they operated a ferry for many years. She wrote,

"I was here eight months without seeing a white woman. There was a man and his wife and two or three sons come here on a fishing trip. I went out and shook hands with her. I was so glad to see a white woman. She only stayed one day. My husband told me he thought she was afraid to stay longer for fear I would talk her to death."

is holding the right of way, and I want a gun to shoot him." We all went back to the station, but no one had a gun. However, one man had a six-shooter, so he got that and we went back and walked to within fifty yards of him without his paying any attention to us until the man began to shoot at him, then he walked off leisurely. There had been a mess-car standing there and he was getting a feed.

We went down to the place where the railroad was to pass through and they were building a saw mill, so we had to wait before we could get lumber to put up a house. Ed went to work clearing a place, laying a wall twelve feet square, then cutting some poles so we could stretch our fly tent over it and we had a little house to go on in. Here I thought we would not have to keep boarders for we had our bed, cook stove and everything we had in there, and surely I thought there will be no room to accommodate them. But in a few days, I had twelve in a twelve foot square. What shall I call it, for it was nothing more than a pen?

Ed went to work and made a round table and some round stools and we put the stools under the table and as the men came in, they would go around to the back of the table, reach under and get a stool apiece and sit down. I could accommodate six at a time and when they had eaten, I would have to arrange the table again for another six.

The monumental scale of the building of the railroad is apparent in these two descriptions from the *Billings Gazette*'s 75th Anniversary Issue, September 1960. One stretch of the railroad was constructed from Minot, North Dakota, west to Great Falls, Montana. Nine thousand men and 7,000 horses moved more than a million cubic yards of dirt and rock in constructing this link. Crews average 3.25 miles per day, with seven miles being the record for one day's work. Supplies filled 11,700 railcars, including 947 containing rail spikes. Wagon trains hauled supplies 100 miles ahead of the track, and up to 30 miles ahead of the land graders. The horses required 590,000 bushels of oats.

In the Northwest, construction progressed slowly, moving from west to east through this area. The tracks reached the south side of the Lake Pend Oreille outlet at the end of 1881. The next year 6,000 men, 4,000 of them Chinese, continued the construction through the Clark Fork division which ran from Sandpoint into Montana. This was the most expensive section to build on the entire Northern Pacific line.

In making the clearing for our pen, Ed had thrown the dirt on three sides, making quite a raise of ground there, but on the fourth side there was a drop. One morning, I jumped up to get breakfast, about four o'clock, and I jumped into about six inches of water. I yelled out and Ed said, "What is the matter?" I said everything is full of water. He had to get up and dig a ditch all around and throw in fresh dirt before I could get breakfast. There had been a heavy rain in the night and it ran in on the depressed side while the ridges make by the other three sides held it in.

105

Ed and Lois Build Another House, Fall 1882

We stayed in that pen until they got the mill running and then we put up a house for ourselves. There Ed went into partnership with a man by the name of Fisher, he too being a carpenter and a good hand around the house. We decided to build a good sized house this time, but they built the kitchen first so I would have a good place to cook. They built the house two stories high. They got it all ready for the roof when it started to snow; it was a soft snow and stuck to the rafters and then froze. It got awful cold, but they finally got the roof on and we moved in. Everything was covered with snow but it appealed to us as better than the pen. Ed took the fly-tent and stretched it over our bed to keep our bed dry and by keeping a fire day and night, we got the snow and ice thawed off the inside of the house. I have often wondered why I did not take sick in that steam and wet.

Before we built our house, there were numbers of people living and doing business in tents. When we built, we went away from the saloons and restaurants some 100 yards, to get away from their influence and noise and also to be near the lake. We had lots of costumers, all we could handle.

One day, two men came right at my back door and began to shovel snow and I learned they expected to put a saloon there. I walked out and asked them if that was their intentions and they said it was. I then told them that we came as far as we did to get away from the saloons and now I said, "Please do not put a saloon here." Then such oaths and foul language as they used! They said they did not care what I said, they expected to put one there. I told them, "Then I give you fair warning, the first man that attempts to put a saloon under my nose, after we have made such an effort to get away from it, I will shoot down and you can depend on it." I guess they thought I meant what I said for after I went into the house, they went away and never came back to carry out their plans as they said.

Sunday evenings, Ed, Fisher and I would start singing and the men would come around the door and windows and listen, even the Chinamen were there. It was all there was that sounded like home to me, as there were no meetings to go to. One man told Ed he was going home where he could go to church. One time, Ed was at work at a bench against the south wall of the house and a man was sitting on the bench. I was feeling a little blue and started to sing "Do They Miss Me At Home" as I was doing my work. This man began to weep and said he wished he could go home but he had spent his money in the saloons and had none. He resolved not to frequent them any more, save his money and go back to his folk. I little thought I was touching a tender chord of another when I was singing for my own pleasure.

There was four feet of snow on the level that winter and bitterly cold. We built on quite an addition to our house so we had a large dining room, but before they got it ready to use, I did all the cooking and dish washing and waiting on of tables and all so the men could work on the house. Before we got the main part of the house done, I had over thirty boarders, accommodating them all in the kitchen. I had five families and it was very cold and the only fires we had was in the cook stove. One family had five children, another had four, another three, another two, and the other family had one. Imagine my trying to do the cooking with all these women and children trying to get around the stove. I could not send them away for there was no place for them to go, and to top it all, Ed was taken very sick.

For a time I did not think he would live from one day to the next. They had built the kitchen a story and a half high, so we could sleep up stairs; he was sick up there and I would run up stairs to see how he was, then down to my work again. We made beds on the floor both up and down stairs for the various families with us. I often look back and wonder how I managed to get through it all. One day a man came in the kitchen to get some hot water and he said, "How do you get around all these children?" I told him I didn't, I just knock one one way and another had to jerk them out of the way, they took so long to move. Finally, they got their houses finished and then I had plenty of room. We lived there until the next spring.

When the snow went off, we had

Do they miss me at home, do they miss me?
'Twould be an assurance most dear,
To know that this moment some loved one
Were saying, "I wish he were here;"
To feel that the group at the fireside
Were thinking of me as I roam,
Oh yes, 'twould be joy beyond measure,
To know that they missed me at home
To know that they missed me at home.

When twilight approaches, the season
That ever is sacred to song;
Does someone repeat my name over,
And sigh that I tarry so long?
And is there a chord in the music,
That's missed when my voice is away,
And a chord in each heart that awaketh
Regret at my wearysome stay?
Regret at my wearysome stay?

Do they set me a chair near the table

When evening's home pleasures are nigh,
When the candles are lit in the parlor,
And the stars in the calm azure sky?
And when the "good nights" are repeated,
And all lay them down to their sleep,
Do they think of the absent, and waft me
A whispered "good night" while they weep?
A whispered "good night" while they weep?
Do they miss me at home — do they miss me,
At morning, at noon, or at night?
And lingers one gloomy shade round them
That only my presence can light?

Are joys less invitingly welcome,
And pleasures less hale than before,
Because one is missed from the circle,
Because I am with them no more?
Because I am with them no more?

Do They Miss Me At Home was a sentimental song that was very popular on the minstrel stage in the mid-1850s. The song was written by S.M. Grannis, and this version was printed in the **Briggs Banjo Instructor** in 1855. Music could indeed affect some people strongly. A young woman in Liberty township, Ohio, was so affected by reading this as a piece of poetry that she fainted. Her mother, believing the girl was dying, became terribly excited, causing a ruptured blood vessel. She died in less than an hour. The girl was insensible for 15 minutes before recovering.

a rather queer kind of sport. As I said, we built our house close to the lake, and we used to throw our scraps out at the back door of our dining room, for we had nothing to feed it to. When the snow went off, the water in the lake raised till it came up to the ground on which the house stood. The lake was full of fish and there was one kind especially plentiful called whitefish. The water rose so high it covered our scrap pile and the fish would seem to gather in schools. This fish was about a foot in length and their meat was white and very sweet, but they were very bony, so much so no wanted to eat them. However, we had lots of fun with them.

As the sun shone hot in June, the snows on the mountains melted again, raising the lake so it came this time in our home and we had to move out for two weeks. It was not long before the work in this part was done and the construction gang moved farther along to make new right of way. We thought we had gotten enough of rail-roading, so as we had a place to live, we would stop there for a time and prospect. We would shut up the house for some days and be gone off on a trip. The first time we crossed the lake, the wind rose and made the lake very rough so that it was hard to get ashore. As the shore rose in most places like a perpendicular wall of rock, it was some time before we could find a landing place. Finally we saw a little break in the wall where we could land. We had to haul our boat up on the rocks where the waves could not beat on it, the lake was so rough. It was too near night to

Every pioneer carried a medicine chest with them; doctors were scarce or non-existent on the frontier.

One of the most popular books published in the early 1860s was written by Dr. A.W. Chase. His *Information for Everybody: An invaluable collection of about eight hundred practical recipes* was available for $1 or $2 in California. He attempted to include all the information a person would need in settling the new territories. Chase had a recipe for every kind of disease known to mankind, as well as treatments for injuries. One such recipe was for "artificial skin" to treat burns, abrasions, and cuts. His recipe for sore throat liniment called for gum camphor, castile soap, oil of turpentine, oil of origanum (oregano or marjoram), opium and alcohol. A sore throat gargle contained sage tea, honey, salt, vinegar, and cayenne pepper. Cayenne was a common ingredient in many stomach, throat, fever and salve recipes. A salve for burns, frostbite, and cracked nipples contained turpentine, sweet oil, and beeswax. If a stronger salve was needed, opium and sugar of lead might be added. One such recipe unfortunately called for four live frogs. This one was supposed to be especially good for rheumatism, sprains, and caked udders.

Toothache was treated with a mixture of alcohol, laudanum, chloroform, gum camphor, oil of cloves, oil of lavender, and a bit of sulphuric acid. If the tooth had to be pulled, this solution would numb the area first. Opium was a very popular ingredient and this book told the housewife how to make her own laudanum and paregoric or "soothing syrup" for use with children. Paregoric was used to treat colic, diarrhea, teething, and sleeplessness. Snakebite could be cured by taking a bottle of whiskey and getting as drunk as possible.

Pennyroyal was one of many herbal medicines used in the attempt to cure disease. Seventeenth-century English herbalist Nicholas Culpepper noted a number of uses for pennyroyal:

"Drank with wine, it is good for venomous bites, and applied to the nostrils with vinegar revives those who faint and swoon. Dried and burnt, it strengthens the gums, helps the gout, if applied of itself to the place until it is red, and applied in a plaster, it takes away spots or marks on the face; applied with salt, it profits those that are splenetic, or liver grown.... The green herb bruised and put into vinegar, cleanses foul ulcers and takes away the marks of bruises and blows about the eyes, and burns in the face, and the leprosy, if drank and applied outwardly . . . One spoonful of the juice sweetened with sugar-candy is a cure for whooping-cough."

Today, we know that pennyroyal essential oil is highly toxic and even a small amount can be fatal. Teas made by seeping the leaves remain popular in some cultures and the leaves are also used to flavor dishes with a strong, mint-like flavor.

Most medicines were compounded using natural substances such as herbs, tree-bark teas, honey, mustard, ginger, and roots such as horseradish. Alcohol was used externally and internally. Causing the patient to sweat was part of the cure for many conditions and diseases. Unfortunately, some of the cures were more dangerous than the disease. One common ingredient for treating stomach and intestinal complaints was calomel, a mercury-containing drug. Mercury, arsenic, antimony and lead were common ingredients in medicines and cosmetics.

Lois nursed Ed through several serious illnesses during their travels. She would have had her own medicine chest and recipes passed down through the family or obtained from friends.

go prospecting, so Mr. Fisher took a little stroll and found a patch of huckleberries, and came back and reported to Ed. We all went with him and picked enough for all the pie and sauce we could use and came back to camp. I got supper while Ed and Fisher cleared a place of rocks and rubble so we could make our beds. I baked a pie and they killed some grouse, which I fried, and we had a fine supper.

Prospecting, July 1883

The next morning, they decided to go to the top of the mountain and be gone for two or three days. We all took our packs. The men took the bedding and provisions and I carried the cooking utensils. When these were all put together, I had a pack of about twenty-five pounds. It went all right for a time though it was a hard load to carry, as it would not seem to lay anywhere I would place it, and had to keep changing all the time. At last, we got up in the pine trees and on the grass. The men had nails in their boots so they could walk all right, but my shoes got so slick I could not walk. Mr. Fisher took my pack and I climbed the mountain on my hands and knees.

I felt well repaid when I got to the top for it was beautiful. We could see so far and the flowers such as I had never seen before, the leaves were like a big tuft of slein grass and the flower stalks came up in the center two or three feet high with a bunch of creamy white flowers in the shape of a sugar-pine-cone and about the same size, a beautifully scented flower; one bunch in a room would scent the house.

The flower Lois found on the mountain was beargrass, *Xerophyllum tenax*. Although it looks like a grass, beargrass is a member of the lily family and bears a resemblance to its cousin, the yucca plant. The leaves grow about 35 inches long and the bloom forms on a stalk that can grow as tall as six feet. Each flower is creamy-white; the lower ones bloom first, creating a knot of buds at the top which creates the cone shape. Native Americans used the grass to make beautiful baskets, and it is, also called "Indian basket-grass." It is thought to be called beargrass because Lewis and Clark began to refer to it in their journals as "a species of beargrass" which was the common name for yucca on the Missouri River plains and eastward.

We could find no traces of copper so we went back and decided to go another route, first going to our home. I told Ed to get me a pair of small boots and he did and had the soles filled with nails, then I could travel with any of them. After our experience climbing the mountain, we decided not to carry so many trappings. For one thing, we decided not to carry anything to mix or bake bread in; we would mix our flour and baking powder at home, then I could mix my bread in the mouth of the sack and bake it on a stick before the fire. However, when we went with our skiff, we carried more utensils to work with. We made a number of trips, some for a week at a time. Several different times, we had what looked like a good prospect in the top gravel, but we could not get down very far because of the water.

Back to Washington for the Winter, 1883

At last, we gave up prospecting and decided to go back to Spokane and buy some lots and build there, expecting to keep boarders again. We all expected to go together to buy the lots but I was sick and told Ed I would stay home, he and Fisher could attend to the buying. They went down and Fisher persuaded Ed to buy lots in Rathdrum, thirty miles above Spokane, so we moved there and rented a small house. It was all we could get and I went to keeping boarders there. We did not get to build that fall, so in the winter, a couple of fellows came in for dinner and Ed was in the dining room. They were a little late and the regular boarders had gone out. In the conversation between the two fellows, Ed made up his mind one of them had struck it pretty rich, so he commenced to wait on them so he would have a chance to talk to them. He told them of our prospecting but that it had not yielded results and asked Mr. Prichard if he had.

Prichard did not seem inclined to talk at first but finally he said, "Well, for your wife's sake, I will show

The *Daily Miner*, from Butte, Montana, carried a story on August 3, 1883, about a party of miners, including the Bobletts, returning to Rathdrum from the Coeur d'Alene gold fields:

"The water was turned into one sluice box for three hours and resulted in $10 in glistening nuggets. The country has been staked off for ten miles up and down the stream and the entire company will return to the gold fields, accompanied by many of our citizens during the latter part of the week. They would not have come in [on] this trip but were out of grub."

you what I have found. A woman that will go prospecting deserves to find something." He told Ed to call me in and said, "I do not want this to be public knowledge as yet, as it is too early." We told him we would say nothing. Then he took out a purse from his pocket and poured about three hundred dollars of high grade gold on a paper. The sight of this awakened in us the old time lust for the yellow stuff, so we decided to go with this party when they started for their claim in the spring. I wanted to get some other woman to go, but no, there was not another woman that was willing to try the trip. I said, "Where my husband goes, I can go."

The Coeur d'Alene Mines, 1884
About the first of April 1884, we arrived at the Coeur d'Alene mines. We put our horses and packs on a steamboat and started from Fort Coeur d'Alene to the Mission by steamer.

When we got [to Cataldo], the water was so high we had to wait three weeks. This was a pretty place, quite a wide grassy bottom. It was an old Indian Catholic Mission. The Indians were not hostile and we felt safe. There were four or five men with us of our acquaintance, so we went over to the left side of the valley and pitched our tents. One day, these men went out and found some wild duck nests and a dozen or more eggs and came in and told us, so Ed and I went out to hunt for duck eggs too. We had not gone far on the side of a hill when I said, "Ed, what kind of a place does a duck build her nest in?" We were right by a little tree top and he said, "Well, just such places as that," pointing to the tree top, and out flew a duck. We got six eggs and looked around for more but could not find them. As there were only three in our camp, we had a good mess of fried eggs. I never could forget how surprised Ed looked when that duck flew off her nest.

There was not much game here because the Indians hunted all the time. The three weeks dragged slowly for there was not much to do to pass the time, but finally we started. We had to get an Indian to take our luggage over the Coeur d'Alene River. Then they put ropes to the horses and led them over. I was to ride one of the horses but I said, "No, I can walk and we can use the animal for provisions." We started walking 50 miles and I led a pack horse. One of our horses, if his pack did not hang just right, would not go far till he would lie down and neither Ed nor Fisher could seem to pack him right. One of the other men was a good packer and he would come over and pack him.

The first day was a hard one for me. I had not done any walking since the summer before and the trail was rough. Our packs had all gotten mixed, so we could not tell where anything was. Being very tired, it was too much work to sort it out. Ed said we better go without dinner rather than take down all the packs to find what we wanted. We were going without dinner when it was noticed by some of the others who could get to their things readily and they invited us to eat with them. How glad I was for I was hungry and tired. It was well we ate for we had a very hard afternoon trip.

The Mission of the Sacred Heart that Lois admired was built on the site selected by Father Pierre-Jean DeSmet in 1844. Father DeSmet was a remarkable man. He was born in Belgium and came to the U.S. in 1821, wishing to become a missionary among the Indian tribes. He founded St. Joseph's Mission at Council Bluffs in 1838, the first of many missions.

One hundred, fifty years before, traveling Spanish priests had converted a number of Native Americans, leaving behind a respect for "black-robes." As early as 1831, a contingent of Rocky Mountain Indians traveled to St. Louis requesting a "black-robe," but there was no one available. After the fourth such delegation in 1839, Father DeSmet was assigned to the mission.

His travels through the Rocky Mountains in 1840 covered 4,814 miles. He surveyed land and selected sites for permanent missions. Everywhere he went, he gained the trust of the tribes. Throughout his career, he brokered peace settlements between warring tribes and between tribes and the U.S. Government. His travels took him wherever he was needed to plead the case for Indians, participating in councils at Fort Laramie and in the Badlands with Sitting Bull. He traveled to Europe 19 times, meeting with popes, kings, and presidents on behalf of the American Indian tribes, calculating his miles traveled at 180,000.

He was particularly successful with the Coeur d'Alene tribe because of one of their legends: Chief Circling Raven's vision of men wearing black robes bringing a great spiritual truth to his people. One of Father DeSmet's deputies, Father Ravelli, was assigned the building of the Mission of the Sacred Heart at Cataldo. Through Father Ravelli's ingenuity and the labor of the Coeur d'Alene Indians, the building was constructed with a broad axe and auger, ropes and pulleys, and a pen knife. Completed in 1853, the building is 90 feet long, 40 feet high and 40 feet wide. Father Ravelli has another unique claim to fame. He was the first person known to use mouth-to-mouth resuscitation when he revived a woman at St. Mary Mission in Montana in 1857.

The mission served as a religious center for the Coeur d'Alene Indians, a resting place for settlers and miners, a supply and post office, and a haven for the sick. It stands today, the oldest building in Idaho, and is visible off Interstate 90.

Prospectors were scouring the entire West in their search for gold. Many of them were looking for the Sioux's "mountain of gold." Lieutenant General P.H. Sheridan wrote a letter to General W.T. Sherman that was published in the *New York Times* on March 27, 1875, in which he discussed the Black Hills and the Army's role in the country.

While on a journey to the Columbia River, General Sheridan met Father DeSmet "from whom I heard an Indian romance of a mountain of gold in the Black Hills, and his explanation of that extraordinary and delusive story of the Indians, frontiersmen, and explorers of the Black Hills country."

Figure 13: Sacred Heart Mission, Cataldo. Historic American Buildings Survey, HABS ID, 28-CATAL v. 1. Library of Congress.

Father DeSmet had lived with the Sioux who showed him nuggets of gold they said had come from several locations in the Black Hills, including the Big Horn, Powder, Rosebud, and Tongue River beds. When he told them the yellow metal had great value, the Sioux told him they knew where there was a mountain of it, but initial explorations found only a formation of yellow mica. Father DeSmet's story was remembered when gold was discovered near Harney's Peak on the eastern slope of the Black Hills of the Cheyenne in 1874.

General Custer's expedition to this area found only small amounts of gold. The Treaty of Fort Laramie of 1868 ceded this area to the Sioux Indians, so the Army had no alternative but to keep prospectors out. Sheridan believed that there was gold in the Black Hills, but much farther west. He proposed a spring campaign:

"If General Forsythe is successful, I will send Gen. Custer with a command from Fort Lincoln, across the mouth of Powder River, thence up on the south bank of the Yellowstone, crossing Powder River, Tongue River, the Rosebud, and on to the mouth of Big Horn. This country is as yet entirely unexplored, and the expedition may develop a very valuable auriferous section, and make the Father DeSmet story to some extent true."

Sheridan's letter continued:

"At present I feel quite confident of our ability to prevent the intended trespass on the rights of the Indians, and the cavalry and the infantry in the Department of Dakota are being moved at the present time to the most available points to carry out my directions of September 3 of last year. Were it not for the precautions on the part of the Government there might be a repetition of California's gold beach and gold lake humbugs, with still greater suffering, as many of the persons now crazy to go to the Black Hills never think of how they are to exist after they get there, or how they will return in case of failure."

Lieutenant Colonel Custer led 750 men of the 7th U.S. Cavalry Regiment out of Fort Abraham Lincoln, Dakota Territory, on May 17, 1876. Custer's division was part of an expedition to find and rout tribes under the command of Chief Sitting Bull. Custer found Chief Sitting Bull encamped on the Little Bighorn River in Montana. Instead of waiting for reinforcements, Custer attacked on June 25, 1876. Over a third of the 7th Cavalry, including Custer and his brother, died in the battle that lasted less than an hour. The Indians won the battle, but lost the war. The Battle of the Little Bighorn galvanized public sentiment against the Indians and troops poured into the Black Hills.

We camped at the foot of the mountain and we learned how to climb it. They packed the horses and started. They tied a long rope to the pack horse, four or five men pulling on the rope as best they could, yet the horse fell down the hill backwards and would have rolled down into the river if the man had not snubbed the rope to a tree and stopped it. They got the horse back and carried part of his load over the worst part of the trail and in this way got him up. Then they took one of our pack horses attempting the climb as before with the same result, the horse too going backwards, rolling down. I was afraid the animal had been hurt. The men took their picks then and dug into the rock so the horses could get a footing, this together with pulling on the rope got them up all right. What a tired crowd we were after such a hard climb. We had to descend on the other side, but it was not so steep and we had to go some distance before we found a good camping site.

The next day, we got to Mr. Prichard's camp on the trail. Here we had to wait for the snow to melt before we could go in. Mr. Prichard had written to some to come and get claims and to come as soon as they could get over the range, as others were coming from Montana over the old Dempsey Trail. There were some forty or fifty men who came over and without provisions, coming on the foot trail over the snow. When some of them got there, they had no shoes and they demanded of Prichard to furnish them foot wear. The mines were twenty-five miles to the north and there was two feet of snow in there. These men threatened to kill Prichard and I guess they would have had it not been for a man by the name of Endicott who lead a party of twelve hunters up there to do some shooting. They took their places in the door of the cabin and told these fellows they would have to kill all of them before they could get Prichard, so they finally cooled down and asked Mr. Prichard to go with then over to the mines. Mr. Prichard went, but not without taking some of the hunters along to check any unforeseen trouble. The water was high and the snow melting and they could do nothing at the mines for a month or so, so they returned to camp.

Before we got up there, we got word from Mr. Prichard that this party was returning and for us to hurry lest the incoming prospectors overpower him and his friends. We went as fast as possible, but no trouble arose. Six men came after a time and when Mr. Prichard heard they were coming, he packed his horse and started for the mountains. It was a fine morning when we started, it was twenty-five miles to make over a rough trail. We camped at noon and while there, a heavy shower came, wetting the grass and brush, so that when we started after dinner, it was not long before I was wet as though I had been in the river. The travel was over logs and poles all the time and my clothes would stick to me till I would have to stop to pull them loose. The sun came out as hot as mid-summer and we had a long hill to climb from the southwest. The little firs were as thick as they could grow and just a pack trail brushed through. It was like an oven in there, not a breath of air.

All but Ed and another man had gone on ahead, I was following Ed while Mr. Hapenstall was trailing behind. I told Ed I would have to rest, but he said to wait until we got a little farther where we could get some fresh air. He hurried on to find an open place and I started to follow, but went only a few steps and fell to the ground. I tried to call for help but could only make a squeaky noise. Mr. Hapenstall called Ed to come back quickly or he would have a dead woman on this hands. He came back and fanned me with his hat for a time, then having rested, I got to my feet and went to the top of the mountain. There was a lovely breeze up there and I went on to camp and felt fairly good.

Silver, 1884

There had been lots of wild goats in the brush as there was long white wool everywhere. Ed was busy panning out dirt and I was watching along the mountain side for goats. We got around to where the face of the mountain was a bare ledge of rock. I looked up and saw a great blue streak in the rock and said, "Ed, what is that?" He was busy panning dirt and said, "What is what?" I said, "Well, look at that big blue streak away up on that ledge of rock." Then he got up and looked at it and said, "Why, that is a silver strain!"

It was too near nightfall to go up to it then, so we started home, resolving to try another route leading to it as it was quite a bit nearer. When we got to the creek and attempted to cross, we found there was nothing to cross on save a pole that was lying from one bank to the other. At the larger end, it was about eight inches in diameter and tapered on the opposite side to a very small pole. The butt end lay up on a high bank where we were, the small end running to the other side near the water's edge. The water here was several feet deep and boiling and foaming over the rocks. If we went back it would take us until dark, so we sat down and studied what to do.

continued on page 117

The Coeur d'Alene gold rush was set off by the 1881 discovery of gold in the Coeur d'Alene River by Andrew J. Prichard, although he did not announce his find until 1883. After Prichard shared his secret with the Bobletts, he told one other person. Frank Dallam had come to Spokane Falls in 1883 because he felt the town needed a Republican-leaning newspaper; he called it the *Spokane Falls Review*. The town of 1,500 already had a newspaper, the *Chronicle* that decidedly favored the Democratic Party and could use a little competition. The new newspaper's future looked much brighter the day Andrew Prichard walked into the office in the fall of 1883 and poured a pile of gold onto a sheet of paper on Dallam's desk.

Frank Dallum had the scoop of a lifetime and he didn't hesitate to take full advantage of it. His story was picked up by the major papers across the country and a massive mining boom was soon underway. Dallum never looked back. He changed the name of his paper to the *Spokesman-Review* 11 years later, and it celebrated its 125th birthday in 2007.

Not wanting to miss a good business opportunity, the Northern Pacific Railroad plastered the country with handbills promising free gold in North Idaho for the price of a ticket on the train. After Prichard put the word out about his discovery, the population of the district increased from 1,000 in 1884 to 10,000 in 1885. Eventually, miners would discover not gold but deep veins of silver, the true wealth of the Coeur d'Alene.

Of course, Prichard continued to search for the mother lode. He named his mining camp Eagle City. Miners were the first to arrive, but they were soon followed by the usual suspects. Wyatt Earp and his brother Jim set up a tent saloon and gambling hall. Three years had passed since their shootout at the OK Corral in Tombstone, Arizona, and they had been forced to make their livings elsewhere. But Eagle City's decline was as rapid as its rise. At its height, businesses were opening at the rate of 20 a week, and lots were going for as much as $2,000. By the fall of 1884, Eagle City was shrinking and Murray was growing.

It isn't surprising that the Bobletts and Prichard would become friends; they had traveled the same trails. Andrew Prichard was wounded in the Civil War, returning home to lose his wife shortly afterwards. He left his children in the care of his oldest son and headed for the mining country in Arizona and New Mexico with seven other men. They found gold, but the Indians were so hostile they had to retreat. Forming a company of 47 miners, they returned, only to be ambushed by Indians. Only Prichard and six other men survived the attack.

Prichard then turned his attention to Colorado, discovering and staking the Dolly Varden Mine, which he sold for $10,000. He prospected through Montana and into Idaho on the old Mullen Trail. His first mine was the Evolution Mine, which he recorded at Pierce City, Idaho, the nearest Land Office at that time. He then moved to Rathdrum, Idaho.

Needing money to develop the mine, he moved to Spokane and went into logging. This is when he took the Bobletts and three or four men who wanted to prospect for placer gold with him. He named his next claim the Discovery. Illness laid him up for the winter and his claims were jumped. He hired a lawyer and went to court; he was to become a fixture in the courts, fighting to regain his claims, one of which was the Widows Claim. One Mrs. A.M. Eddington, a 45-year-old woman, swore the claim belonged to her. Mrs. Prichard called her an "out and out imposter" and said she sought to secure an interest in it by inducing Mr. Prichard to marry her. This he had refused to do, and the real widow, Mrs. Mary H. Lane, arrived from Illinois in time to be an important witness for his lawsuits.

An article in the Saturday, March 30, 1901 issue of the *Idaho Daily Statesman* records the transfer of Prichard's first mining claim:

"Oldest Coeur D'Alene Claim Has Been Sold. A Wallace correspondent sends the following to the *Spokesman-Review*: Deeds were recorded yesterday transferring the Evolution and a number of adjoining claims to the Evolution Mining Company, although the articles of incorporation of the company are not yet on record.

"The claims are situated on the north side of the South Fork, a little over a mile west of Osburn. They are but little developed, a crosscut tunnel on the Evolution, in which a large body of carbonate ore was cut a year and a half ago, being the most important work.

"The Evolution is commonly known as the oldest claim in the Coeur d'Alenes, Andrew Pritchard having first staked it in 1881 or 1882. Returning to the region later to look after it, he went north from there and discovered placer gold on the creek which has since borne his name, and the rush to the Coeur d'Alene gold fields began."

One of the men Prichard became involved with in the courts was Wyatt Earp. In January 1884, Wyatt and Jim Earp and Wyatt's third wife, Josephine Sarah Marcus, arrived at the Mission on the steamer *Amelia Wheaton*. Everyone but Wyatt called Josephine "Josie." He called her Sadie because she hated the name and he liked to tease her. Another four days of travel brought them to Eagle City. The next night, January 31, Wyatt and Jim checked out the Acion Saloon, where Wyatt was elected deputy sheriff of Kootenai County by an impromptu vote. Prichard had covered the area with claims by proxy for people living outside the area, an illegal practice. In retaliation, Wyatt and Jim, with some locals, staked claims over the top of Prichard's. The legal fights began. Local courts then had to determine how many claims a person could register and whose claim was legal.

Wyatt quickly made his presence felt. April was a particularly busy month for him. William Payne sued Earp and associates over possession of some town land in Eagle, alleging that two men armed with revolvers had forcibly taken possession of the land. Payne received a $25 judgment, which the judge trebled, and regained possession of the land. Wyatt filed the Eagle Creek Placer claim. He and Jim invested in real estate in Eagle City. Wyatt paid one dollar to W.H. Carroll of Fort Coeur d'Alene for a share in the Point of Rock claim in Eagle Creek. He also purchased five acres of land and bought a round circus tent, 45 feet high and 50 feet in diameter, for $2,250 and started a dance hall. Later, Wyatt and Jim opened the White Elephant Saloon,

which an advertisement in the *Coeur d'Alene Weekly* called "the largest and finest saloon in the Coeur d'Alenes."

William Payne was involved in another gun incident, in which he was a willing participant. The April 5, 1884, issue of the *Spokane Falls Review* carried a lengthy description of "A Shooting Scrape" in which 50 shots were fired and one disinterested bystander was wounded. This fight, also, was over property in Eagle City.

Philip Wyman said he located a lot the previous fall on the east side of Eagle Street and placed a building foundation on the lot. Four weeks later, he sold the lot to Jack Enright, Alfred Holman, William Payne, and Danny Ferguson. These real-estate investors erected a tent on the lot, which remained occupied thereafter.

However, Sam Black claimed to have located the lot in November, erected a tent on it, and occupied the same all winter. In January, Black sold the property to William Buzzard, who built a cabin on the back of the property in January. Buzzard claims to have recorded the lot in his name on November 27.

Enright's party countered, declaring the tent and cabin were not actually on the lot, but across an alley at the back. Each party then began to build on the lot.

That Friday morning, when Enright approached the property, Buzzard was waiting for him, backed up by his Winchester. Enright said the Winchester was good for the time being, but he would be back, prepared to argue the question. He also told the bystanders they might want to find a healthier part of town, as there was going to be some "unpleasant work in the neighborhood in a few minutes."

Soon, Enright, Ferguson, Payne, and Holman were seen walking down the street, armed with a Winchester, shotgun and revolvers. Buzzard and two or three partners awaited their arrival with a Winchester, a shotgun and a Sharps. Bystanders were again given fair warning to leave.

The Buzzard party fired two shots before ducking behind a rude fortification of hewn logs. Within minutes, approximately 50 shots were fired. Buzzard's company was forced to retreat into the cabin. "Everybody praised his grit, and accords him great credit for standing his ground manfully." Bullets left three holes in his hat.

Buzzard returned the compliment, praising Enright's bravery in exposing himself "with reckless disregard of consequences." One of Buzzard's shots almost grazed Enright's face. Another bullet kicked snow up into Ferguson's face, momentarily blinding him.

Finally, Deputy Sheriff W.E. Hunt and Wyatt and Jim Earp arrived at the scene. While the Earps dealt with Enright's men, Hunt entered the cabin to disarm Buzzard and his partners. "With characteristic coolness, [the Earps] stood where the bullets from both parties flew about them, joked the participants on their poor marksmanship, and although they pronounced the affair a fine picnic, used their best endeavors to stop the shooting. After Mr. Hunt had disarmed the parties in the cabin, the Earps announced the fact to the outside, and told them to put up their guns as the fight must end." Afterwards, Enright and Buzzard "took a smile together, and each complimented the other upon having made a square fight."

The only injury was to John Burdett, a carpenter, who was shot through the upper leg. "The unfortunate man who was wounded has the sympathy of the entire community. Messrs. Enright, Payne and Buzzard have each called upon him, and signified their readiness to render him any assistance in their power, pecuniary or otherwise. He will be cared for until he has completely recovered."

Wyatt continued to file claims in May, starting with the Golden Gate claim, as well as the Consolidated Grizzly Bear, the Dividend, and the Dead Scratch. He and his partners located a number of claims and a lawsuit was filed charging them with claim jumping. This suit ended in a victory for Wyatt in July. Meanwhile, Wyatt's brother, Warren, arrived in town and moved in with Jim.

On June 9, 1884, Prichard filed suit against Wyatt for claim jumping and won. When Wyatt wasn't busy filing claims or contesting law suits, he fulfilled his duty as a lawman. Two months later on June 19, Danny Ferguson, 23, one of Wyatt's associates, was involved in another shooting, and this one ended with a fatality.

According to the *Spokane Falls Review* of April 20, 1884, one Thomas Steele "met a fallen woman, with whom it is said, he was intimate, and in her company visited several saloons, he drinking but little and she drinking to intoxication. At about 1 o'clock this morning the deceased endeavored to induce the woman to go home, but she refused; finally however he took her by the arm and got her out of the saloon, and after going abut fifty yards she lay down in the street and declared her intention of remaining there all night. This, it appears, so provoked Mr. Steele that he slapped her face several times."

It was at this point that Ferguson arrived on the scene and thought that Steele was abusing the woman. When he intervened, Steele turned on him and said "Maybe you want some of this – damn you, I'll fix you." Pulling his gun, he stuck Ferguson over the head with it causing the gun to discharge. Ferguson had also pulled his gun and the two rapidly exchanged shots. Even at that close range, Steele was the only one to be hit.

Ferguson rushed to Earp's house to turn himself in, a wise precaution since Steele had many friends in the area. Ferguson was ordered to stand trial in July and released on a $3,000 bond. When Earp began hearing rumors that Steele's friends were planning to lynch Ferguson, he sent Ferguson a warning to disappear. Years later, a man named Danny Miller wrote a letter claiming to be Danny Ferguson. True or not, Danny Ferguson never stood trial for the killing of Thomas Steele.

Jack Enright's temper proved to be his undoing a few weeks later. According to a story in the *Idaho Sun*, July 8, 1884, he marched into the office of the Eagle City Pioneer and began shouting at the manager, Henry Bernard. Bernard pulled his gun and shot Enright in the chest, killing him. Bernard was sentenced to eight years in the state prison for the shooting.

The Earps didn't stay long. By September the gold was panned out and the miners were moving on to other towns. Wyatt, Josie and Jim pulled up stakes, closed the Elephant Saloon, and headed back south. Many of their hard-fought claims went for taxes and the Earps were financially worse off than before.

A new, permanent town was developed just up the creek from Eagle City, the town of Murray. The gold that Prichard had found on the North Fork of the river soon ran out, but silver found on the South Fork of the Coeur d'Alene was so rich the area gained the name "The Silver Valley."

I suggested we get down and crawl across the pole. We did, but I would not want to try it again, for if either one would have fallen in, we would have both gone and no one would ever have known what had become of us. We got across all right but I had to sit down for a time and rest, for I was so weak. We went on to camp and told the boys what we had seen, so the next day, we all went up to see what we could find. The rest went on ahead but Ed and I hunted our own route. We found a series of benches on the ledge, like a winding stairs. Sometimes we had to hug the ledge pretty close and hold on with both hands to get around a point of rock. I was very anxious to get to it, and as I was ahead, Ed would sometimes say, "Lois, do not go any farther, we may fall." I would answer, "Come on, there is no danger if we are careful." If we had made one misstep, we would have gone down hundred of feet among the loose rock. Finally, we got to a place where we could go no further and had to turn back. We did not get near enough to get any of the blue rock, but the rest of the party did and it was as pretty rock as I ever saw.

Endicott and his party went on to Prichard's Creek to prospect and, as there was an old silver miner there, Ed and I took some of the rock and started up to see him. We had gone about two miles when we met him coming down to our camp. We met at a little side branch of the creek and we sat down on a log to rest and talk. This miner said if we could only find the lode, he thought it would be rich, so we went back to camp. The next day a number of us started out to find the lode and locate the claims, this miner being with us.

We decided to go up from the other side of the mountain, and as it was very hot weather with no breeze stirring, I had an awful headache. We had our lunch with us but no water and I was very thirsty and tired. I wanted to sit down and let the rest go on, but Ed said, "I am sure when we get to the top there will be plenty of snow and you can get a drink, then we will eat our lunch and you will feel better." At the thought of getting snow I pushed on and reached the top, finding plenty of snow to quench my thirst. On coming to the open, I went immediately out on the snow and it seemed like standing over a radiator, so warm did the air seem from the sun as it shone and reflected back from the snow.

We got a snow ball apiece and went back a few steps from the snow under a tree and ate our lunch. After this refreshment, I felt all right again. After an hour's rest, we hunted all afternoon for the ledge, finally we set some stakes and all signed their names on a paper that we put up and went back to camp. The boys went up several times and brought down rock, but they could find no lode. The rock looked like blue glass more than anything else that I can describe. There were several who begged for specimens of the rock as they were going out. I did not have a piece left. I thought I was on the ground and could get plenty, so I gave mine away. The Endicott party finally reached the bed rock and they came to the conclusion that it would not pay to mine, so they all came out to our camp to go back home.

Ed and I went out to catch some fish and as we got to talking about the parties return, I said, "I wish too we were going out." Another party came in and they were especially rough and as I did not know them, I felt it was not safe there with them. If there had been another woman in the party, I would not have cared. Ed said, "Well, let's go."

Ed had some rock in his pocket he had taken up there from Pend Oreille Lake, and he showed it to the silver miner. He looked at it and said, "Well, if I had a claim on a ledge like that, I would get on it and go to work." We went back to camp about five o'clock in the evening and got everything picked up and at six in the morning, we started for home. As we were going up the hill from Prichard Creek, we met a party going in, led by a man called Dream Davis. I will refer to this party later.

We had our horses and as we had only our clothes and bedding and enough provisions to last to Fort Coeur d'Alene, we decided to ride. However, I believe riding was more tiresome than walking, for my

continued on page 123

Miners literally dug everywhere looking for gold and silver. Lois and her group went out on a ledge, others dug into the sides of deep ravines. One enterprising party at a bar in Murray didn't want to go out into the cold, so they cut a hole in the floor of a vacant bedroom and dug down 30 feet to bedrock and mined it with some success. The Bedroom Mine Bar still stands in Murray.

The Bunker Hill Mine was one of the most productive mines in Idaho. Its discovery is one of the best stories from the gold-rush days. Details vary from one tale to another, but all agree that a jackass deserves the credit for finding gold. Noah Kellogg arrived in Eagle City with $5, a suit of ragged clothes, and a roll of blankets; and he was determined to find someone willing to give him a grubstake. Two storekeepers, Peck and Cooper decided to give him a chance and staked him for supplies and tools. One version of the tale says that an old jackass, owned by Peck, was annoying the citizens with its constant braying, so Kellogg said he would take it, loaded his supplies on its back, and walked out of town.

He wandered around in the mountains until he made camp one night on a hill near the site of Wardner. That night the jackass strayed, and in the morning Kellogg had to search for the animal. Following the jackass's braying, he finally spied it high on a hillside. As Kellogg approached, the jackass kicked up a piece of glittering rock. Looking closer, Kellogg realized that the animal was standing near a large outcropping of galena (lead-silver ore).

Wardner was named for James Wardner, a man perhaps more interested in money than ethics. He owned a grocery store in Murray and, as soon as he heard of the strike, threw a couple of bottles of whiskey into a saddle-bag and hastened to the camp where Kellogg and his partner, O'Rourke, were busy working their claim. After generously sharing his whiskey, he asked for a hatchet and walked around the valley blazing trees. When they asked him if he had staked a claim, he replied that he had, but it was for the water rights in the valley. Kellogg and O'Rourke were forced to take him on as a partner.

The first partners sued and a judge ruled that "from the evidence of the witness, this Court is of the opinion that the Bunker Hill Mine was discovered by the jackass, Phil O'Rourke, and N.S. Kellogg."

Since the jackass was owned by the first partners, they got half the mine. This is the only jackass ever credited with discovering, owning, and operating a mine. There was an old dance hall song about the jackass that went "When you talk about the Coeur d'Alenes, and all their wealth untold, don't fail to mention Kellogg's jack, who did the wealth unfold."

Wardner described the jackass in *Jack Wardner of Wardner, Idaho*:

"Kellogg's Jack – A diminutive but pure bred specimen of the Spanish Jackass. He was mouse colored, his head was nearly as large as his body, his ears, when laid back in obstinacy, reached his withers, and he was noted all through the Coeur d'Alene as the best pack animal, although the most cunning and tricky brute that was ever cinched."

In 1900, Jim Wardner sold his interest for $100,000, a fortune at the time, to Simeon G. Reed of Portland, who had the capital to exploit the mine. Wardner moved to Fairhaven [Bellingham], Washington, and lived just 20 miles from the Bobletts.

He purchased a nearby island named Eliza, imported black cats from as far away as San Francisco and told the local citizens he wanted all their stray black cats. The horrified citizens discovered that he was raising the cats for their fur, selling the hides to Easterners as "hood seal" fur, for $2 a pelt. Even worse, he was committing "catabolism," feeding the meat to the other cats. The good people promptly shut his operation down. Then he went into banking, lumber, and a water business and made enough money to build himself a castle. Soon, he lost the castle and the money and moved across the border. In Canada, he went back into mining and lumber and had another town named after him, Wardner, British Columbia.

Two articles in the *Fairhaven Herald* [Washington], mentioned Wardner. In the March 11, 1890, issue:

"Among the residences the finest building is for Mr. J.F. Wardner, on the corner of Fifteenth and Knox Streets. This house is a combination of the Queen Anne and Eastlake styles. It will be wired for electric bells and lights and heated by the return system of steam. The windows will be of French plate glass. The interior will be finished in polished redwood, and all fittings and the plumbing will be of latest improved patterns. When finished, this residence will cost about $15,000."

The second article is dated September 5, 1903:

"James F. Wardner is reported dying in a Milwaukee hospital from the effects of blood poisoning caused by drinking cyanided water in Nevada last spring."

He was still searching for gold. Somehow, Wardner survived his illness in Milwaukee but did die in El Paso in 1905, according to the *Washington Post* [Washington, DC] on March 31, 1905:

"Milwaukee, Wis., March 30 – News was received here today of the death at El Paso, Tex., of James F. Wardner, widely known as a mining prospector and promoter of gigantic enterprises. Mr. Wardner was an eccentric man, and during his lifetime had made and lost fortunes. Among Wardner's most celebrated 'schemes' were 'the National Candy Bank,' operated in St. Louis, and the 'Consolidated Black Cat Company, Limited' with its ranch for raising black cats in the state of Washington. Other pursuits to which Wardner by turns addressed himself included such widely different occupations as hog-raising in California and gold mining in Arizona."

Several other projects of Wardner's were mining deals in the Klondike, the Isthmus of Panama, and a quicksilver mine in Mexico. Not everyone believes that the cat ranch really existed, rather that it was just a joke perpetrated by Wardner, but descendants of early residents believe he at least attempted to start a cat-fur business.

A *New York Times* reporter, Frank Wilkeson, traveled to the Coeur d'Alene mining area in 1887, just three years after Lois and Ed returned to western Washington with even less money than when they started. He had an easier trip into the mines since the addition of the narrow-gauge railroad, but his report bears out Lois's opinion of the people that made up the second wave into the mines. He visited Wardner, which lies 12 miles east of the old mission at Cataldo, and about 20 miles west of the old site of Eagle City. Wardner did not exist when Lois and Ed first traveled through tthe mountains on the way to their camp.

"Spokane Falls, Sept. 5 – In the Coeur d'Alene Mountains and close to the region where the placer mines about which there was such intense excitement among miners a few years ago were found there rages today a fierce mining excitement. Gold-bearing quartz and agentiferous galena have been discovered in several places. Two of these discoveries were recently sold for $700,000. I understand that the purchaser of these mines, the Sullivan and Bunker Hill, is about to stock them.

"The trip to the Coeur d'Alene mining camps is not a hard one. From Spokane Falls, a station on the Northern Pacific, a railroad runs to the northern extremity of Lake Coeur d'Alene where there is a shabby little town. The journey from Spokane Falls to Coeur d'Alene City is short, and if it was shorter, the travelers would be happier. At the lake, the passengers are transferred to a steamer which belongs to D.C. Corbin's Coeur d'Alene Railroad and Navigation Company. The steamer is clean and good meals are served on it . . . The steamer follows the narrow, winding lake for 25 miles, then enters the Coeur d'Alene River and ascends that beautiful stream for 35 miles to the old Catholic Mission, which was established 40 years ago, and which is still in charge of the priest who established among the Indians before Idaho was named. A very pure man is this priest, of whom every one speaks well. A narrow gauge railroad runs from the mission to the mines, and the ride on it is similar to that over any narrow gauge mountain railroad.

"Alas, the romance of mining towns has departed! They are no longer picturesque. They are no longer the homes of men who wash golden gravel and talk drawlingly of "bars," meaning the ferocious grizzlies, and not an aquatic deposit of gravel. One no longer hears interesting tales relative to the strange doings of Poker Jim or Seven-up Jack or Farro Pete. There are no campfires under the pines; no donkeys grazing on the flanks of the foothills; no pack train of heavily laden mules which follow a white mare that wears a bell on a leather collar around her neck. The open-handed, red-shirted, hairy miner who used to sit by the open door of his log cabin is almost extinct. A mining camp of today is a nasty, squalid, pretentious village and the working miners are generally foreign-born blackguards.

"I was in Wardner, which is the largest camp in the Coeur d'Alene district, for two days. I put Wardner into my notebook. Here it is: In a narrow gulch, flanked by steep mountains over which a fierce forest fire ran a few years ago, is a 40-foot wide street, the grade of which is exceedingly steep. On each side of the street there is a row of small buildings, all of which are built after the same pattern and all have false fronts nailed to them to give them a more imposing appearance than they would have if their gable ends were exposed to the street. Almost every other building on the main street is a saloon.

"In two of the saloons are gambling tables, around which unwashed and mean-faced men sit and smoke and pretend to gamble with ten-cent checks. Tall fire-blackened stumps stand close to the street on vacant lots which are held for sale for hundreds of dollars. All the shabby stores and squalid hotels and dirty eating houses have a row of barrels, which are supposed to be filled with water, standing on a plank that is nailed to their ridge poles. The water in these barrels is to be used in case of fire, and would be fully effective as a stream of water shot out of a small-sized squirt gun. The sidewalks on the main street are made of two-inch plank and are ten feet wide. At short intervals are steps, sometimes two, sometimes four, to overcome the grade and to trip the unwary or alcoholically disabled. Nightly, men roll down these steps, and nightly they profanely denounce the sidewalks and evoke Devine wrath on the men who built them.

"It is evening, and as the sun sinks behind the mountains, men gather in groups in the hotels, on the walks in front of these foul dens, in eating rooms, in billiard rooms, and in drinking saloons and they talk. Almost all of them are dirty. They have red faces and swollen noses, and there is a network of bright red veins in their cheeks. They are poorly dressed. They talk of mines and talk for the benefit of strangers. They lie and brag and lie again. They spin long yarns relative of free-milling, gold-bearing quarts, and exceedingly rich but remote placer diggings, and of immense veins of silver ore. They covertly watch the unsophisticated stranger to judge the effect their marvelous tales have on him. They eye him hungrily, as though to see in which pocket he carries his money. Finally, one approaches him, chair in hand, and seats himself at his side, saying in mellow tones: 'How are you, Colonel?' which remark being quickly supplemented by saying, 'It is a beautiful evening, eh, Colonel?' This one-sided conversation is considered in all the Coeur d'Alene mining camps as an introduction, and as a vouching for the respectability of the unwashed mountaineer, which should be more satisfactory than a letter from – say, a Bishop. Then he asks you your name and presently you are introduced to a mob of Colonels and judges and saloonkeepers, none of whom, to judge from their personal cleanliness and puffy faces, ever use water, and all of whom have evidently had a serious misunderstanding with their washerwomen. These men ask impertinent questions as to who you are, where you came from, where you are going and what you are doing. They thrust their hands deep into trouser pockets and draw forth specimens of ore, which have served their useful purpose in many mining camps, and these they moisten with their tongues and hold close to your nose for inspection, saying 'Colonel, just look at that. It runs $1,200 to the ton and is free-milling.' And they lie as lightening rod men when you look at the specimen.

"As twilight rises out of the valley and climbs up the brush covered mountain flanks, women who know how to ride appear on the streets on horseback, and they ride briskly up and down the narrow street, and the groups of men make remarks about them. Presently, these women, most of whom are respectable, disappear. It is a little darker, twilight has passed away, and it is early night in the camp. Then a swarm of hard-faced and old women parade the streets for a short time, and then they too disappear. By 9 o'clock, night is fully established in Wardner. Drunken men stagger along the streets, or lean against posts and vainly endeavor to light cigarettes. Rocky Mountain miners smoking cigarettes is a spectacle I never saw before! A swarm of laboring men are engaged in cheaply imitating the wickedness and profligacy of the old-time mining camps. Men play billiards for cigars. Others try to play whist for drinks. And more reckless men, who have heard tales relative to the old placer mining days when men wasted fortunes in a night, rush into gambling rooms and lose as much as a dollar. By 11 o'clock these roisterers become beer-laden and they then indulge in noisy, wordy rows. I lay in my bed one night at 12 o'clock and heard a row in a saloon directly opposite my open window. I judged from the savage talk that pistols would presently crack, and I tried to curl up in a corner of the bed, knowing that a 44-caliber pistol ball would tear clear through the frail house. I waited patiently for the pistol shot, and waiting fell asleep to awake at 3 o'clock to hear the row still in progress. Then I was easy in my mind and turned over and slept soundly.

"When I was in Wardner word came into town that a new mineral region had been discovered in the Bitterroot Mountains, about 25 miles from Thompson Falls, on Clark's Fork of the Columbia. This intelligence excited the more energetic of the young miners and presently a score of them left town on horseback, driving a few pack horses before them. The prompt movement of these men was the only thing I saw while on this trip which reminded me of the days when the glories of pacer mining had not passed away."

Unfortunately, Lois doesn't mention Dream Davis again, but this article printed in the *New York Times* on July 28, 1884 tells the story of Dream Davis.

"THE COEUR D'ALENE MINES – OVER THE TRAIL TO THE CAMPS IN THE GOLD GULCH – CLAIMS WHICH ARE SADLY IN NEED OF CAPITAL TO DEVELOP THEM – A RICH CLAIM REVEALED BY DREAMS

"Things were 'booming' because of a rich find in a side gulch just below the town [Murray], which is known far and wide by the name of 'Dream Gulch.'

"Dream Gulch has been worked for more than six weeks. It has been, and is still, the best paying streak yet opened and has been a source of considerable profit to its owners. According to popular report a series of unusual occurrences led to the discovery of its gold. As the story runs, its richness and the lay of its ground, the contour of the mountains, and even the minutest points connected with its situation, were revealed in a dream to an old man named Davis, who was a plain farmer living with his wife and children in the neighborhood of Palouse, on the line of the railroad. He thought nothing of the dream the first time, but when it recurred to him the two following nights, he put faith in it and actually mortgaged his farm for $1,000 to obtain money to go in search of the treasure. The Coeur d'Alene excitement was agitating the country, and he naturally made for that section.

"On the journey, he met one or two miners, and on telling them his wonderful dream so often repeated, was taken in by them, and the party set out in search of the gulch. Davis asserted that he would know it as soon as he saw it, and assured them that if he could strike it not only would gold be found in the gulch's bottom, but a quartz bed would be struck but a short distance below the surface by digging down at the foot of a pine tree on the hillside. The men did not believe in his vision, but they were willing to be led by him.

"When they came to the gulch in question, Davis walked up to it, remarking, 'If this is the gulch, you will find quartz by digging right here.' The men dug down about ten feet, and to their surprise found a large ledge of pure white quartz. Davis then asserted that the lead had been broken across the gulch, but would be found on the other side, running obliquely with the side of the mountain. The ground was dug up where he directed, and sure enough, the same ledge of pure white quartz was found. Work was then begun at the bottom of the gulch, and when bed rock was struck a few feet down, nugget gold was found in all its richness.

"As soon as the snow was sufficiently gone work was begun on the claim. There was no water to be had nearer than Alder Gulch, more than a mile away, but the men had such confidence in the claim that they dug a ditch the whole distance and, at an expense of $7,000, brought water around the side of the mountain. They have been amply repaid for their outlay. Just how much gold has been taken out is impossible to learn, but the figures say between $40,000 and $50,000 thus far.

"But I must go on to Eagle City and finish up the district. It is four miles from Murrayville [Murray]. One sees men at work in ditches as one leaves Murrayville, but they grow fewer and fewer as he nears Eagle City. Osborn, the point where the trail from Kingston and the country tributary from Spokane Falls and Rathdrum comes in, is one mile this side of Eagle City. It has only a few tents, probably five, and is little more than a name. Eagle City is called 'dead' by the people in the other towns in the gulch, and I must confess it has something of that appearance, though it is the most

substantially built of any. It is much more concentrated, has fewer tents, more wooden houses, and more of the air of a business center. But it has many vacant houses and not so many people by two-thirds as Murrayville. In Eagle City the streets are quiet; in Murrayville they are full of people. When 'Dream Gulch' was discovered, the people stampeded from Eagle City to Murrayville and they stayed there because some claims are there working and things are more lively."

As is true with any legend, there are several descriptions of Dream Davis and his mine. In 1966, Russell A. Bankson and Lester S. Harrison published *Beneath These Mountains*. Their goal was to prove or disprove the legends that had grown up around the Coeur d'Alene gold rush. Their research showed that Floyd M. "Dream" Davis and his mine were even more mysterious than previously thought.

He arrived in Murray dressed as a traveling preacher, introducing himself as a "circuit-riding gospel peddler." He wasn't in town to preach, however; he wanted to learn all he could about mining. After several weeks of interviewing the other miners, he purchased an old jackass and supplies and headed out of town. In the weeks that followed, no one ever saw him on the trails or in the mountains. He seemed to have vanished.

When, long-haired and bearded, he led his jackass into town in early October, he went directly to the Courthouse to file his claim. The agent spread out the map and Davis placed his finger on a spot. That was the place, he said, Dream Gulch and the Dream Gulch Mine. Next stop was the bank. He opened his pouch and poured out $3,210 in gold nuggets and dust. He assured the bystanders that he would be bringing in more.

Naturally, the editor of the *Sun* wanted the story, and Davis was happy to oblige. He repeated his story of being a farmer and preacher until the dreams started. Three nights in a row, he experienced the same dream or vision. On the third night, a voice told him to follow the landmarks and he would find great riches. In this version of the story, Davis goes off alone, follows the clues, and finds his mine. After the story was printed, other miners joined him on his trek back to the gulch.

The first snow sent the miners back to Murray, where Davis deposited enough gold to bring his total to about $10,000. Speculators offered him $10,000 for the claim and he promptly sold out. He had cleared $20,000, but none of the other miners had found any amount of gold in their claims in the gulch. Davis headed out of town. The next, and last, word of Floyd Davis was a newspaper article in the *Sun* in February, 1887 that read:

Figure 14: Dream Gulch. Photo courtesy of Murray-Idaho.com.

"The body of F. M. Davis, known to everyone in the Coeur d'Alenes as 'Dream Davis' has been discovered. He disappeared from Portland about two months ago. His body was identified beyond doubt in Los Angeles, California. He had lost all his money and, destitute, he had committed suicide."

horse was the hardest I ever tried to ride. When we got down to the Mission where we had waited for the water to recede, we met some of our crowd who had been after more provisions.

We all camped together and in the night I was awakened by someone groaning. I shook Ed and wakened him and he raised up to listen. He got up and followed the sound and not far as a man by the name of Frank Robertson was nearly dead with cramps. Ed came back and I got up and we took our bedding and put it over him. We made a fire and, going to the water, got some good sized boulders. These we put into the fire and heated, then poured water on them, rolling them in clothes and put them around him. It was not long before we got a sweat started and he got better, but he was not able to travel.

The party he was with wanted to go on to their places as they knew the rest would be out of provisions. The Endicott party wanted to get out and go to their homes in California, so that left only Ed and I to stay with him. He said for us to go too, but we would not leave him looking more dead than alive, so we stayed there for three days. He continued to improve, so he thought he could stand it to ride. We started for Rathdrum where Ed and Fisher had bought three lots formerly. Ed and Frank decided to build a hotel as Rathdrum was on the road into the mines and we felt sure there would be a big rush in there by the following spring.

They went to Ellsport and took down the houses we had left there, but before leaving, we got a house and opened up. We had all we could do all the time. Frank was a splendid helper and we got along fine, but when we commenced to build, he had to help Ed on the house and I had to get a girl to help me. I thought I could get along alone and so I did for a time, but it was too much for me. A widow with one son, by the name of Mrs. Whisler, came along and wanted work, so we hired her and she proved to be good help. She stayed several months until we moved into our house. She finally did all the cooking and washing of the dishes and we gave her and her son $60 a month and their keep.

Ed and Frank put up a large two story building and we paid for lumber and the carpenter work out of the receipts of the hotel. As soon as they got it up and enclosed so we could use it, we moved in. We had no rent to pay and seemed to get along fine. We put every cent into the house as fast as we made it. As fast as a room was finished and furnished, we got an occupant. In fact, after every room was ready and occupied, they still came to us, so we finished up the garret and made shingle bed stands, putting them so there was just room enough between to dress.

There was a lodging tent near by and they all boarded with us, as well as the man who was in charge of it. They got to drinking and gambling and did not pay their board so that finally we had to take their bedding for their board bill. Now we had bedding for over a hundred beds and we made beds on the floor in the dining room, office or any place possible.

In the winter, Mr. Prichard came to our house and he found we had a widow cooking for us, and of course he had to have an introduction to her, and it was not long before we had a wedding in our house and had to hire another cook. We had to get a regular hotel range costing $150. We had one hundred and fifty for every meal for several months. During this time, Michael Rosbrough, Ed's brother-in-law, and Charley Rosbrough, Ed's nephew, came out from Iowa and stayed with us, working on the house and helping until spring.

> Lois might have needed a larger kitchen range, but it didn't necessarily save her time or labor. The new cast-iron stoves included reservoirs to heat water as well as ovens and cook tops. The heat produced by the stove was welcome in winter, but stifling in summer. In six days, a coal burning stove consumed 292 pounds of coal, 14 pounds of kindling, and 27 pounds of ash that had to be sifted out.

We had nearly everything paid for: the furniture, bedding, lumber and work, but we owed a grocery bill of $750. However, we had back board bills due us to at least that amount. We had our land at the boundary line of one hundred sixty acres and we felt we could easily meet our obligations. The grocer learned we had acreage and he kept at Ed to give a mortgage on the same to cover the grocery bill. At first, he tried to make Ed believe that he could force this on him, but we knew differently, as our land was in the territory, then the Territory of Washington, and our house and the grocery store in Rathdrum, Idaho.

However, Ed thought it would be best to mortgage our land and when the notary-public came to have me sign the document giving the same, I was very much tempted not do it, even if it was Ed's wish. However, I signed it against my better judgment, hoping for the best.

The men came back from the mines, not having made good on their claims and as there were Ed, Mike, Charley, Frank and a cousin of Ed's, Jake Boblett, and Joe Kagey, all out of work, the men took a contract to furnish ties to the railroad some ten or twelve miles out, so we rented our house and went. Since there would be 12 men, I told them to take along a cookstove and I would go as cook, to which they all agreed. We were going to camp out, so I took nothing more than my rough clothes as did Ed.

A Case of Arson, September 27, 1884
A new route and closer had been found to the mines so the party who had rented our house at $75 per month could not meet the rent and had to give it up, going to Spokane. A family moved in near where we

were camping and as the teamsters went to town on Saturday night, I said, "Let us go and bring some of our clothes so we can call on our neighbors." Ed said he wanted to go hunting with a party and that we could go to town the following Saturday night and bring some trunks of clothes. That very night our house burned to the ground with all the contents save a little bedding. We learned the fire was set in a little carpenter shop right by the side of the house. The neighbors said they smelled coal oil very strong as they were passing that afternoon.

We knew the grocer well; he ran a general merchandise store and had a big insurance on his goods, and we learned he had just gotten through invoicing his goods that day and had gone to Portland, Oregon. Also, a consignment of goods had been taken out of the store and sent to Fort Coeur d'Alene and a new store started there. We could easily see why he did not want to take a mortgage on our house. I then told Ed we had better go home now, but he would not consent and said, "We will stay right here and get it back."

Lois wasn't the only one who believed the fire was caused by arson, but whether or not the grocers, Woonacott & Glass, were at fault is unknown. The Rathdrum fire made headlines as far away as Portland, Oregon, including this article in the *Morning Oregonian*:

"Pacific Coast – Eighty-five Thousand Dollar Fire at Rathdrum, Idaho – THE TOWN NEARLY ANNIHILATED – Many people homeless and without food.

"Rathdrum, Sept. 28,- Special – Fire broke out at 10 P.M., the 27th, in a small unoccupied building in the rear of Rector's drug store, destroying the entire business portion of the town – fifty-five buildings. Losses aggregate $85,000, as follows:

Lee & Jackson, saloon,	$4,000
Harry Gordon, saloon	4,000
Woonacott & Glass, General Merchandise	19,000
J.H. Smith,	3,500
Dr. C.W. Weaver, Coeur d'Alene Hotel, including office and instruments	4,500
Rector Bros., drugs	2,500
John W. Smith, liquors in storage	2,500
George W. McCabe, livery and stage company	2,500
J.G. Brophy, saloon	2,000
E.A. Boblett, American Hotel	2,000
Sibley & Ish	2,500
C.M. Benson	2,000
C.W. Wood, livery	25,000
John McCrea, hardware	2,000
Sun Chung Co.	2,000
S.C. Cramer	2,000
Thomas Ford	2,500
T.K. Hireen	2,000
A.P. Powell	1,000
John Russell	1,000
Oliver Edmond	1,000
Henry Keiser	1,500
Branch of Sprague Brewery	1,500
W.A. Hart	1,100
George Stafford	1,000
M.W. Musgrove, on residence and office of *Kootenai Courier*	1,000

And others in smaller amounts. No insurance is known, except on Woonacott & Glass' property. Over twenty families are destitute. Not a business house is left in town, and no provisions are on hand. Temporary relief is promised from Spokane. The fire is supposed to have been the work of an incendiary."

Chapter 11
Washington Territory
1884-1899

𝒥 knew we could not do it as we had lost everything and we had to begin all over. Mr. Frank Robertson, who was a boss in the camp, knew my feeling in the matter and said to me, "Do you want to go home?" I said, "I do." He further said that when we got pay for the ties we were all going to go to the Sound and that he would get tickets for the entire crew. I was afraid he would not do it, but it pleased me thinking that I possibly would soon again be with my relatives: my father and mother and sister Eliza and her husband, who was like one of our own brothers. No wonder I was glad when Frank got the tickets for Tacoma and brought them in and handed Ed our two. Ed read them and looked up at Frank and started to say no, but Frank told him not to decline as we were all going. Ed smiled and said, "Well, if you all are going, I might just as well go with the crowd."

In 1884, some time of that fall, we took the train for Tacoma. We stopped at a hotel there and the men tried to get work. We knew it would be no use to go on the ranch in the fall so they all tried to get work. We stayed at the hotel a week and things looked pretty blue. I learned the landlady was a Methodist and I felt we had a friend in her, so I told her we had just been burned out and had lost everything and I was ashamed to go out on the street. Mr. Boblett had done his best to find work, he being a carpenter, but there was no work to be had that was honorable. She asked me what I could do and I told her I could cook and do any work a woman could do. She told me there was a man looking for a cook. I talked with him and soon had a job for Ed and myself for $75 per month. Now I said, "There are four men with us looking for work and as you are hiring men, could you not employ them?" He said he could and we felt pretty well pleased at hav-ing found work. We went nine miles out of Tacoma and Ed and I cooked for forty-three men that winter who were bringing the water into the townsite of Tacoma.

Ed and the other men found work on Tacoma's first municipal water line. Tacoma became a town almost overnight when the Northern Pacific Railroad began construction on the western terminus of its transcontinen-tal line. In fact, the population grew from 1,098 in 1880 to 36,006 in 1890. A house-to-house delivery system run by Tom Quan, a Chinese immigrant, with barrels and a mule cart, was sufficient for a short time. As demand grew, earthen water reservoirs were built in the city, with water piped through bored logs down Pacific Avenue. In 1884, the City Council grant-ed a franchise to Charles B. Wright to build a system that would bring water into town from Tule and Spanaway Lakes and Clover Creek. His company, The Tacoma Light and Water Co., built a 10-mile-long system that carried water through open flumes made from hollowed-out logs into a reservoir in town. Unfortunately, the open system was accessible to thirsty animals, storm debris, and playing children. The result was an outbreak of typhoid fever that killed several people, including two city councilmen. The company failed, the city of Tacoma took it over in 1893, and Tacoma Water was created.

Back to Blaine, 1885

The last week of February 1885, we started for Blaine on a steamer which went as far as Seattle. There we had to wait till the next day when we got aboard the *Evangel*, run by Captain Beecher, a son of Henry Ward Beecher. He ran by Port Townsend, then on to Blaine, coming across the Straits. There, waves burst in the door

continued on p. 129

The *Evangel* was a well-known ship in the area; although "infamous" might be a better description. This article appeared in the *Blaine Journal*, October 22, 1891:

"THE EVANGEL

"Last week the steamer *Evangel*'s boiler blew up at the Whatcom dock causing the death of four men and injuring several others very badly. The steamer's upper works were torn to pieces, but the hull was uninjured.

"The *Evangel* was for a long time the only steamer making regular trips to Blaine, and was as well known to most of us as our own houses. Capt. James Tarte ran her most of the time, but Capt. Beecher also came here in her for a number of months. The steamer has had an eventful history, which we clip, as below, from the *Seattle Post-Intelligencer*:

"It is doubtful if there ever was another vessel built on the coast with a history as peculiar and interesting as that of the steamer *Evangel*.

"She was built in Seattle at the foot of Cherry street in 1882, by Rev. J.P. Ludlow a Baptist preacher. She was a propeller, 100 feet long, 17 feet wide, 7 feet deep and of 77 tons burden. As originally built, she was only eighty feet in length and was designed by Ludlow as a gospel ship. Ludlow was at the time clerk of the court in the third judicial district and had for a long time before cherished the idea of building a gospel ship for the purpose of conveying preachers and workers in the cause of Christianity around from place to place on the sound, holding services at mills, logging camps, etc., where no other opportunities for church work existed. Shortly after his appointment as clerk of the court, a rich relative died, leaving him several thousand dollars. This gave him an opportunity to put his ideas into practice, and he started to do so, and frequently express the belief that the Lord had sent the money to him for the purpose of aiding him in the undertaking.

"He made known his intentions through various channels of the churches of the country, and in a short time subscriptions began to come in from church societies all over the world to help on the work of building the ship, subscriptions having been received from Henry Ward Beecher's church at Brooklyn, and various other churches in the east especially.

"Before the vessel was finally completed, Ludlow became interested in an Alaska mail contract. The Pacific Coast Steamship Company had been carrying the mail up to this time, but a company was formed, with John Leary at the head, for the purpose of bidding for this mail contract, and when the time came for examining the bids the Pacific Coast Steamship Company was surprised to find that it had lose the plum. The steamship company then went to work and chartered or subsidized nearly every available boat on the coast, so the new contractors were at a loss for a vessel to put on the route to carry out their contract. They finally succeeded in purchasing a steamer named the Yaquina at Portland, which was owned by Captain Hatch. She was loaded with lime when they bought her, and was to be brought around to Seattle and delivered to them as soon as discharged, but the night after the purchase was made she took fire and was completely destroyed. The new company was determined to carry out its contract, however, and induced Ludlow to cut his boat, then almost ready to launch, in two in the middle, and make her twenty feet longer, and put her on the Alaska route instead of using her as a gospel ship. Ludlow returned all the contributions received from church organizations, as far as he could when he decided to divert the boat from the original object in view. Her name, *Evangel*, meaning good news, had already been selected and was suggested by the name 'Good Tidings,' which Mr. Ludlow was advised to call her . . .

"When the boat was ready to launch invitations were sent out to all the churches and church societies in the surrounding country requesting their members to be present and witness the ceremony. Nearly everybody in the city and the surrounding country and towns was present on the occasion. Instead of breaking the usual bottle of wine over the bow, a little girl dressed in white was stationed on the bow, and as the vessel slid down the ways into the water the child scattered religious tracts in profusion, which fell like snowflakes. A number of old steamboatmen who witnessed the affair prophesied that the vessel would be ill-fated on account of the unusual manner of conducting the ceremonies launching her.

"When the steamer was on her way to Alaska on the first trip, the sheet-crown of her boiler burned out when a short distance north of Victoria, and she had to return to Seattle for repairs. This laid her up several weeks, and in consequence of the delay and the general ill luck, the new company gave up the mail contract and it reverted to the Pacific Coast Steamship Company. There was some suspicion that the engineer had been bribed to cripple the vessel. Just before she started out on the trip Ludlow was offered $24,000 for her, but he refused. The object of making the offer was to keep her off the route.

"By the time the boat was put in condition again she had cost Ludlow so much that he found it necessary to put her to work carrying freight and passengers on the Sound in order to save himself from financial ruin. Captain Tarte, Ludlow's son-in-law, was placed in command of her, and Reverend Karnes, a broken-down minister, was a deck hand on her. The rest of the crew was made up of some of the foremost members of the Baptist church of Seattle. Karnes finally became disgusted with his lot as a roustabout, and settled on a ranch near Green lake and in time became quite wealthy. Business for the steamer was dull, and she was not successful. After dragging along for two or three years, she was chartered by Herbert F. Beecher, of Port Townsend, son of the noted divine. Beecher ran her about a year, but evidently was not successful, as he never paid the charter money, though suit was brought for the amount. Ludlow became disgusted with steamboating, as it had about ruined him financially, so he sold the gospel ship to Morgan & Hastings, of Port Townsend. This firm afterward dissolved and Morgan took the boat and sold a half-interest in her to Captain Winn Mann, of Port Townsend, and those two gentlemen owned her at the time of the accident, and was running her between Port Townsend and Whatcom.

"As originally designed, she was a neat little craft with ample machinery but when lengthened out it made her too large for her power and this, no doubt, has had much to do with her ill luck, though she was regarded as a very substantial and safe boat. Ludlow is now in Japan doing missionary work. He is described as a very eccentric man. He hated tobacco, and when a man entered his office smoking he would throw open every window and door. His younger son was named Pilgrim Stranger Ludlow, the father giving as a reason for the odd name that he wanted to boy to be constantly reminded that he was a pilgrim and a stranger on earth, whose only home was in heaven."

Lois and Ed sailed on the *Evangel* when it was captained by Herbert Foote Beecher, the son of Henry Ward Beecher and nephew of Harriett Beecher Stowe. Captain Beecher's name was associated with several ships. He purchased the steamer *Brick* from Captain Tarte. In 1889, he arrived in Seattle from San Francisco with a large steamer called the *Point Arena*, with the intentions of running it between Blaine, Port Townsend, Whatcom, and Victoria, B.C. Beecher gave up the *Evangel* when he was appointed collector of customs in 1885.

Beecher's term of duty with the customs lasted two years and ended with serious questions raised about his conduct. No further reference appeared in the *New York Times* after this one, dated July 9, 1887, so perhaps no charges were ever filed. The article is especially interesting in regards to drug smuggling.

"AGAINST H.F. BEECHER. AFFIDAVITS AND LETTERS LEFT BY THE LATE ABNER L. BLAKE.

"San Francisco, July 8. – The *Chronicle* devotes two pages to letters and affidavits found among the effects of the late Abner L. Blake, formerly Deputy United States Collector at Port Townsend, Washington Territory, who died under what were considered mysterious circumstances, at Chicago, last May, while on his way to Washington. The article says that Blake, who had been removed from the Custom's service, held to the opinion that H.F. Beecher, son of the late Henry Ward Beecher, who was Collector at Port Townsend, and who is now Treasury Agent there, had defrauded the Government, and in one instance had withheld from an informer the money due him, growing out of a large opium seizure. The alleged seizure is said to have consisted of 14 barrels of opium, which were found hidden in a bog on the Alaska coast, having been placed there by the Captain of the steamer *Idaho*. The seized opium was sold by the Government for $80,000, of which the informer, G.M. Rouse, was to have received about $16,000. In the papers of Mr. Blake it is shown that Rouse received no money, but that a Chinaman, Ah Coy, of Victoria, was substituted as a "dummy" informer, and was given $133, although he signed as having received $3,000.

"These and other serious charges were made by Blake to the officers at Washington, but no attention being paid to them, Blake started East with the documents in person, but was induced to stop at Chicago, where he died. The affidavits include those of every person connected with the opium seizures, including that of Ah Coy, together with transcripts of the 'seizure book' at Port Townsend. Other affidavits among Blake's papers, made by people at Port Townsend and elsewhere, charge Mr. Beecher with collecting from the government money, for expenses and for the construction of boats for the use of the customs service, in each instance larger in amount than actually paid by him.

"In the letter written by Rouse from Chicago, he expresses the belief that Blake there met 'Bill' Minty, formerly employed on the Steamer *Evangel*, of which Beecher was Captain, and was by him induced to remain at Chicago, and that while there Blake met foul play, to prevent his proposed exposure, resulting in his life."

One hundred years and more have passed, and the police are still involved in fighting the same types of criminal activity. Drug smuggling was a problem then as today and the authorities were always on the lookout. This item appeared in the *Blaine Journal* on Thursday, January 9, 1890:

"Inspector Reilly, of Whatcom, had noticed several times lately a man hire a horse at a livery stable in that place and ride out of town towards the north, and he did the same one day last week. After the man had been gone a sufficient length of time Inspectors Reilly and Buchanan procured a buggy and took the road toward Nooksack crossing, and just before reaching the crossing they met their man in the road with a large gunny sack filled with something on his horse. They stopped the man, and upon looking through his baggage discovered that he had a large quantity of opium on board. Man and opium were both taken over to Port Townsend, from where Mr. Buchanan returned home last evening."

near the engine room and the men on the boat had to spike it. It upset the darkey's cook stove and the water would come into the dining room windows by the bucket full. Everything breakable in the state rooms was scattered over the rooms in pieces. The windows in the pilot house were broken and even the smoke stack dipped water a number of times. Finally, we got in behind an island and how glad I was, for I had made up my mind we would never get across. I was so sick I could not be up at all and nearly every man on the boat was sick. Finally, we got to Semiahoo Spit, for that was the only steamboat landing for Blaine at the time. We all went to Darters and stayed there for a few days and, on the fourth of March, we came home to Blaine and in a few days we went over and brought Father and Mother over to make their home with us.

Aretas Whitcomb died June 25, 1888 at the age of 75. Amos Dexter died April 29, 1895 at the age of 73. My sister, Mrs. Eliza Dexter, died August 29, 1897 in Blaine. [Lydia Priest Whitcomb, Lois' mother, died September 25, 1898 at the age of 95.]

Our mortgage would soon be due and we knew property values would soon come up in a few years on the Sound, so Ed went to Tacoma to borrow money to lift the mortgage, getting another so as to put off the payment until he could pay it by the increase in value. However, he could not find the money to borrow for our land in Blaine, so he sold 80 acres of the north part of our land to Mr. A. J. Martin and a Mr. A. W. Steen for $1000 and in less than two years, we could have sold it for $10,000. That is the way signing a mortgage went with us.

The Caines came in March, 1872 and bought out Mr. Crampton and in September 1884, they had the first map of Blaine plotted and recorded. January, February, March and April 1890 was the time we had a land boom in Blaine. It seemed everyone had gone crazy. We had 40 acres unplotted land that Mr. Boblett was offered $900 per acre and he would not take it. He thought he could get lots more than that for it.

At about that time, an evangelist was holding meetings in the M. E. Church and one day we had eighteen in our house to buy property. One man stepped up to me and asked if the meeting was to be there. I said, "It looks that way, doesn't it?"

When the meeting closed, Ed said to me, "Don't you think we ought to go over to Victoria, B.C.?" I said, "Yes, but not now for I think we ought to stay home and sell property." Ed said he wanted to go to get rid of selling it. He said if we went away, then Dave Miller would sell so much higher that he could get more when he wanted to sell. My mother was living with us, so we fixed up and went, taking Mother with us. This was sometime in March, 1890; I think the first part, for there was good sleighing. We went to Victoria and stayed with our daughter for a month and when we came home, the bottom had fallen out of the boom, but Ed still thought it would come up again. Men that he sold property to would come back with a pitiful tale and Ed gave them back their money till we had none left.

Lois made one trip in 1890 that she failed to mention. She, Ed, the Pauls, and nephew Rosbrugh decided to climb Mt. Baker, 30 miles east of Bellingham in the Cascade Range. The 10,778-foot glacier-covered volcano is still active although it has not had a highly explosive eruption in the last 14,000 years. A minor eruption occurred in 1957. The mountain set a record for snowfall in a single season in 1999 with a total of 1,140 inches or 95 feet of snow. It is no wonder they would stop at the snow line.

The *Blaine Journal* reported the trip on September 11, 1890:

"Blaine will not be behind, so far as climbing the great white robed mound, Mt. Baker, is concerned. A party of seven, consisting of Mr. E.A. Boblett and wife, Charles Paul and wife, Victor Paul, Charles Rosbrugh and John Wagner, leave this morning for the foothills. Messrs. Boblett and Charles Paul, who have some knowledge of the country around the north side of the mountain, feel confident the mound can be scaled from the side, although the little party will not go farther than the snow limit. The male members will prospect, and their friends here will look expectantly for their return to examine the rich specimens of quartz they will bring with them. They will be gone two or three weeks."

The paper noted that the party returned on September 26, 1890:

"A party consisting of E.A. Boblett and wife, C. Paul and wife, V. Paul, C.C. Rosbrugh, Fred Schultz and John Wagner have returned from a visit to Mt. Baker. They report having spent a most enjoyable time and say that bear hunting is a very exciting sport with a good trail to follow."

Chapter 12
Alaska District and the Yukon Territory – The Klondike
1899

*H*ard times came on and we had difficulty in making ends meet. Mother was helpless and this kept me from earning much, as I had to care for her. Ed was getting along in years as he was 15 years older than I and was hardly able to do a days work. About this time, my sister died, leaving me her estate as she had no other relatives, and on this property was a mortgage of $800.00. We sold some of the land to lift the mortgage. The Alaska excitement was running pretty high at this time and Ed had a desire to go. He was too old to go alone, so I told him if he could raise the money, I would go with him, otherwise he should not make the trip. He finally got a chance to sell forty acres and then we got ready and started April 17, 1899. I kept a diary of the trip but by some mishap part of it has disappeared, so I will do my best to remember the most important happenings.

We started for Atlin [British Columbia] from Blaine on April 17, 1899 at 3 P.M. We went to the train at two o'clock with a host of friends. The train being late, we had a visit with the folks. When at last we heard the whistle, we bade them all goodbye and boarded the train. We then went to Westminster, BC. Being late in starting, we missed the train and stayed all night at Wise's Hotel, had a fine supper and got up in the morning feeling very much refreshed. Then we took the train for Vancouver, BC. When the train came, Ed was not ready so Mr. and Mrs. Paul went on to see that our freight was all right and one hour later we followed up, finding them in the depot to Vancouver. We started in search of the Carter House where we stayed three days with nothing to do.

We had to go around and get the things needed for the trip. One night, we went to the Salvation Army Barracks. There were nine conversions and we had a fine meeting. They sang many of the old familiar songs. We wanted one piece called "The Shelf Behind The Door."

On April 24, decided to stretch a tent for we did not know how long we might have to stay. The men went to the depot to get Mr. Paul's tent, as it was all ready to use. Mr. Openhammer told them they could stretch it right by his store on a nice grassy place, so we were soon keeping house for ourselves. The men hunted around and found a little stove and two benches belonging to the Salvation Army, then we thought we were all right. We camped this way for a week, visiting around Vancouver, taking in all the sights while waiting for the boat that would carry us to Alaska.

On Thursday the 27, we took boat and started for our destination. The first night out the water was very calm but when we came to Queen Charlotte Sound it was very rough and I got sick again. The next place of note was Seymore Narrows. For thirty miles we watched the mountains with their snow peaks and glaciers. We reached Skagway [Alaska] April 30. We stayed here until May 2. Skagway is quite a little town though rough looking. We went about and on our way saw a sign saying "M.E. Church". It being Sunday afternoon, we went on and came back to the evening service, hearing a fine sermon.

When first I came to Jesus
With my load of guilt and sin
I asked him to fergive me
And he freely took me in
He cleansed my soul from idols
And filled my heart with joy
And give me peace and happiness
Old Satan cain't destroy
CHORUS The shelf behind the door
The shelf behind the door
Tear it down, throw it out
Don't use it any more
For Jesus wants his temple clean
From ceiling to the floor
He even wants the corners clean
Just in behind the door
VERSE 2: There's many people of today
Profess to love the Lord
They say, their doing all his will
And trusting in the word
But yet their always grumbling

Do you know the reason why?
T'is, because they have some idols
That their keeping on the sly
VERSE 3 Some love the filthy weed, you know
An' some the social glass
Some say, they'd rather dance than eat
Some idolize their dress
And 'er they get their hearts put right
They give the consant o'er
And put them on that little shelf
That's in behind the door
VERSE 4 O, how the gospel chariot would
Go sweeping thru the land
O, how the Christian soldiers
They would fight at Gods command
O, how the work of Jesus
Would spread from shore to shore
If it were not for that little shelf
That's in behind the door

There are at least two versions of *The Shelf Behind the Door* and it isn't known which one Lois sang. This version was recorded by Max Hunter, as sung by W.H. Shelly, Cabool, Missouri, on May 14, 1958, and is part of his extensive collection of folk songs. The audio materials in this collection were given to the Springfield-Greene County Public Library, Springfield, Missouri.

Another, somewhat more militant, version was printed in **The Reverend Martin Wells Knapp's Bible Songs of Salvation and Victory** published in 1902 "for God's people of every land: suitable for revivals, the Church, Sunday-schools and the home."

～～ ～～

Lois didn't describe the accommodations on their boat, and by 1899 ships going to Alaska were both more plentiful and comfortable. Noah N. Brown, a miner and newspaper reporter, was on a trip to Seattle when the *Portland* steamed into the harbor, loaded with gold. The fever struck him that night, but try as he might, there were no tickets to be found for anything sailing north. By luck, he was standing at the ticket counter when a man discovered he would not be able to take his horse on board. Refusing to go without the horse, he sold his ticket to Noah for double the original price. Noah sailed on the *Mexico* on July 19, 1897.

"I shall never forget the event of that memorial occasion when we pulled away from the dock, opposite the foot of Yesler Way. Sun shades, hats and handkerchiefs were waving, vessels in the bay were whistling, bells were ringing, and voices of thousands of people were strained in bidding us a successful voyage."

He found the accommodations on the nearly derelict ship left much to be desired.

"The *Mexico* was packed to its gunwales. It booked many more passengers than the law allowed and my berth – did I say my berth? Well, it was in the passage way of the steerage. Three bunks high on each side, with orders not to sleep on the deck. A few hours for me in the 24 down were sufficient. I tried to purchase a place somewhere outside of that roasting hole. Nothing doing. Though walked over, trampled over, accompanied with foul air and loud, boisterous language, I had to stay – we had to stay. But what of that? We were going to the Klondike, that would help toughen us…This vessel, it was said, cleared $20,000 on this voyage of seven days. It was its last trip, it sunk in Wrangle narrows on its return voyage."

Ed was 71 and Lois about 55 when they joined the Klondike Gold Rush in Yukon Territory. Within a six-month period, 100,000 miners, known as "stampeders," started for the gold fields, but only 30,000 actually arrived. The Boblett party followed the most common route, up the West Coast to Skagway, Alaska. The fares from Seattle to Skagway ranged from $25 to $55 a person.

Among those miners was a man named "Soapy" Smith, of Denver fame. He came to Skagway in 1897, looking for a new way to make a fortune. He opened a saloon/casino called Jeff's Place and staffed it with his "lambs," also known as the Soapy Smith Gang. Any man lucky enough to win a game of chance in Jeff's Place was usually met by one of the gang in the alley and relieved of his winnings.

Soapy built the first telegraph station, opening for business after just a few weeks of construction. Unbeknownst to the miners, the wires extended into the harbor and ended there. The lack of wire didn't stop requests from coming in to the miners asking for money back home. The money flowed into Soapy's new enterprise.

The good citizens of Skagway tried to run Soapy and his gang out of town, but he retaliated by taking over the town. He coerced or bribed 300 residents to form a law and order committee and name him chairman. He rode at the head of the Fourth of July Parade as Grand Marshal. Soapy did have his soft spots and gave generously to charities, particularly those benefiting the widows of men who died at the hands of his gang.

Three days after the parade in 1898, a miner carried $3,000 in gold into Skagway. Soapy's Lambs convinced him to put the gold in Soapy's hands for safekeeping. Tricked into a game of three-card monte, the miner began losing and felt he was being cheated. When he tried to take his gold back, a mock brawl was staged, during which the gold disappeared, and the miner was thrown into the street. The miner's plight stirred a vigilante group called the "Committee of 101."

The Committee ordered Soapy to return the gold or else by the next day. Soapy refused. The Committee held a meeting that night in a warehouse at the end of the wharf to discuss their next step. Word of the meeting reached Soapy, and he decided to crash it with his armed men.

Armed with two revolvers and a double-barreled rifle, Soapy rushed out onto the wharf, only to be met by Frank Reid and three other vigilantes. Reid was armed with a revolver. Soapy swung at Reid with the butt of his rifle; Reid blocked it, and got one shot off, missing Soapy. After a short struggle, both men fired at the same time and fell to the ground. Soapy was dead, and Reid was fatally wounded. Witnesses claimed to have heard eight shots and Soapy had more than one wound. Whatever the truth, Reid was given credit for killing 38-year-old Smith. Letters from J.M. Tanner, one of the other three men on the wharf that night, showed that another guard shot Soapy. According to the *Skaguay News*, July 15, 1898, Soapy's last words were "My god, don't shoot."

The souvenir business was brisk in after-death photo-graphs of Soapy. Even society women were not immune to the lure of such a souvenir. Mary E. Hitchcock left her privileged life in New York seeking adventure in the cold North. She took along her friend, Edith Van Buren, two Great Danes, a portable bowling alley, an ice cream maker, and a full-sized circus tent. Her book detailing their adventures, *Two Women in the Klondike*, described their purchases.

"Having purchased in Skaguay photographs of 'Soapy Smith at rest,' 'Soapy Smith sleeping with shoot-ing-iron,' and 'Soapy Smith's grave,' his story interested me greatly, but it was told in many different ways." The photographs she purchased showed Soapy in his coffin; others were available showing his autopsy.

Twelve days later, Reid died and was buried in the Skagway Cemetery. His headstone reads "He gave his life for the honor of Skagway." Not faraway is the tomb-stone of an infamous prostitute, which reads "She gave her Honor for the life of Skagway."

Other camp followers to arrive in the Yukon were Wyatt Earp and his wife, Josie. Wyatt and Josie arrived in Alaska aboard the *S.S. City of Seattle*, spending their first winter in Rampart City, in 1897.

Earp and C.E. Hoxsie built the Dexter Saloon in Nome, the first two-story wooden building, that opened in September 1899. It measured 70 feet by 30 feet, with 12-foot ceilings, and was Nome's largest and most luxurious saloon. Wyatt was arrested June 29, 1900, for interfering with an officer while in discharge of his duty. He claimed he was only trying to assist the officer and was released without charges. The Earps sold out and left Nome in October 1901, with $80,000 – a fortune at that time. The Earps returned to Nevada to work on their claims, and eventually settled in California, where Wyatt became involved with the movie industry, meeting such actors as Tom Mix, William S. Hart, and John Ford. Wyatt even appeared as a movie extra.

The Earps had a stormy relationship, with Josie angry about his womanizing and Wyatt unable to stop her gambling, but they were together for 47 years. Wyatt died in 1929 and Josie died in 1944. In all his years as a gunfighter and law-man, Wyatt was never so much as grazed by a bullet.

Tuesday morning, May 2, finds us aboard again with calm weather. We could not find one of our valises so we had to go on. We took the train to the summit and on the way we had some experiences of the hair-raising order. One place, our train ran into a snow drift and had to go back over a place that made us all feel uncomfortable. I began to think I would rather walk, but at last we got to the Summit Station at the end of the road. Here we all expected to walk, but Mr. Hainey said no, that Mrs. Paul and I might ride, as he sent a team to take our baggage free for sixteen miles to Log Cabin. Here we stopped for two days for our freight to have it inspected. We rode over the snow in a sled and the driver said it was fifty feet deep.

Leaving Skagway for Bennett, British Columbia, May 4, 1899

Thursday, May 4, we started for Bennett City. We reached there about four o'clock. We put up at the best hotel in town, meals 75 cents and beds 50 cents. They were the worst beds I ever slept on. They were single beds or bunks with canvas covering. They sagged till they were like troughs. They had a bar in the house with the landlady as bartender. Such proceedings were not irregular for that country. On the 5th of the month, we rented a house and thought we would open it up, but we changed our minds after making a table and buying a cord of wood for $10.00. The men looked around and came to the conclusion we would not make much keeping boarders, so we gave up the house. Then we bought a pony, harness and

continued on page 139

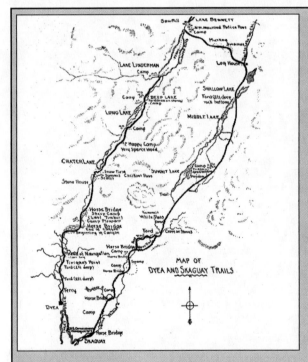

Figure 15: Dyea and Skagway Trails. En Route to the Klondike: A Serious of Photographic Views, Part III, People's Series. Chicago: W. B. Conkey Co., 1898. University of Washington Library Archives.

Once in Skagway, Stampeders had a choice of routes, all dangerous and challenging. White Pass, the trail on the right, looked more direct on the map than Chilkoot Pass, but looks were deceiving. The trail was so rocky, muddy, and steep that thousands of pack animals died along the way. One section of the trail became known as Deadhorse Gulch, it was so littered with carcasses.

The Bobletts chose to take White Pass out of Skagway. Fortunately, by the time the Bobletts arrived, a narrow-gauge railroad had been built. They didn't have to climb the Golden Stairs, a half-mile stretch near the middle of the pass that rose more than 1,000 feet, and consisted of 1,500 steps carved out of snow and ice. Too steep for packhorses, stampeders had to "cache" their goods, making numerous trips until they had moved all their supplies. This is where many stampeders gave up, discarding their goods along the way.

Disembarking at Summit Station, the Bobletts traveled another 16 miles to Log Cabin (also known as Log House), where they went through an inspection of their goods by the North West Mounted Police. The stampeders were required to have one-year's supply of goods before they were allowed into Canada. This was roughly one ton of goods per person. Most of the money made in the gold rush was made by the outfitters.

On December 31, 1897, the *Skaguay News* printed *When and How to Outfit*. It cautioned the miners to bring plenty of food.

"Man requires more food in a cold country than in a warm one. The half of a yearling calf only makes a meal for the men of a certain Siberian tribe. Miners in the Yukon district require strong and rich food and they will drink bacon grease like so much water."

The article suggested that four or five miners band together to share the work and collect necessary supplies, which is exactly what Lois, Ed, and the Pauls did. Supply cost estimates varied from $150 to $500 per person.

The paper supplied a list adequate for a party, including these necessities:

1 tent, 10 x 12 feet	1 Yukon stove
1 frying pan	2 cooking pots
Eating utensils for 6	2 butcher knives, 1
2 hatchets	drawing knife
200 feet of rope	1 handsaw and 1 whipsaw
32 assorted files	1 brace and bits
25 pounds of assorted	15 pounds of oakum
nails	10 pounds of pitch

The tools, rope, oakum, and pitch were used to build boats the miners would need for the second leg of the trip to the mine fields.

A number of publications were available to the miners with suggestions for supplies. McDougall and Secord, suppliers out of Edmonton, had a list for the Chilkoot Trail in 1898 that was widely used:

3 suits heavy knit	12 pairs wool socks
underwear	1 pairs heavy moccasins
2 pairs german stockings	4 heavy flannel overshirts
1 heavy woollen sweater	1 pair overalls
2 pairs 12-lb. blankets	1 waterproof blanket
1 dozen bandana	1 stiff brim cowboy hat
handkerchiefs	1 pair hip rubber boots
1 pair prospectors' high	1 mackinaw, coat, pants,
land boots	shirt
1 pair heavy buck mitts,	1 pair unlined leather gloves
lined	1 duck coat, pants, vest
6 towels	1 pocket matchbox, buttons,
30 yards mosquito	needles and thread, comb,

netting/1 dunnage bag	mirror, toothbrush
1 sleeping bag/medicine	pack saddles, complete
chest	horses
flat sleighs	100 lbs. navy beans
150 lbs. bacon	400 lbs. flour
40 lbs. rolled oats	20 lbs. corn meal
10 lbs. rice	25 lbs. sugar
10 lbs. tea	20 lbs. coffee
10 lbs. baking powder	20 lbs. salt
1 lb. pepper	2 lbs. baking soda
1/2 lb. mustard	1/4 lb. vinegar
2 doz. condensed milk	20 lbs. evaporated potatoes
5 lbs. evaporated onions	6 tins/4 oz. extract beef
75 lbs. evaporated fruits	4 pkgs. yeast cakes
20 lbs. candles	1 pkg. tin matches
6 cakes borax	6 lbs. laundry soap
1/2 lb. ground ginger	25 lbs. hard tack
1 lb. citric acid	2 bottles jamaica ginger

A second article in the 1897 *Skaguay News* was *From Woman's Standpoint* written by Annie Hall Strong.

"When our fathers, husband and brothers decided to go, so did we, and our wills are strong and courage unfailing. We will not be drawbacks nor hindrance, and they won't have to return on our account.

"There are a few things, however, a woman should carefully consider before setting out on this really perilous journey. First of all, delicate women have no right attempting the trip. It means utter collapse. Those who love luxury, comfort and ease would better remain at home. It takes strong, healthy, courageous women to stand the terrible hardships that must necessarily be endured."

Strong stressed the need for proper shoes.

"Get a shoe that fits, and if the sole is not very heavy have an extra one added." She then suggests carrying house slippers, walking shoes, gum boots, and felt boots. Moccasins can be purchased from the Indians and are very comfortable. Among her suggestions for wearing apparel are "2 short skirts of heavy duck or denim to wear over bloomers, arctic mittens, 1 hat with rim broad enough to hold the mosquito netting away from the face, snow glasses, and some sort of summer wear gloves to protect the hand from the mosquitoes."

Figure 16: Stampeders and Supplies on the Wharf at Skagway. Yukon Archives, Anton Vogee fonds, #114.

Figure 17: North West Mounted Police and Stampeders Waiting to be Checked Through. Yukon Archives, Anton Vogee fonds, #114.

Strong had nothing but disdain for sleeping bags. She suggested a piece of 5 x 14-foot heavy canvas.

"Fold half the strip of canvas on the ground, place your bedding on it and draw the other half over. You are then protected from the dampness and wind and have something doubly useful, for if you are caught in a blizzard without a tent you can stretch your canvas over a pole and made as a tent at a moment's notice.

"An old miner would no doubt laugh me to scorn for suggesting a little satchel or handbag, but the comfort derived from the hundred and one little ictas a woman can deftly stow away in it will doubly repay the bother of carrying it."

Besides the suggested items, Lois took enough dishes, silverware, and cooking utensils to set up and run a boarding establishment.

After clearing customs, they followed the trail to Lake Bennett. Here the stampeders had to build boats for the 500-mile run down the Yukon River to Dawson City, or sail through Windy Arm, Taku Arm, and Atlin Lake to the town of Atlin.

The winter of 1898-99 arrived just before the stampeders, and the lake froze and cut off access to the interior. On May 29, the ice melted enough to allow boats onto the lakes and rivers. Thirty thousand men and women in 8,000 boats set sail in a two-day period. Many miners died when their boats struck the rapids and rocks and broke apart.

Noah Brown and his companions also stopped on Bennett Lake to build a boat. He wrote home:

"Crafts of different designs and descriptions were roughly made but staunchly constructed at the head of Lake Bennett, either from lumber by the little saw mill there, or else made by the crude way of whipsawing. My partners and I were fortunate to secure our boat with the order given, as Billie Wimmer struck out on our landing at Dyea, to Bennett, and being successful in presenting our order at the little saw mill, put us in readiness to start as soon as we got our equipage there. The craft was 29 feet in length, four feet in the bottom and six feet at top, costing us $180."

The trail into the gold fields was dangerous and graves and animal bones marked the way. One reminder of the dangers the party faced was the grave on Deadman's Island. It was named for two men who drowned close to shore. Luc Richard and Thomas A. Barnes, who, with all the dogs in their sled team, died when they fell through the ice near the B.C.-Yukon border on May 10, 1898. They were

Figure 18: Boat Building on Lake Bennett, 1897-1898. E.A. Hegg, Eva Davies Collection, Library and Archives Canada / C-004688.

freighting material to Caribou Crossing to build a pair of steamboats.

This obituary from Volume 1, Number 1, of the *Caribou Sun* is reproduced as closely as possible to the original. Throughout it, Luc Richard's name is spelled incorrectly as "Lue."

"TWO MEN DROWNED
Lue Richard and Thomas A. Barnes meet with
Death in Lake Bennett.

"Last Tuesday a serious accident took place near the Island about midway of Lake Bennett which resulted in the death by drowning of Lue Richard and Thos. A. Barnes. They with O.S. Felton and H.M. Buck were on their way to Bennett with Richard's dog team for supplies. When near the island the party became alarmed at the poor condition of the ice and started toward the shore when the ice gave way; Richard at once sank to the bottom but Barnes hung on to the ice for about ten minutes and made a gallant struggle for life, but sank for the last time when the rescueing party had almost reached him. The accident was seen from the shore by a number of Yukoners who rendered all aid possible and succeeded in rescuing Messrs. Felton and Buck, who lay flat on a small patch of white ice which barely sustained them. The dog team and sled were lost. All valuables on the bodies were recovered. The body of Mr. Richard was recovered the next day, but the searching party did not find the remains of Mr. Barnes until the day following. A reward of fifty dollars was paid for the recovery of the bodies.

"The funeral took place on Friday afternoon when Mr. C.A. Walsh read the Episcopal burial service and a choir sang Rock of Ages and Nearer My God to Thee. A very large attendance of men and a number of ladies were present and contributed a profusion of wild flowers. The burial took place on the island about forty feet from the water line among a garden of wild roses. Headstones were placed on the graves properly inscribed and a picket fence will enclose the Island's first cemetery.

"Mr. Richard was about thirty-eight years of age, of French descent, and came here from Frenchtown, Montana, in company with Will P. Brayton, Mike Beaulieu and Charles Bouchard also of Montana.

"Thos. A. Barnes was about thirty-five years of age, an Englishman by birth, whose residence was in Axtell, Kan. He was a member of the Iowa-Alaska Mining company who are in camp here."

Figure 19: The Richard-Barnes Grave on Deadman's Island. Photo by Murray Lundberg, *Explore North*, 2003.

sled for $20.00, and piling our stuff on it, started down the lake on the ice. I was glad to leave the city for I think it was the filthiest place I ever saw; dead horses and dogs and filth of every description everywhere all around the lake and yet this lake was the water supply.

Joining the Rush, 1899

With our load of about 2500 lbs., we started down the lake, so of course we all had to walk. They told Mrs. Paul and I to go ahead, which we did, and after walking some four or five miles, a gentleman with a light load overtook us and gave us a free ride to Deadman's Island. He divided his lunch with us and left us to wait for the men with the goods. The load being heavy, they did not get along until about four o'clock, then they stretched the tent as it was all ready and we camped for the night.

The next morning when we got up, there was about three inches of snow on the ground and it was still snowing. It continued to snow until about eight inches deep. As the ice was getting thin, and so much soft snow had fallen, we decided to divide the load. Mr. and Mrs. Paul and Victor started on to the mill where we could get lumber to build a boat. The next day, Victor came back after Ed and me and the rest of the goods. Seeing him coming, I went down to the lake to get some water and went through the ice nearly to my knees. I did not want much of that and began to scramble out. I went to the tent and put on dry shoes and stockings and hung the others up to dry. I soon had dinner ready and then we started on our way to the mill, arriving all right. We crossed on a crack in the ice where it went up and down some several inches and it made me feel uncomfortable.

On the 13th of the month, we went up Wheaton River prospecting and found several specimens. It being late when we started, we did not have time to go far as it was very hard traveling on foot and there was no small boat. It being Saturday, we came home early to bake our bread; that night there was a heavy Chinook wind all night and all day Sunday.

Monday was as warm as summer and the men were busy preparing our boat while Mrs. Paul and I busied ourselves gathering small vines to make our beds. Tuesday the 16th was another lovely morning. That night, Victor killed a nice fat pheasant and we made a pot-pie for dinner. Mrs. Paul and I took a walk up the mountain and found high bush cranberries and crocus and snow all together. Of course, the berries were last years berries but they were fresh and nice. The beautiful scenery I can never forget, the high snow peaks, the glaciers and the ice-bound lake made a most magnificent sight to behold.

The 27th was another fine day and after finishing our pheasant, together with the dumplings which I made, Mrs. Paul and I went down to the beach where the men were busy building our boat. We asked them if we could not help, but Mr. Paul said they did not want any women fingering in the pie.

We sat there for a while and then someone said there was a lot of nails in some old lumber around the point, so Mrs. Paul and I started to draw them with a hatchet and a hammer. We split and pounded out nails until she said, "Look here." I looked around and she held the hammer in one hand and the handle in the other. We decided to go back and get another hammer, but not until we had gotten several pounds of nails. We told Mr. Paul they were glad to get our fingers in the pie. Then we hulled some corn and boiled it, made a dried apple pie and cooked some rice for dinner.

On the 18th, Mrs. Paul and I took a stroll up on the mountain. Mrs. Paul concluded it was too hard work so she sat down to rest while I went on to the top. I had not been up there long when I heard Mr. Paul call to Mrs. Paul that there was a job for us. I hastened and told them they could not get along without our help. We then went to picking oakum to cork the boat and it took us all day as some of it was very hard, having been used once.

May the 19th, we were still having fine weather. A little excitement happened on this morning as three muskrats come out of the ice. The men got after them and Victor killed one. We had no fresh meat, so he proposed we cook if for dinner, which we did, and it tasted good, but the name rat spoiled it for me.

May the 20th was another beautiful day. Mr. Paul and Victor started up Wheaton River in the morning prospecting. Ed stayed to work on the boat till noon and quit with his hands all swollen and sunburned.

Mrs. Paul and I persuaded Ed to go with us to the river to see if we could catch some fish, but we had no luck. However, we found some dry-land cranberries. They grow on the ground and look like cranberries, only they are smaller and have no seeds. We stewed them and they were fine.

Lois and Mrs. Paul certainly deserved Mr. Paul's thanks for picking the oakum for the boat, which wouldn't have been seaworthy without it. Picking oakum dates back to the early 1600s.

Marine historian Ted Kaye describes oakum as "loose fibers obtained by unpicking old ropes which were then sold to the navy or other shipbuilders – it was mixed with pine tar and used for caulking (sealing the lining) of wooden ships. Picking oakum was done without tools of any sort and was very hard on the fingers. Oakum is a recycled product. Before wire ropes, all rigging on ships was hemp. In running rigging, uncoated hemp rope for standing rigging was tarred, parceled, and served. The pine tar and varnish coating wears out in time and since untreated hemp goes slack when wet, worn rigging had to be replaced."

Historically, oakum picking was performed by slaves, poorhouse inmates and prisoners, because few people would willingly perform such tedious work. The *Pall Mall Gazette*, London, England, printed a series of articles written by W.T. Stead during his incarceration at Coldbath Fields Prison in 1885-86. Stead wrote in *My First Imprisonment*:

"Then I set to work to pick oakum. It was not the proper oakum, but coir fibre. I had to pick from ten ounces to one pound. It is an excellent meditative occupation. But it is hard at first on the finger-nails. Mine wanted trimming; for, if the nails are not short, the leverage on the nail in disentangling the fibre causes considerable suffering."

Stead was fortunate. He had to pick one pound of oakum daily, while a man sentenced to hard labor had to pick three pounds daily. Picking was introduced into prisons as a punishment for men in 1840:

". . . prisoners were given a weighted quantity of old rope cut into lengths equal to that of a hoop stick. Some of the pieces are white and sodden looking . . . others are hard and black with tar upon them. The prisoner takes up a length of junk and untwists it and when he has separated it into so many corkscrew strands, he further unrolls them by sliding them with the palm of his hand until the meshes are loosened. The strand is further unravelled by placing it in the bends of a hook fastened to the knees and sawing it smartly to and fro which soon removes the tar and grates the fibres apart. In this condition, all that remains to be done is loosen the hemp by pulling it out like cotton wool, when the process is completed . . . The place is full of dust . . . the shoulders of the men are covered with brown dust almost as thick as the shirt front of a snuff taker . . .the hard rope cuts and blisters their fingers."

On May the 21st, Ed's hands were still hurting him some. I was tired for I had done a big washing. Mr. Paul and Victor returned home, having found nothing worth staying here for, so on the 23rd we commenced on the boat again to be ready to sail for Atlin as soon as the ice went out. I thought it would not take long as it had rained a little during the night. On May the 24th, it rained again.

Ed's hands were getting a great deal better, so Victor and Ed started making oars for the boat while Mr. Paul was making camp chairs. He made a chair for Mrs. Paul and myself and now we would not have to break our backs sitting on the boards and benches. Mrs. Paul made a mosquito net for her face and I made one for Ed and myself. On May the 28th, the wind was blowing. Mrs. Paul and I went down to see a pile of ice the wind had blown up on the shore. It looked like a mountain of ice and certainly was beautiful, frozen in long icicles.

Mrs. Headland, a lady who was stopping here while her husband was hauling for the mill, came over and told us they saw lots of fish in the river the night before, so our party decided we would go out and try to fish. We had no luck, as they played around our hook and would come to the top of the water and seem to say, "You can't catch us."

Victor went up the river some five miles and he managed to get them to biting and brought home ten fine ones. However, I did not learn the name of them. We had them for breakfast the next morning and they were very good. We tried our luck again but all in vain. However, we found the ice all gone and then launched our boat, and we were all ready to sail as soon as the wind went down. In trying to get the fish to bite, we tried everything we could get for bait. First Victor caught a big miller, then we tried green flies and Mrs. Paul hooked on a mosquito. You can well imagine that a mosquito must be large to be used as bait!

In his letters home, Noah Brown also mentioned the mosquitoes.

"On reaching here, you are cut off from society and its advantages; you live upon what you are able to procure and that cooked or prepared by your own hands after a hard days toil and you are nearly eaten up by the greatest pest in the world, the festive and gay mosquito or the little black gnat, that we found so plentiful at White Horse Rapids . . . We have been told of people going crazy from the mosquito on some of the streams here."

On June 1st, the wind was still blowing. The wind continued blowing the next day and we still had to wait. The men partly loaded the boat, but had to unload again and draw the boat out of the water to save it being dashed to pieces. We all had to work hard to keep our stuff from getting wet and to save the boat.

Atlin Mining District, Summer 1899

On June the 4th, we got up at three o'clock, got our breakfast, loaded our boat and started across the lake about five o'clock. We had not gone far before the wind came up, but we made it all right by hard work. It got pretty rough and of course I had to get seasick. We traveled until eleven o'clock, then we had to stop because of the ice. There were a number of boats at this place waiting for the ice to go out. We thought we were elected to stay here for some time, but to our surprise, it was all gone the next morning, as well as most of the boats also. It rained all afternoon and softened the remainder of the ice so that a little gasoline boat pushed its way through and the rest followed. We were so tired we did not hear them leave. We got up about five o'clock, got our breakfast and pulled after them. With a fair wind, we sailed through the narrows at Caribou Crossing and came down to Windy Arm.

We were told we would have trouble at this place, but we found it fine until we got nearly across, when the wind came up and began to blow pretty hard. However with fair sailing, we came on to Taku Arm, a distance of about twenty-five miles, and there we camped for the night. It was a sight to see so many boats all over the lake, it looked like a fleet.

We soon started on again and the first thing we were aware of was that we were again surrounded by ice. We went on and when we got up the lake, we saw the steamer that had passed us in the morning. I looked up the lake and saw something; some said it was ice, others that it was rough water, and Victor said it was fog. We took Victor's glasses and found it was ice. We then camped for dinner and the ice came down and we were fearful we were going to be icebound. Mr. Paul and Victor thought we could get through as it was not more than a hundred yards wide to open water, so we started. I felt afraid as we approached it but when we got into it, it was but a mass of small icicles and the boat rode through nicely.

The wind raised again and blew the ice to the other side, so the steamer, as well as ourselves, could proceed again. We went on till night, sometimes rowing, sometimes pulling. We traveled this way until two o'clock, when the wind came so strong against us we had to stop. On going to shore, we found the ground covered with caterpillars, so we called it Caterpillar Camp.

At eight o'clock the next day, the wind was still contrary, though not so hard, and we started again, keeping close to the shore. That night when we camped, we decided to get an early start the next morning and start across Windy Arm before the wind got too strong, as some had been lost by taking the risk.
I got up and got breakfast and called the men. Victor wanted to know what we were getting breakfast for. The sun was two hours high. He said, "I don't care if it is, look at my watch." We did and it was only two o'clock. We waited until three, then tried it again, eating breakfast and getting an early start and we could sail pretty close to the wind and we traveled nearly one hundred miles in a few hours.

I do not remember how we got to Taku City, but I know it was a hard trip on me as Ed was sick all the way. I had to take his place poling and sometimes rowing, and again towing with a rope at the same time using a pole to keep the boat off the rocks, while the rest of the party were walking on the shore pulling on the rope. We traveled many miles that way.

One evening, we camped and got our supper and just as we got through, Mr. Paul said, "Hurry up and clean up the dishes as I believe we are going to get a wind." And we did. We could feel the breeze blowing. We loaded up, I do not remember just what time we started, but we went a hundred miles, traveling until midnight before we stopped. There was no moon, but we could plainly see Taku City. Victor said, "I believe I could read a newspaper." We handed him some printed matter and he could read it plainly.

The next morning, we went across to Taku City and there had to have the boat hauled overland some nine to fourteen miles to Atlin Lake. When we got there, they had passed an ordinance no more tents to be put up for business purposes. We had taken a good-sized tent, cook stove, dishes, etc., with us expecting to run a tent restaurant, but they would not permit this. We went around the lake prospecting for a time, but could find nothing worthwhile. We saw claims that had been jumped, some as high as six times. Everything was tied up, so we could do nothing, so we went back to Atlin.

In a few days, a man that knew Mr. Boblett in Blaine came to our tent and told of a man [with claims to lease] about thirteen miles away, up on Pine Creek, and wanted Ed to go with him. They planned to go the next morning and I asked if I might go

Figure 20: Men Hauling a Scow at Windy Arm. University fo Washington Special Collections, E. A. Hegg 2147A.

along. The man said it was all right if I could walk that far. I told him I could walk as far as Ed. As Ed was not very strong, I suggested we start out ahead. He said that was all right but not to go beyond Pine City. We got there first and waited for the rest of the party. But when we found the man who had the claims to lease, he backed out and said, "We will go up to the mines and possibly we can find some good claims that can be worked on." We went on, climbing a very high mountain going over the trail.

We came to where some were working and some wanted to lease. Ed said, "Have you a gold pan? I would like to try some of the dirt." One went and got a pan and brought it full of dirt and panned it himself and as he was panning, he spit in the pan. Ed and I cast glances at each other without the rest of the party taking notice. The man had quite a sprinkle of gold when he got through, but we had lived too many years among miners to be taken in so easily.

We then started down the stream and did not get very far before we came to where some more men were running a sluice-bore. They had the dirt pretty well washed out and there was quite a little gold to be seen. Ed asked the man where he got the dirt that the gold came out of. He said, "Do you see that wheelbarrow there?" pointing to one not far away. We looked at the dirt in the barrow and saw it was not the same dirt at all and we again started down the creek. We met a man and Ed, in talking with him, asked where they were getting the dirt they were washing that was giving the gold. The man said it was not bottom dirt as represented, but came out of the hillside.

Figure 21: Claim on Pine Creek Near Pine City. Yukon Archives, Anton Vogee fonds, #3157.

Everybody wanted to lease us his bottom claims, but not any of the high land. They would tell us no one had as yet gotten to bottom rock and had proved it sufficiently. But as we went on down the creek, we came to a crew and they told us there was nothing there, the gold was all on the high ground. Of course, we concluded we did not want any bottom ground, and as no one would lease us the high ground, we started out to go back to camp. Victor went out hunting and we started for the road. We had a high mountain to climb and the road was steep. We had to help ourselves up with the brush, but finally we got to the top and sat down to get our breath.

Freedom in America at this time meant very different things for men and women, particularly in rural areas. Many women were free to do what a man told her to do, whether it was her father, brother, or husband. A woman's life was complex. She was expected to bear whatever children God gave her, work on the farm, weave cloth and make clothes, prepare foods to be stored against winter needs, and do all this while taking care of daily chores of cooking, cleaning, and caring for family members, including the elderly and infirm.

These expectations were set against the view of many men that women were childlike beings with brains too small for complex thought. Historian Hubert Howe Bancroft summed up these beliefs:

"Give her a home, with bread and babies; love her, treat her kindly, give her all the rights she desires, even the defiling right of suffrage if she can enjoy it, and she will be your sweetest, loveliest, purest, and most devoted companion and slave. But life-long application, involving life-long self denial, involving constant pres-sure on the brain, constant tension of the sinews, is not for women, but for male philosophers or – fools."

The upheaval that swept the county during the opening of the West and the Civil War freed women, and, in many cases, forced women to make their own decisions and seek their own futures. Independent and resourceful by nature, Lois was born at a time when she could exercise her inclinations and live a life of her choosing.

Claire Rudolf Murphy and Jane G. Haigh wrote in their book, *Gold Rush Women*, about the unique challenges women faced in the North. "But the pioneer movement on the Plains was more often a family affair, with the promise of free land and a new home at the end of the trail. In the North, disease and Indian attacks weren't the greatest challenges facing stampeders: the experience of women in that wilderness was shaped by the brutal cold, rugged territory, and vast unpeopled distances."

The Gold Rush was an equal-opportunity employer. Anyone with enough nerve and spirit could try their luck, whether they were men or women. Many women went as homemakers to see to their husband's needs rather than as partners working a mining claim.

Some single women came simply looking for a chance to support themselves. They worked as cooks, store clerks, laundresses, waitresses and seamstresses. Money could be made by any woman willing to work in the dance halls, so much a dance and a percentage of the drinks. Other women chose careers as prostitutes, dance-hall girls and actresses. Any woman with stamina could qualify as a dance-hall girl. For a dollar, a miner could dance with one of the girls. She earned $40 to 50 a week, plus a percentage of the drinks. The dancers and variety girls wore revealing costumes on the stage, and then changed to fashionable gowns to mingle with the crowd and sell drinks. Mining camps broke many women, particularly the prostitutes. Alcohol and drugs took their toll as did poor diets, filthy living conditions, and venereal diseases.

Fannie Sedlacek Quigley

But some of the women who came to make their own fortune did succeed. Fannie Sedlacek Quigley and Lois had quite a bit in common. Fannie credited her upbringing on a Nebraska farm, battling blizzards, locusts, and financial stresses, as strengthening her mentally and physically. Fannie had no formal education and didn't speak English until she was a grown woman. She struck out on her own at 16, following the railroad west. She was 27 when she joined the stampede to the Klondike.

She hiked in dragging her sled laden with her tent, Yukon stove, and supplies to Dawson City. She pitched her tent and hung her sign, "Meals for Sale." Like Lois, she didn't mind a good, long walk, and her long hikes through the country earned her the name "Fannie the Hike." Fannie picked up extra money working as a dance-hall girl and housekeeper. She said, "I reckon I've set up my tent and hung my Meals-for-Sale sign at most every strike in the North."

Fannie married Angus McKenzie, and they operated a roadhouse at No. 18 Below on Hunker Creek. Fiercely independent, Fannie and Angus had their differences, often fueled by alcohol. Fannie left Angus and hiked 800 miles down the Yukon to Rampart, then on to Tanana, and eventually to the town of Chena, still looking for a strike.

Fannie met Joe Quigley in Fairbanks when she nursed him back to health after he became gravely ill with typhoid fever. She married Joe in 1918, although there is no record of a divorce from McKenzie. They staked their claims at The Silver Pick on Quigley Ridge, the Hard Luck Association claim, and the Golden Eagle Claim. Fannie died at the age of 74 in 1944.

Nellie Cashman

Nellie Cashman was another woman formed in the same mold as Lois. She had already tried her luck searching for gold throughout the western US, including Nevada and Arizona, south into Mexico, later into British Columbia, finally joining the rush to the Yukon.

In Nevada, Nellie and her mother opened a miners' boarding house on Panaca Flats, then one of the roughest mining camps in the west. She and her mother were among the few respectable women in a town with 72 saloons and 32 brothels. Whenever Nellie had extra money, she supplemented it by canvassing miners for matching funds and then built schools, churches and hospitals from the Mexican border to Alaska.

A flip of the coin in 1874 decided the next move for Nellie. She went to British Columbia and the Cassiar district. At Dease Lake, Nellie opened a combination saloon and boarding house, dealt in mining claims, and grubstaked miners. The 1874-75 winter was a particularly bitter one, and Nellie heard that miners who had elected to winter over on their claims were starving and suffering from scurvy.

Nellie and several others assembled emergency supplies, including limes to fight the scurvy, and snowshoed hundreds of miles to rescue the miners. This exploit and others like it earned her the nickname "Angel of the Mining Camps."

Nellie returned to Arizona in 1876 to nurse her ill mother. From 1877 until 1898, she worked her claims in Tucson, Tombstone, Bisbee, and Baja. While Nellie was in Tombstone, she became acquainted with the Earp family and ran restaurant and retail businesses, including selling boots manufactured by her brother-in-law. When the brother-in-law died at the age of 39, leaving a widow and five children, Nellie moved the family to Tucson. Her sister died of tuberculosis and Nellie assumed the full care of the five children.

Nellie may have fallen in love in 1889. The *Phoenix Daily Herald* noted that Nellie and Mike Sullivan had left to get married. Something must have transpired on the way to the preacher, because the wedding never took place.

Always restless, Nellie traveled with her teenage foster children to Prescott, Jerome, Yuma, and Kingston in New Mexico, Montana, Idaho, and Wyoming. At some point, she supposedly made a trip to Africa.

Nellie was the same age as Lois when she returned to Alaska, landing at Skagway in March 1898. Nellie was accustomed to being the only woman in a mining town to open a restaurant, but she found others ahead of her in Dawson; women like Ethel Berry and Belinda Mulrooney who were as driven and tough as she was. Nellie returned to mining and filed a claim on Bonanza, later selling it for $100,000.

Nellie arrived at White Horse in 1904 and continued on to the Alsek district where she purchased several claims. Returning to White Horse for supplies, she took the Dawson trail. One day she walked 21 miles alone in a temperature of 61 below zero. Her chin was "frozen a little," but she declared that the "dry, bracing frigidity of the Arctic Circle was more attractive to her than the sunshine of Dixie land."

In 1907, at the age of 60, Nellie moved one more time. She packed her sled and moved 600 miles upriver into the Yukon to Nolan Creek. The placer gold on Nolan Creek was buried by more than 100 feet of frozen, boulder-rich glacial overburden. Needing steam boilers for thawing the ground, Nellie returned to Fairbanks and purchased boilers and piping for herself and other miners.

Nellie continued to mush her dogs hundreds of miles on her trips in and out of Nolan Creek. On one trip to Anchorage in 1923, she completed a 17-day, 350-mile trip from Nolan Creek to Nenana in December. She was 78 years old. Nellie realized she was losing her health and in 1924 returned to Fairbanks. She died in Victoria in 1925.

Belinda Mulrooney
Belinda Mulrooney was 25 years old when she stepped off the ship and tossed her last half-dollar in the Yukon: "I vowed I'd never need small change again." She brought silks and hot-water bottles that she sold to Natives along the way.

Her trip up was exciting in more ways than one. A passenger went into labor and Belinda was chosen to act as midwife. She delivered the baby while the captain read instructions from a medical textbook.

Belinda preferred to make her money off the miners rather than mine herself. In Skagway, she set up as a broker, buying furs from Indian women and selling them to steamship passengers. She spent her $5,000 in profits on silk, cotton goods and hot-water bottles which she then sold in Dawson for $30,000.

She opened the Grand Forks Hotel at the junction of Eldorado and Bonanza Creeks. An instant success, she invested the profits in mining claims and built the Fairview Hotel in Dawson. She ordered and personally escorted over White Pass a shipment of silverware, china, linen, brass bedsteads, and cut-glass chandeliers to make the Fairview a first-class hotel.

According to Murphy and Haigh, Belinda was not a woman to be trifled with.

"Belinda had signed a contract with packer Joe Brooks in Skagway, paying him $4,000 to ferry her goods over the pass. Brooks, looking for easy money and figuring a woman wouldn't be hard to cheat, dumped her freight on the trail. Furious, Belinda immediately returned to Skagway and seized Brooks' pack train, retrieved her goods, and arrived in Lake Bennett riding Brooks' own horse!"

After Belinda gained a one-third interest in Big Alex McDonald's Eldorado and Bonanza Mining Co., she started telephone companies in Dawson and Grand Forks, the town she built. Belinda was married in 1900 to Charles Eugene Charbonneau, a champagne salesman from Quebec.

It took him just four years to squander her fortune. After he was indicted on charges of selling a salted gold mine, he snuck out of Dawson with all of Belinda's jewels and furs, and she never heard from him again. He commuted each winter to Europe, working as a bank director and steamship magnate, with her fortune bankrolling him. He died in World War I. She pulled up stakes and headed for Fairbanks, where she staked claims and opened a bank in Dome City.

Confirming the prejudice facing women at the time, she once said, "I only hired a foreman because it looks better to have it said that a man is running the mine, but the truth is that I look after the management myself." She returned to the States in 1908, built a mansion in Yakima, Washington, called Mrs. Charbonneau's Castle, and supported her family on her fortune. She died in 1967 at the age of 95.

Harriet Pullen

Harriet Pullen was living in Washington State when the news of gold swept through Seattle. Determined to improve her life, she left her husband and children and arrived in Skagway with $7 in her pocket. She did what many women had done before her — taking work as a cook, earning $3 a day. Tons of dried apples were shipped into Skagway in the miners' supplies. Taking advantage of materials at hand, she made pie tins out of discarded cans and baked apple pies.

When Harriet had accumulated enough money, she sent for her three sons and some horses and went into the freighting business on White Pass Trail. Lois may have used their services. Harriet not only survived the rough trail conditions, the business competition, and the cor-

ruption imposed by the Soapy Smith gang; she actually thrived. She made enough money to build the Pullen House into one of Alaska's most memorable hotels and to send her children to the States for their education. She died at the age of 87 and was buried near the site of her hotel.

Isabelle Cleary Barnette

Lois and Ed arrived in Skagway with just enough money and supplies to get started. Isabelle Cleary Barnette arrived with a ship holding $20,000 worth of goods she and her husband had brought from San Francisco to sell to miners. Isabelle was 36 when she married E.T. Barnette in Helena, Montana. She was a woman who wasn't afraid to travel, making more than 13 trips in and out of Alaska while setting up their trading post in the Tanana Valley. With each trip lasting one month, Isabelle and E.T. drove dog teams over the Alaska Range to Valdez. One man remarked after one of the trips, "They looked like they had been on a Sunday drive."

When the Barnettes reached Seattle, they purchased a new steamboat and supplies. On their return, they discovered that gold had been found just 16 miles from their trading post. They named their trading post and the area around it Fairbanks. As miners rushed in, food became scarce. Some miners claimed E.T. was hoarding food to drive prices up. When they threatened to storm the Barnette's cache, Isabelle was able to defuse the confrontation and the miners left without doing any harm.

Isabelle gave birth to a daughter in 1904 in the still-primitive town. When she became pregnant again at the age of 48, she moved to San Francisco to be near a doctor in case of a difficult delivery.

The Barnettes made their fortune on the trading post and by investing in several claims. Burnette was indicted for embezzlement when a banking firm he developed collapsed, bankrupting many Alaskans. He was never convicted, but the marriage floundered and Isabelle divorced him in 1918. With a settlement of $500,000, she moved to Los Angeles with her two daughters and lived comfortably there until her death at the age of 80.

Ethel Bush Berry, the "Bride of the Klondike."
Ethel Bush Berry was named the "Bride of the Klondike."

Just as Lois began her married life searching for gold with her new husband, so did Ethel. But Ethel's story turned out quite differently – she found the mother lode. She married Clarence J. Berry when he returned from his first trip to the Yukon. She spent her honeymoon crossing Chilkoot Pass with a dog team, and then lived alone in a tiny cabin in Forty Mile for the next two months while Clarence prospected in the creeks.

"When I got there the house had no door, windows or floor, and I had to stand around outside until a hole was cut for me to get in . . .We had all the camp-made furniture we needed: a bed and stove – a long, little sheet-iron affair, with two holes on top and a drum to bake in. The fire burns up and goes out if you turn your back on it for a minute. The water we used was all snow or ice, and had to be thawed. If anyone wanted a drink, a chunk of ice had to be thawed and [the hot water] cooled again."

Clarence was unsuccessful in his search for gold and was tending bar in Bill McPhee's saloon in Forty Mile to augment their income when his luck changed. He was there on the August night George Carmack announced his discovery at Bonanza Creek. The Berrys immediately set out and staked their own claim on nearby Eldorado Creek. It would become one of the most valuable claims in the Yukon. Soon the Berrys were making $140,000 a day. Whenever Ethel needed money, she went outside and smashed a few dirt clods and pulled out the nuggets.

Newly rich, the Berrys returned to the States to buy Ethel a diamond ring and a farm. Ethel also wanted a real honeymoon. She was 23 years old when their ship, the *Portland*, docked in Seattle, and announced that gold had been found in the Yukon. Ethel arrived wearing men's clothing and in possession of a bed roll that was too heavy for her to lift. Rolled up inside was nearly $100,000 in gold. Ethel became as famous as the ship, with its "ton of gold."

Her story spread around the world, and everybody wanted to read about the "Bride of the Klondike." Her advice to other women who were thinking about going north was this:

"Why, to stay away, of course. It's much better for a man, though, if he has a wife along. The men are not much at cooking up there, and that is the reason they suffer with stomach troubles, and as some say they did, with scurvy. After a man has worked hard all day in the diggings he doesn't feel much like cooking a nice meal when he goes to his cabin, cold, tired and hungry, and finds no fire in the stove and all the food frozen."

Ethel did more than just cook for her husband, though. She panned the miner's pay dirt in a washtub and did her share of digging.

She also described her clothing in the newspaper articles:

"I put on my Alaskan uniform . . . the heavy flannels, warm dress with short skirt, moccasins, fur coat, cap and gloves, kept my shawl handy to roll up in case of storms, and I was rolled in a full robe and bound to the sled, so when it rolled over I rolled with it and many tumbles in the snow I got that way."

Money wasn't the lure when they returned to Skagway in 1898; they had plenty of that. The adventure of searching for gold was just too strong to ignore. She, Clarence, and her sister, Tot, joined the thousands of miners climbing the treacherous Chilkoot Pass. Again, they struck gold, and when the 1909 Alaska Yukon Pacific Exposition took place in Seattle, Ethel loaned $70,000 in gold nuggets that she had collected herself. Clarence later sent the nuggets to Tiffany & Co. to be made into a dresser set for his wife.

Although Ethel declared she would never go north again, she couldn't stay away. Each year she traveled up the Yukon River by boat, horse, and wagon over Eagle Summit to visit their claims, stopping only when Clarence died in 1930. Ethel lived in Beverly Hills, California, until her death in 1948 at the age of 75.

Mattie Crosby, Miss Tootsie

Although few African-Americans went to the Yukon, some did and some were women. Mattie Crosby went north with a family from Maine and did not see another African-American for 30 of the 72 years she lived in Alaska. Since race was not a deterrent to owning mining claims, Mattie staked her own and managed them along with a café, a brothel, and a bathhouse.

Mattie's brothel, the Crosby, featured running water, thick straw mattresses, lace curtains, flowered wallpaper, and lavender-glassed lamps run by a carbide generator. Her home-brew became Iditarod's most popular drink.

She would see a need for a new business and branch out. One was a boarding house for dogs. Since dog teams were indispensable to life in the Yukon, she had a steady base of customers.

Noah Brown couldn't help noticing the Alaskan dogs that filled the towns.

> "The approach of daylight here is not signaled by the crowing of the cock as is usual in most countries, but is more especially noted by the howling of the native canine, whose general appearance is like that of a coyote or wolf, and as the first note or howl is signaled, all join in the chorus and thus they pass it down the line for a period of several minutes; this being the case only in cold weather."

Lois and Ed were in Alaska just one summer and never had to use dogs, but many of the miners did, especially during the bitter winters when lakes were frozen over. Brown wrote,

> "Although a nuisance in a great many ways, the dog could not be very easily disposed of, as they are used to pack with, carrying on their backs in a pouch as much as 20 to 50 pounds in a load. They draw in harness heavy sleighs, and it is no unusual sight to see eight or ten hitched tandem to a sleigh drawing several hundred pounds. They are also used in the chase for moose, bear, and caribou."

Mattie soon became known as Miss Tootsie, and her trademarks were a red wig and glass eye. She nearly drowned three times getting to her mining claims and lost the sight in one eye when she froze her face driving a dog team. She was also known for her sense of humor. She stopped for dinner once at a remote camp where a boy looked her over closely and remarked that his family always washed up before eating. She replied that her skin wouldn't change color no matter how much she scrubbed. Mattie died October 11, 1972 at the Pioneer Home in Fairbanks at the age of 88.

Lucille Hunter

Another African-American woman who went to Alaska was Lucille Hunter. She was 19 and pregnant when she and her husband, Charles, traveled to Klondike. Lucille knew all about hard labor as she had worked in the fields in the Deep South since she was 13. She named her daughter Teslin after the baby was born on the shores of Teslin Lake. The Native people had never seen a black person before and called the Hunters "just another kind of white person."

Lucille, Charles, and the baby made a mid-winter trek by dog team in sub-zero temperatures to reach Bonanza Creek by early spring so they could stake their claim before others arrived. They also staked claims on the Stewart River. Lucille continued to work the claims after Hunter's death in the 1930s. Each year she walked more than 150 miles from Dawson to Mayo and back again to do the assessment reports needed on her claims. She died in Whitehorse at the age of 97.

Chapter 13
Home
1899-1922

I began talking about going home. I wanted to go to Dawson and down the Yukon, but the rest of the party did not. As we were going back to camp, Ed and I talked of selling what we had: our big tent and stove, dishes, home-made mattress, together with a lot of provisions, and start for home.

In Atlin, there were bulletin boards all over town announcing meals for twenty-five cents. I told Ed we could get that at home and be where we could get something to cook. Ed said, "Yes, and if we can sell our stuff for enough money to get home, we will." There was a man that was with us and he said, "I have $40.00 left yet and I will divide with you if you don't have enough to make the return trip."

We returned to Atlin that day pretty well worn out and the next morning we began selling our stuff so as to return. I ran all over town before I could sell my dishes. I had an outfit to seat a table for twelve of earthen dishes and silver plated forks, knives, and spoons. I could only get five dollars for the outfit. Our tent we paid twenty-five dollars for, we sold for twelve dollars. Our stove and mattress together with the cooking utensils, we received twenty-five dollars. I had one hundred fifty pounds of dried fruit together with a lot of dried corn that I had dried myself. It all went cheap, but with what we got, together with what we had, we had enough to get home on.

The morning we were to start, this man that offered to help us came to see if we had enough to get out on. We thanked him and told him we thought we could make it all right.

On the morning of July 3rd, 1899 we started across Atlin Lake. We were told we could go down the Atlin River to Taku City but we would have to watch out for the reefs. We found it pretty swift and I did not have to pull on the oars, Mr. Paul and Victor guiding the boat through the rifts. It was so swift, I was afraid, and then the water seemed so smooth, we got a little careless and all at once someone shouted, "There are the falls!" Victor was steering and Mr. Paul was pulling and we barely escaped going over a four-foot falls, and the side of the boat was scrapping on the rocks. If we had gone over, we would have lost all our stuff and possibly our lives. I thank God for His protecting over us.

We had no more trouble and went some eighteen miles in sixty minutes. When we got to Taku City, we camped out and got our dinner, then started down Taku Lake for several miles and camped out for the night. The trip up Pine Creek, running all around through Atlin trying to sell our stuff, and then down the Atlin River was too much for me, so I could not get supper nor eat any.

However, in the morning, I felt better and then we proceeded to return much the same as we came, sometimes pulling on the oars and sometimes towing and then sometimes using sails. All along the lake, the scenery was beautiful and we felt repaid for our efforts even though we were disappointed in our plans.

One place we saw, there had been a fire on the side hills in the timber of evergreens and some were burned so as to turn the tops red while others were yellow and still others were black.

The next thing of interest was when we got back within twenty or thirty miles of Bennett City. The wind was blowing fearful hard toward a rocky shore. Ed had been quite sick for several days and Mr. Paul and I were pulling the boat while Victor was steering. The wind was blowing hard toward the shore which was a wall of rocks. We were pulling with all our might but the wind was too strong and it seemed we were doomed. I commenced to pray and pulling at the same time to help answer that prayer. Just as we were nearing the rocks, the wind shifted and took us out into the lake again, out of danger. Victor said, "I have heard of miracles but this is the first one I have ever witnessed." I then told them I was praying as I saw the danger and God had answered my prayer.

The wind carried us that evening to Bennett City. Here we stayed until we sold the boat, then we took the first train for Skagway, then a boat to Vancouver, BC. I missed three meals in succession on account of sea-sickness. I believe we were two weeks getting to Vancouver.

On the way down, Ed joked with some of the passengers that he was going home to chicken gravy and potatoes, and others said so are we. We had not had any potatoes, and no chicken and very little fresh meat of any kind until we got home on the 4th of August, 1899.

Mrs. Wade, one of Ed's sisters, had company that day and we got home in time to have fine chicken dinner.

After we were back a little while, we sold the rest of the land that was willed to me by my sister and built us a home. It was a two-story house built a purpose to keep boarders and roomers. One Sunday not long after we got the house finished, Ed and I went to church as usual, never dreaming what we would agree to do before we came home.

Fred, Lois's and Ed's Third Adopted Child, 1902

There was a man came and sat down in front of us and turned to us and said, "We have a boy at our home that needs a home and you need a boy. He is a good worker and I want you to have him." I had said many a time I would never take any more children to raise as we had raised two orphan children and I felt we had done our duty, but before he had gotten done talking, I felt we ought to take him. So, the 2nd of April, 1902 we got the boy. They called his name Gussie Anderson. I never liked the name Gus, so I

Figure 22: Fred (Gussie Anderson) with Lois and Ed, 1902. Photo courtesy of Marlayne Boblett.

said I will call his name Fred, so he goes by that name now and he is grown.

Ed Dies, August 17, 1903

It was not long after we took him till Mr. Boblett took sick and died.

Not long after he died, a Congregational Minister and his wife came and rented some rooms and one day

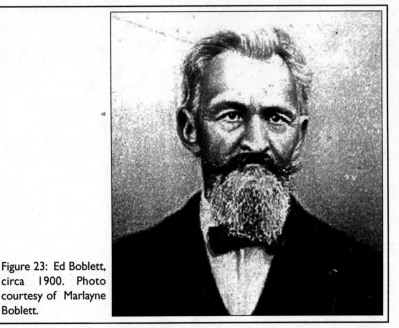

Figure 23: Ed Boblett, circa 1900. Photo courtesy of Marlayne Boblett.

I said to the wife, "I would like to go to Gettysburg [Washington] and visit my son Charley." She said, "Why don't you go? There is nothing to hinder you. We will take care of your chickens and if anybody comes and wants a room, we will let them have them."

Well, I got ready and took Fred and we went from here to New Westminster on the train, then we took the boat to Gettysburg. After we were there about a week, I said to Charley, "Isn't there a trail from here to Port Townsend?" He said, "Yes, why?" I said, "Well, I am going to walk in, for I won't take that steamer. It makes me so deathly sick, and I won't go down that rope ladder either."

So one morning after Charley had gone to work, I said to Agnes, "I am going to start for home." She said, "Why don't you wait, for Charley will be so mad?" But I started just the same. It was twenty-five miles into Port Townsend and part of the way was just a blind trail. After we went quite a long way, Freddie said, "Ma, I'm hungry." I said, "It isn't dinner time, so we'll walk a little farther and when we come to a place where there are some cows, we will stop and get some bread and milk." We hadn't gone much farther when we came to a place where there were lots of cows, so we stopped and got some bread and milk. I asked if she could keep us all night and she said, "No, but about five miles farther there is a place you can stay." So we started again and it was just about supper time when we got there. We had a good supper, and when we went to go to bed, she gave us some warm water to bathe our feet in and we sure enjoyed it, as we were very tired.

The woman told us she thought if we got up real early in the morning and got over to the main road, we probably would get a ride in. The next morning, we were up early and got over to the main road. After we went down the road two or three miles, a milk wagon came along and I asked him if we could have a ride into town. He said, "I can't take both of you." Then I asked him if he would take my boy and my

Edward A. Boblett may have spent his youth as a miner and carpenter, but he spent his later years immersed in public service in the town he literally helped build, as a real-estate investor and builder.

When Ed ran for City Council in Blaine on May 7, 1891, the voters showed their confidence in his abilities, as reported by the *Blaine Journal*.

"Saturday was a beautiful day for the city election, but the fine weather and interest did not seem to bring out a very full vote. Nearly 350 were registered, and only 275 ballots were dropped in the box. Of course, incorporation carried, and the last council was elected by a good big majority. Following is the vote:

For Mayor -   N.A. CORNISH, 153;
                  E.S. CLARKE, 117.
For council -   E.A. BOBLETT, 227.

"E.A. BOBLETT, the oldest member of the city council, was born in Bedford county, Virginia Nov. 24, 1828. He has since lived in Ohio, Indiana, Iowa, Minnesota, Kansas, Colorado, Arizona, and Idaho. He came to Seattle in November of '66, and about a year later to Blaine, where his principal interests have since been. He was one of the pioneers at this place, and his standing among the people is shown by the final vote he received on election day. He was a member of the late town council."

Ed died of paralysis and is buried in the Blaine Cemetery, Blaine, Whatcom County, Washington.

His obituary appeared in the *Blaine Journal* on August 21, 1903.

"BLAINE PIONEER IS NO MORE

"Edward Alexander Boblett – One of the First Settlers of this Section Passed Away at His Home in this City Monday Night After a Protracted Illness. On Monday night August 17, 1903 E. A. Boblett died in this city as the result of paralysis which first manifested its dread presence in his system sometime last winter.

"Edward A. Boblett was a native of Virginia where he was born November 24, 1828 in Bedford County. In the course of his life he lived in all parts of the United States, making his home at different times in the states of Virginia, Ohio, Iowa, Kansas, Colorado, New Mexico, Arizona, Idaho, Minnesota, and Washington. He first came to the Territory of Washington November 8th, 1868, where Seattle now is. About a year later he came to Blaine, where he erected the first house in this vicinity. Since that time he resided in Blaine until the time of his death. Here he followed the carpenters trade, and became an extensive owner of city property. In honor of his high standing in the community one of the streets was named Boblett street.

"Mr. Boblett was married June 17th 1860, in Colorado to Miss Lois A. Whitcomb. Besides his wife the survivors of his family are his three sisters, Mrs. Roberts, and Mrs. Wade of Blaine, and Mrs. Schwartz, of St. Joseph, Mo.

"Mr. Boblett was a respected member of the Masonic Order, which took charge of the funeral arrangements. The funeral was held at the Congregational Church on Wednesday at 2 o'clock Rev. O.H. McGill, Rev. L.M. Hutton and Rev. Whitfield of Kent conducting the services. To the memory of this departed pioneer Blaine will ever bear respectful gratitude. The pall bearers were T.H. Dearborn, G. Pennington, O.D. McDonald, J.W. Hunter, J. Ortell and Dr. McDonald."

valise, and he said he could take them all right and I said, "All right then, I'll make it in on foot."

When I got into town, Freddie was there to meet me and I asked him how he felt and he said, "I am sick." I said, "For goodness sake, don't get sick for we are here among strangers and away from home. Come on and we'll look around town and maybe you'll feel better." So we started and we hadn't gone far until he said, "I want to go back to the hotel." We went back and he wanted to go to bed and I told him to undress, and when he went to unlace his shoes, he couldn't stoop over, so I unlaced them for him, but he couldn't undress, so I undressed him. Then I said, "You can get into bed, can't you?"

He tried and couldn't, then I picked him up and when I went to lay him down, he let a scream out of him that you could hear for almost three blocks. So I ran down to the landlord and asked him if there was any good doctors in town and he said yes. I said, "Send one up as soon as possible for my boy is awfully sick and I think he has appendicitis." He called up three or four places, but the doctor wasn't there. So I said, "Send him up as soon as you can get him." Then I went back up to Fred. Pretty soon the doctor came and the minute he looked at Fred, he said, "It is a case of appendicitis." I just broke down and cried. He said, "There is no use crying, he'll be all right." So he fixed him all right, but we had to stay a couple of days so Freddie would feel all right to travel. We got home all right and he hasn't been bothered with it since.

After Fred was big enough to work, he went with Frank Bice up to the mines in the Wenatchee country. After a while, I went over to Winthrop to visit a nephew by the name of Aretas Hotchkiss. I told them Fred was working in the mines with Frank, so one day Reta asked me if I wanted to go over to the mines to see Fred and I said, "Yes, I would like to go so well." Then he said, "I'll take you over and Olive will go with us." We had to go around Dead Horse Point and it was almost straight up and down with just a little trail to walk around. When we got there, we stayed overnight and came back the next morning. Then a little while afterwards, I came back home.

I have done a great deal of traveling, mostly in a hard way and a very slow way but I was young then and did not mind. Now I am contemplating going to the World's Fair at San Francisco in 1915 in an auto and camp out all the way if I am permitted to do so. I think it would be a little faster and much easier than traveling in an old lumber wagon drawn by an ox team.

There is no evidence that Lois ever made it to the World's Fair in San Francisco, but over her lifetime she traveled thousands of miles, walking much of the time. Walking is maybe what she missed the most when her health failed her.

That was the last trip I ever took. Fred is a grown man now and works in the logging camps. As I am the only one left in our family, I lead a pretty lonesome life. The only place I go is to church, as I am seventy-eight years old and that I can't walk and do like I used to. I tend my garden and do my own house work.

$\mathscr{L}$ois A. Boblett
1922

Figure 24: Lois and Her Roses, circa 1920. Photo courtesy of Robert Mix.

Lois's obituary in the *Blaine Journal* on March 19, 1925, read:

"LOIS A. BOBLETT, FIRST WHITE WOMAN HERE, DIES

"Mrs. Lois A. Boblett, the last of the two or three first white women to land in Blaine 55 years ago, passed into the Great Beyond Saturday evening. She had been sick for many months and perfectly helpless, hence the end came as a relief. Funeral services were held Monday afternoon at 2:30 o'clock in the M. E. church, Rev. F. M. Bushong officiating.

"Lois A. Whitcomb was born in Milwaukee, Wisc., Feb. 1, 1844. When seven years old she moved with her father's family by ox team to Iowa, where she lived until 10 years old. She again moved to Nebraska, and from there to Colorado, where she was married to Edward A. Boblett, this being the first white couple married in that state. They had no children, but raised three orphan children.

"In November, 1869, Mr. and Mrs. Boblett left Prescott, Arizona, on a government train for California, and took a boat from Wilmington for San Francisco, where they stayed a week before they could take a boat for Seattle. They arrived in Seattle in December, 1869, and in 1870 they came to Semiahmoo on the steamer *Libby*. Mrs. Bice, now residing near Custer, was one of the women who came on that boat, we are informed. Mr. Boblett took up a homestead where a part of Blaine now stands, one boundary of which, we understand was Boblett Street, named after him. Mr. Boblett passed on about 21 years ago.

"Mr. and Mrs. Frank Bice, the latter a great-nephew, have cared for the deceased during the past two years. With the passing of Mrs. Boblett there is removed from our midst the only woman left of those early pioneers who landed here in 1870. She had lived most of her life on the frontiers of this country and many were the interesting tales she could tell about her experiences during those years. The deceased was a life-long member of the M.E. church and a regular attendant up to the time she became helpless to get about."

In the End

*W*hat happened to the folks that peopled Lois's journal? Where did they go when they "settled down" and left their youthful adventures behind them?

Aretas Whitcomb, Lois's Father

Lois inherited her wanderlust from her father, Aretas Whitcomb. A man of many talents, he operated a hotel, the Wind Palace, and a saw mill, worked as a miner, a farmer, and a carpenter, and built one house after another. His failing health was mentioned in the April 5, 1888, issue of the paper: "Grandpa Whitcomb has had a very bad spell of hiccoughing and choking, so bad, in fact that it was thought that in his old age (86) that he could not withstand it, but we believe he is some better to-day." On May 31st, "Grandpa Whitcomb passed a very miserable night last night, and consequently is lower than ever to-day."

Lois nursed him through his last illness, as she would other family members. He was the first person to be buried in the Blaine Cemetery. His obituary appeared in the *Blaine Journal*, June, 1888:

"– DIED – At the residence of Mr. E.A. Boblett, in Blaine, at 3 a.m. Monday, June 25th, 1888, Aretas Whitcomb, aged 86 years 6 months and 29 days.

"Grandpa Whitcomb belonged to one of the oldest New England families. He was born in Lisbon, Grafton county, New Hampshire, December 26th, 1801. He was married to Miss Lydia Priest, with whom he has lived over 63 years, at about twenty-five years of age, and soon after removed to Pennsylvania. Since then he has lived in Wisconsin, Iowa, Nebraska, Colorado, Arizona and Washington Territory. He has lived here eighteen years. He leaves an aged widow and three daughters, Mrs. E.A. Boblett and Mrs. A. Dexter, of this place, and Mrs. P. Hodgkiss [Hotchkiss], who resides in Colorado. His only son, Josiah Whitcomb, was killed by the Apache Indians in Arizona about twenty years ago. Mrs. E. Holtzheimer, Clarence Whitcomb and Mrs. Byce are children of Josiah Whitcomb. Grandpa Whitcomb was a Free Will Baptist, and was a consistent Christian during his life. Death took him early Monday morning after having consumed his strong body by nearly half a year of confinement to his bed. He knew he was going when the last moments came, and was glad. He died without a struggle, just falling quietly away, his breath gradually ceasing. The world has moved since this aged man was born. Thomas Jefferson was just entering upon his first term as president. There have been twenty-two presidents since. Napoleon I rose and fell. The United States has passed through three wars. Four million slaves have been freed. The locomotive, telegraph, telephone, reaping machine, sewing machine and steamboat have come since he first saw the light of day. The funeral service was held Tuesday afternoon, conducted by Rev. A. Warren."

Lydia Priest Whitcomb, Lois's Mother

Lois's mother, Lydia Priest Whitcomb lived to be 95 years old. She lived with the Bobletts and enjoyed visits from her other daughters, both of whom eventually moved to the Blaine area.

On the occasion of her 88th birthday, she was the honored guest at a surprise birthday party. The Bobletts took Grandma Whitcomb to Victoria, B.C. to visit Isabelle and her family in 1890. Lydia had an exciting adventure in August of 1891, her first train ride. She and Lois attended a reunion and she found the train much quicker and more comfortable than the old wagon.

Her 90th birthday was marked by a February 2, 1892 article in the *Blaine Journal* that read: "Monday last Grandma Whitcomb celebrated the 90th anniversary of her birth. But few of us are allotted to reach this ripe old age, and possess their mental faculties to such a remarkable degree as Mrs. Whitcomb, and her reminiscences of Blaine since early in 1871, are exceedingly interesting. When the old lady landed on these shores the following families came with her, viz: M.A. Upson, C.C. Kingsley, Mr. and Mrs. Henspeter and B.H. Bruns. A few of her pioneer friends were with her on this anniversary, making it a memorable occasion." Lydia celebrated her 95th birthday with a party at the Boblett home.

Her obituary appeared in the *Blaine Journal* and she was buried beside her husband in the Blaine Cemetery.

"WHITCOMB, Lydia (September 30, 1898)

"After a lingering illness Lydia Whitcomb departed this life, Sunday night, Sept. 25th, 1898, at 10:05 o'clock. She was born in New Hampshire, August 27th, 1804, hence at the time of her death was 95 years and 20 days of age. When 14 years old – 80 years ago – she was converted, through the instrumentality of the Christian church. Until 26 years ago, she was a member of the Free Will Baptist church, since which time she has been a faithful and consistent member of the M.E. church. In 1825 she was married to Aretas Whitcomb, with who she lived happily for 63 years.

"She was the mother of four children two of whom survive, Mrs. Boblett of this city, and Mrs. Hotchkiss of Colorado.

"Grandma Whitcomb knew much of the hardships of a pioneer life. She has traveled, practically, across the continent in a wagon, leaving New Hampshire many years ago on her western journey. She was in Wisconsin in an early day in the history of that country, having cooked in the first hotel ever erected in the city of Milwaukee. She has been a resident of Washington for 28 years.

"The funeral services were held in the First M.E. church last Tuesday at 1:30 p.m., the pastor, Rev. J.W. Kendall, officiating. The sermon, an impressive one, reviewed the life of the deceased – her long Christian service, and the beautiful lesson taught by those years of unselfish devotion and fidelity to the Christian cause - if the reward was limited to the labor performed in the Master's vineyard, what a glorious reward would be hers."

Gus Anderson/Frederick Boblett, Lois's and Ed's Son

Lois and Ed raised three children, Isabelle "Belle" Jane and Thomas "Charles" Kerr and Gus Anderson/ Frederick Boblett. Fred was living with Lois at the time of the 1920 U.S. Census and working in a shingle mill. He worked in lumber mills, mines and on a ship, the *Border King*, in 1928. The ship sailed between Bellingham and Powell River, B.C. Whether Fred died or perhaps moved to Canada, no record is found after 1928. There is no doubt that Lois loved him as her son.

Isabelle "Belle" Jane, Lois's and Ed's Daughter

Isabelle married William Douglas Ferris, Jr. on November 2, 1878, while the family worked at the lumber mill in New Westminster, B.C. She was 17 years old. William worked as a teamster and farmer, although he is listed on the 1880 U.S. Census as a printer. Belle and William followed Lois and Ed to Spokane, where their first child, William Edward, was born. Their daughter, Maude Lavinia, was born during a brief return to Canada. Their third and last child was Charles Addison, born in Idaho in 1884.

Belle and William decided to return permanently to British Columbia. Belle became a dressmaker, and in the 1901 Canadian Census was listed as the head of house with her son, Charles, in the home, as well as her widowed son-in-law, Charles Esnouf, and two-year-old grandson, Clarence. Her daughter, Maude Lavinia, married Charles in 1898, gave birth to Clarence in December of 1898, and died in December of 1899. Missing from the household is Belle's husband, William, although he did not die until 1928 while living in Vancouver, B.C. Belle never identified herself as divorced, only as widowed. In the 1911 Census, Belle was living with her grandson Clarence.

Belle lost two of her three children. Charles Addison died at the early age of 27 from complications of diabetes mellitus. He was a respected member of the cigar makers union. Belle adopted and raised her grandson Clarence.

Belle's obituary was carried in the *Victoria Daily Times* on December 5-8, 1930, page 15:

"FORMER POLICE MATRON DIES Funeral Here To-morrow For Mrs. I. J. Ferris, Victoria Pioneer

"Funeral services will be held at St. John's Church tomorrow at 2:30 o'clock for Mrs. Isabella Jane Ferris, former police matron of Victoria, who passed away in Vancouver Tuesday after a lengthy illness. Interment will be made in the Ross Bay Cemetery.

"The late Mrs. Ferris was born in Arizona [Missouri] seventy years ago, and came to this province as a child with her parents. She was married in 1878 at New Westminster, her husband, who predeceased her by many years, being prominent in public affairs in British Columbia in the early days.

"For nine years Mrs. Ferris was police matron in Victoria and since 1920 had acted as relief matron at Oakalla Provincial Jail. She is survived by one son, William Edward of Hollywood, Cal.; a brother, Charles Kerr, Port Angeles, Wash.; a grandson, Clarence Ferris of the staff of the Bureau of Provincial Information, and several great-grandchildren.

"The remains were forwarded from Vancouver yesterday and are resting at Thomson and Fetterley's Undertaking Parlors."

Thomas "Charles" Kerr, Lois's and Ed's Son

Thomas Charles Kerr, Isabelle's brother, married Viola Belle King in 1882 when he was 20 years old. They had two daughters, Idora [Isidora] and Lotta, before divorcing.

His second marriage was to Agnes Jane Crawford around 1890. Charles and Aggie had a large family: Gordon Charles, Edward Alexander, Agnes Martha, Katherine Sarah, James Bernard, and Norman Crawford Kerr.

Charles and Aggie lost one child, Edward Alexander, who died at the age of 11 from juvenile diabetes. He was buried on the homestead. Charles worked in the lumber camps and farmed. He died April 25, 1950 in Port Angeles, Washington.

Eliza Miller Whitcomb Richards, Lois's Sister-in-Law

Eliza Miller Whitcomb Richards is the most tragic figure in the family story. She and Josiah Whitcomb were married in 1855 in Auburn, Iowa. Josiah and Eliza's first child, Sarah, was born in 1856 and died at the age of six. Their second child was Lois Almena, named for Josiah's sister. She was born in 1858 in Aowa Creek, Nebraska. John Sanders was born December 3, 1861 and died October 3, 1862. Florence Irena was born June 26, 1863. Their last child, Clarence, was born May 27, 1866. Clarence is the baby they thought had died and were preparing to bury when he began breathing again. Clarence died in 1894.

Eliza was 34 years old when Josiah was killed. She married Richard S. Richards in Prescott in 1869. They traveled to Washington Territory with the Bobletts. They built a double house with the Bobletts in Seattle and Dick worked as a carpenter with Ed. They moved to Blaine with the Bobletts. Dick and Eliza had three children: John Henry, born April 8, 1870; Clara Ida, born June 5, 1872; and Amy Kate, born August 11, 1875. It is difficult to say which epidemic struck the Richards home, but all three children died in a three-week period. Clara Ida died May 31, 1881; John Henry died June 4, 1881; and Amy Kate died June 18, 1881. Sadly, it was not uncommon for a family to lose all of their children to epidemics that regularly swept through a community.

After the deaths of the children, Eliza and Richard divorced. Eliza lived with her daughter Florence and her husband, Edward Holtzheimer. Florence and Edward had four children, Ernest, Francis, William and Paul. Eliza's other daughter, Lois "Minnie," married Thomas Henry Bice, her senior by almost 20 years. They had eight children: Frank, Annie, George, Albert, Olive, Alice, Edith, and William.

Eliza died January 4, 1902. in Blaine and is buried near her daughter Florence in the Blaine Cemetery. Her obituary hasn't been located, although there were obituaries for Florence and Ed Holtzheimer and Lois and Thomas Bice.

Lois Bice, Lois's Niece and Josiah's Daughter

"LOIS MINNIE BICE, PIONEER, CALLED, The *Bellingham Herald*, July 23, 1940

"Lois Minnie Bice, aged 82, 1433 Moore street, passed away at her residence Monday. Mrs. Bice, who had been a resident of Bellingham the past year, had previously resided in the Custer district for fifty-nine years. She was a member of the Cardinal Rebekah lodge, the Methodist church of Custer and the Whatcom County Dairymen's association.

"Surviving her are four sons, Frank and Bert, both of Blaine, George and William, both of Custer; three daughters, Mrs. Annie Bainter, Bellingham, Mrs. Olive Bainter, Blaine, and Mrs. Edith Eckrem, Custer; one sister, Mrs. Florence Holtzheim[er], Blaine; nineteen grandchildren; six great-grandchildren and two great-great-grandchildren. Funeral services will be held at the Monroe chapel at Ferndale Thursday afternoon at 2 o'clock with Leslie Kagey conducting. Interment will follow in Enterprise cemetery."

Thomas Bice, Husband of Lois Bice

Two articles appeared for Thomas Bice, in the *Blaine Journal*, December 1 & 8, 1911:

"BICE, Thomas H. (d. 1911) - Thomas Bice passed away at his home near Custer Wednesday morning from cancer, at the age of 73 years, 7 months and 9 days. He has suffered from cancer of the face for the past five months. Thomas Bice was one of the earliest settlers in this part of Whatcom County, first coming to this section from California in 1858. He lived on the old place where he died for about 37 years, and was esteemed by every one who knew him. He was a native of Cornwall, England. An aged wife, four sons and three daughters are left to mourn the loss of husband and father, all of whom reside near the old home place just north of Custer. The funeral services will be held at Custer this afternoon at 1:30 o'clock and the burial will take place in the Enterprise cemetery."

"TO MEMORY OF THOMAS H. BICE E. Holtzheimer Pays Tribute to His Old Friend and Neighbor [and brother-in-law]

"The following tribute to the memory and life of Thomas H. Bice, was written by his friend and neighbor, Ernest Holtzheimer, who is perhaps better qualified to do so than any other person in this section. Owing to its being received too late last week it could not appear in last week's *Journal*.

"With the death of Thomas H. Bice, which occurred November 29th, another of the few remaining pioneers who prepared the way in the wilderness many years ago, has crossed the divide from whence no mortal ever returns, and his face will be seen no more. Stricken by a malignant disease several months ago, medical attention and solicitous care proved of no avail, until enfeebled by long suffering, peacefully the end drew near, and with the birth of the new day, on the wings of the morning, his spirits took flight to the eternal realms above.

"When a mere boy, deceased emigrant with his family moved from England to the United States. untold privations, he at last succeeded in the establishment of a comfortable home noted for thrift and hospitality. During his long sojourn among us he affiliated with the Methodist church.

"He attained the age of 73 years and seven months, and leaves behind him to mourn his loss, his wife, four sons and three daughters, besides one brother and two sisters who reside in California. Respected by all who knew him, Thomas H. Bice will long be remembered by his pioneer associates as a true friend, by his neighbors as an honest man, and by the present generation as an exemplary citizen."

Florence Whitcomb Holtzheimer, Lois's Niece and Josiah's Daughter
Florence Whitcomb Holtzheimer was the daughter of Josiah and Eliza Whitcomb. She survived whatever killed her three younger half-siblings and offered her home to her mother after Eliza divorced Richard Richards.

"HOLTZHEIMER, Florence (d. 1949) The *Blaine Journal*, April 28, 1949

"Mrs. Florence Whitcomb Holtzheimer, one of Blaine's oldest pioneers passed away Friday night, April 15, in a Bellingham hospital. Born in Fayette county, Iowa, June 26, 1863, she came to the Pacific Northwest when a child of seven years, with her family and landed at the Semiahmoo Spit in September, 1870. It was an event that marked the arrival of Mrs. Holtzheimer and her sister Mrs. Minnie Bice as the first two white girls to arrive in Blaine.

"On June 26, 1879 she married Edward Holtzheimer who owned a homestead on California Creek. They resided on the creek for a number of years before moving into town. Her desire to start a Blaine hospital never materialized. To this couple, four sons, Ernest, Francis, William and Paul were born and remain to mourn her with nine grandchildren, 10 great grand-children, four nephews and two nieces.

"Pallbearers were Garrett Holtzheimer, Erman Holtzheimer, Theodore Holtzheimer, Jack Holtzheimer, Willis Loop and Carl Patrick, four of whom are grandchildren of the deceased. Internment was made in the California Creek cemetery, following the services conducted Monday, April 18, by Rev. Evan David at the McKinney Funeral home."

Edward Holtzheimer, Husband of Florence Holtzheimer
The obituary for Florence's husband appeared in the *Blaine Journal-Press*, May 3, 1928.

"HOLTZHEIMER, Edward - Edward Holtzheimer, One of Earliest Settlers, Goes On

"Edward Holtzheimer passed away at 10 a.m. yesterday, May 2nd, at his home in this city. He had been in a feeble condition for several months following a stroke of paralysis and the end did not come unexpectedly. Mr. Holtzheimer was born in Germany April 4, 1842, and was a little past 86 years of age. He came to this country when a lad of 16 years. Later he served his adopted country in the Civil war, and was a member of the G.A.R. He came to this section in 1871 and was among the few earliest settlers. In those days the settlement started along the bay and the creeks and it was on the bank of California creek that he selected his homestead. In the years intervening he made his home here continuously and loved to talk of the old days among his friends.

"Deceased secured in his younger days an excellent education and was probably as fluent and as interesting writer as this section ever boasted. Many times he has written for the *Journal-Press* and a number of times his writings were eagerly snapped up by magazines of wide circulation, one series of articles in particular being his experiences as a young man with an expedition in Colorado, we believe. He was a man of strict integrity and was honored and respected by all who had the good fortune to know him. There are left to mourn his passing a wife and four sons, Earnest of Oregon, Francis and Paul of Blaine, and William of Vancouver, BC. Funeral services will be held Saturday afternoon at 2 o'clock at the Purdy chapel under the direction of the International Bible Students. Burial will take place at Hillsdale cemetery at California creek, near which he spent so many years of his life."

Eliza Dexter, Lois's Sister
Lois' sister, Eliza, married her first cousin, Amos Dexter. The Dexters accompanied the Whitcombs and Bobletts until they settled in Blaine, Washington. Since the Dexters had no children, Eliza left her property to Lois.

Eliza's obituary was printed in the *Blaine Journal*, on September 3, 1897.

"DEXTER, Eliza (d. 1897)

"The death of Mrs. Eliza Dexter, relict of Amos Dexter, which occurred at the home of her sister, Mrs. E. A. Boblett, in this city, last Sunday, August 29th, 1897, removes one of the earlier pioneers of Whatcom county. For several years past this devoted Christian woman has been a constant sufferer from a complication of diseases, which finally triumphed over life, and the gentle patient, suffering spirit, with calm, supreme Christian resignation, succumbed to the inevitable and winged its flight to that far away land from whose borne no traveler has ever returned.

"Deceased was born near Concord, N. H., April 7, 1827, therefore had passed her seventieth year.

"She was married to Amos Dexter on Sept. 8th, 1848, near Madison, Wis. Soon after their marriage they removed to Iowa, from whence they emigrated to Nebraska, then to South Dakota, then westward to Colorado, from whence they were soon attracted to the promising territory of Washington, locating on the place at the head of Drayton harbor, where they resided continuously for a period of 28 years.

"In the true sense of the word they were pioneers, precursors of western civilization, and had experienced all of the excitements, adventures and thrilling incidents that enter into the life of the frontiersman. They had tasted the joys, experienced the disappointments and suffered the self-denials of the pioneer. They had seen the great western wilderness by the magic touch of civilization transformed into a great industrial empire. Even more marvelous than all this, they had witnessed the wonderful development of peerless Washington. When they first settled in Whatcom it was almost an unbroken, trackless forest. Now the homes of an industrious people dot hill-side and valley, and on the shores of the inland sea growing cities eloquently attest the commonwealth's vast wealth of varied natural resources. To contemplate the national development, the thrilling events and the remarkable advancement occurring during the period closing a biblical lifespan – three score and ten – seems almost miraculous. Since 12 years of age she has been a devoted Christian, embracing the Free Will Baptist persuasion. During the past five years she accepted the faith of her husband – that of a Seven Day Adventist. To the faith of a Christian she clung with a fidelity, zeal and steadfastness, that impressed all with whom she came in contact that with her it was genuine, abiding conviction. Her life was one of truth, of earnestness, of sincerity. Her conception of duty lofty – to it she proved faithful to the end.

"The funeral services were conducted at the home of E.A. Boblett by Rev. A. Warren, Monday afternoon at 2 o'clock. The services were impressive. The speaker paid a touching tribute to the memory of the departed. Her remains were interred in the city cemetery by the side of the remains of her husband, the late Amos Dexter. Her departure is mourned by a mother, who recently passed her 93rd year, two sisters, Mrs. E.A. Boblett of this city, and Mrs. Preston Hotchkiss of Ouray, Col., and a host of old-time neighbors and friends, who extend sympathy to the sorrowing family in the hour of bereavement."

Amos Dexter, Lois's Sister's Husband

Eliza lived just one year after the death of her husband, Amos. His obituary was printed in the *Blaine Journal*, April 24, 1896.

"DEXTER, Amos (d. 1896)

"Amos Dexter, one of the old pioneers of this section, died at his home on Drayton Harbor last Saturday morning, April 18th, 1896. His death resulted from a complication of diseases, chief of which being rheumatism and a trouble of long standing with his lungs and heart. He had been confined to his bed for about four weeks prior to his death. The best medical aid was summoned, but all efforts to arrest the progress of the disease and restore his health were futile. Amos Dexter was born in the year of 1821 in the state of New Hampshire. After leaving the state of his birth he resided in Wisconsin, and there married Miss Eliza Whitcomb, the maiden name of Mrs. Dexter, who has been his life companion since. Mr. Dexter and our respected townsman, Samuel Wade, while young men, worked together in Wisconsin, way back in the forties.

"After leaving Wisconsin the deceased lived in Colorado, Nebraska and Dakota. In company with Preston Hotchkiss he operated a saw and grist mill for a long time at Elk Point, Union county, Dakota. In 1870 Mr. Dexter and Mr. Hotchkiss came to Washington territory and entered more than 500 acres of what was known as 'offered land' that is situated on the south side of Drayton Harbor. The greater portion was purchased by Mr. Dexter, and with the exception of a few acres that have been sold, most of the original tract now forms the estate left to Mrs. Dexter, as there are no children. Mrs. Dexter is the daughter of Grandma Whitcomb and sister of Mrs. E.A. Boblett and Mrs. Sarah Hotchkiss. The *Journal* voices the sentiment of the whole community in expressing sympathy for Mrs. Dexter in her hour of bereavement. While she mourns the loss of a kind, noble and faithful husband, the community regrets the loss of an estimable, enterprising and industrious citizen. Mr. Dexter has been one of the pioneers of this new commonwealth and has assisted in blazing the way that lead to the formation of a new state. The greater portion of his life has been spent upon the frontier battling with the rugged forces of nature. By hard labor and close economy he has carved out from a wilderness of woods a substantial and serviceable home on Drayton harbor. He devoted a great deal of attention to horticulture, and was instrumental in rearing an excellent orchard on the home place. He has been a constant visitor to Blaine ever since there was a Blaine. His familiar figure on our streets and at our places of business, marketing his products and purchasing his supplies has gone into history.

"The passing away of an old pioneer, born in the rugged hills of one of the old New England states and moving along 'Westward as the course of Empire takes its flight,' opens up a field for reflection. Mr. Dexter was a young man when the war with Mexico was fought, he was in the zenith of his manhood when the Confederates commenced firing on Fort Sumter. He has seen the steam locomotive supplant the old stage coach and the pony express from ocean to ocean. He was attending to his humble duties as a husbandman, while a dozen new states west of the Mississippi river were admitted into the Union. He has said 'Good bye old world I am going home' just at a time when the forces of electricity are about to revolutionize the social business and commercial world. He was one of the great legion of American citizens whose industry and patriotism permit us to call this country the greatest nation on earth. He has joined his ancestors in the 'Undiscovered Country.'

"Deceased was buried from the Methodist church on Sunday morning last, the edifice being filled to overflowing to pay the last sad tribute to the deceased. The remains was (sic) brought to the church at 11 a.m. M. Rosbrough, I.M. Scott, A.J. Loomis, Jas. Cain, John Wagoner and S.P. Hughes acting as pall bearers. The services opened with a reading of a scriptural selection from the fifteenth chapter of first Corinthians by Rev. Mr. Whittlesey of the Congregational church. This was followed by an eloquent and telling sermon from Rev. Mr. White of the M.E. church, who dealt feelingly upon the many virtues of the deceased, and held forth the pattern of his life as an example to the many in our midst on the declining side of life. The remains were conveyed to their last resting place by a large number of sorrowing friends, who had been his associates through a decade of years.Michael Rosbrough [or Rosbrugh] acted as a pall bearer at Amos Dexter's funeral. His name did not appear in the paper after 1896. Michael married Ed Boblett's sister, Amanda, and had four children: Charles, Mary, Elizabeth, and Elmer. Three of the children, Charles, Mary [Mott], and Elizabeth [Gott] moved to Blaine. Michael searched for gold with the Bobletts in Colorado and Arizona, traveling with them to Washington Territory. He also farmed with them and worked as a carpenter."

The adventures that Lois and Ed shared with their family and friends ranged across a vast area at a time when the West was in its infancy.

According to the *Arizona Miner*, Ed and Lois were the first white couple married in Colorado. Lois didn't feel that she was doing anything extraordinary; she was just living her life one day at a time. The events she witnessed and the ones in which she participated had ramifications far beyond her imagining.

She was there for the birth of governments, states, and cities. She fed legislators and governors, soldiers and miners, gunslingers and conmen.

Earp, Prichard, Wardner, Yesler, and Maynard were just neighbors and friends.

Who would have known they would become famous in their own ways, or even become legends, representatives of an entire era in American history?

Lois faced each challenge with faith and courage. She firmly believed she could do anything Ed did and had complete faith in his ability to protect her in an emergency. After all, *if you had to do something, you might as well just get started and do it.*

Lois led an active life in the community, with her name appearing regularly in the local paper. She was faithful to her church and an officer in the Women's Christian Temperance Union, never forgetting her experiences in Arizona with alcohol. Perhaps Josiah would have lived if the soldiers hadn't stopped to drink. She traveled to B.C. to visit her daughter Isabelle and hosted weddings and birthday celebrations in her home.

When Lois developed dementia late in life, her nephew Frank Bice and his family moved into the Boblett home to care for Lois. Frank's son, Ralph, who was three years old when the family moved into the big, white house on 4th Street, remembers how closely everyone had to watch Lois. She would leave the house and go in search of a home, a wanderer to the end.

Those days are long gone. Some historians refer to the Klondike Gold Rush as the Last Great Adventure. Gamblers and adventurers to the last, Lois and Ed wouldn't have missed out on such an experience. They were at the beginning of the migration across the western half of the United States and participated in events that formed the country as we know it today. Lois, in her memoir, turned the "romance" of the West into the reality of a day-to-day struggle to survive whatever life or nature demanded of her. The passing of Lois, Ed, and the other pioneers put an end to one of the most turbulent, fascinating chapters of American history.

Bibliography

Acts Adopted by the First Legislative Assembly of the Territory of Arizona. Prescott, AZ: Arizona Territorial Government, 1865.

Anderson, Kraig. "Cape Flattery Lighthouse, Washington." Lighthousefriends.com. http://www.lighthousefriends.com/.asp?ID=120 (accessed February 2, 2008).

Andreas, A.T. *History of the State of Nebraska*. Chicago: Western Historical Co., 1882.

Arizona Miner, "Bobletts Leaving Prescott," September 11, 1869.

Arizona Miner, "Editorial – Death of Josiah Whitcomb," editorial, October 31, 1868.

Arizona Miner (Arizona State Library, Archives and Public Records), "Fight at Montezuma Saloon," June 24, 1866, Hayden Biographical Files, History and Archives.

Arizona Miner (Arizona State Library, Archives and Public Records), "George W. Holaday," January 24, 1866, Hayden Biographical Files, History and Archives Division.

Arizona Miner (Prescott, AZ. Courtesy of Sharlot Hall Museum), "Grief Hill," February 1870. www.sharlothall.lib.az.us. (accessed January 12, 2008).

Arizona Miner (Hayden Biographical Files, History and Archives Division), "Judge Holaday Arrives," August 22, 1866, Arizona State Library, Archives and Public Records.

Arizona Miner (Biographical Files, History and Archives Division), "Pine Tree Saloon Ad," September 12, 1866, Arizona State Library, Archives and Public Records.

Bankson, Ressell A., and Lester S. Harrison. *Beneath These Mountains*. New York: Vantage Press, 1966.

Bates, George W. "Interview. November 22, 1938, American Life Histories." Library of Congress, American Memory– Manuscripts from the Federal Writers' Project, 1936-1940. http://memory.loc.gov///.html (accessed February 10, 2008).

"Battle of the Little Bighorn, 1876." Eyewitness to History.Com. http://www.eyewitnesstohistory.com/er.htm (accessed March 10, 2008).

Becker, Paula. "Maynard, Catherine Broshears (1816-1906), Seattle Pioneer." History Link.org Online Encyclopedia of Washington State History. http://www.historylink.org/ (accessed February 9, 2009).

The Bellingham Herald (Bellingham, WA), "Lois Minnie Bice, Pioneer, Called," July 23, 1940.

Berger, Mrs.Will H. "Interview, Nov. 21, 1938, American Life Histories." Library of Congress, American Memory–Manuscripts from the Federal Writers' Project, 1936-1940. http://memory.loc.gov///.html (accessed January 29, 2008).

The Billings Gazette (Billings, MT), "Billings Gazette's 75th Anniversary Issue Sept.-1960," September 1960.

Billington, Ray Allen. *America's Frontier Heritage*. New Mexico: New Mexico Press, 1974.

Blaine Journal (Blaine, WA. Courtesy of Whatcom Genealogical Society), "As They Found It–Early History of Blaine, WA," December 12, 1889.

Blaine Journal (Blaine, WA. Courtesy of Whatcom Genealogical Society), "As They Found It–Early History of Blaine, WA," December 19, 1889.

Blaine Journal (Blaine, WA. Courtesy of Whatcom Genealogical Society), "Blaine Pioneer is No More," August 21, 1903.

Blaine Journal (Blaine, WA. Courtesy of Whatcom Genealogical Society), "Blue Canyon Explosion," April 12, 1895.

Blaine Journal (Blaine, WA. Courtesy of Whatcom Genealogical Society), "Boblett's Church Donation," March 14, 1889.

Blaine Journal (Blaine, WA. Courtesy of Whatcom Genealogical Society), "Charles Gott," May 3, 1895.

Blaine Journal (Blaine, WA. Courtesy of Whatcom Genealogical Society), "Charles Gott Critical," May 17, 1895.

Blaine Journal (Blaine, WA. Courtesy of Whatcom Genealogical Society), "Charles Hinton Gott Dies," May 24, 1895.

Blaine Journal (Blaine, WA. Courtesy of Whatcom Genealogical Society), "Death of Charles Anderson," September 26, 1889.

Blaine Journal (Blaine, WA. Courtesy of Whatcom Genealogical Society), "Died–Aretas Whitcomb," June 28, 1888.

Blaine Journal (Blaine, WA. Courtesy of Whatcom Genealogical Society), "Died–Eliza Whitcomb Dexter," September 3, 1897.

Blaine Journal (Blaine, WA. Courtesy of Whatcom Genealogical Society), "Drug Smuggling," January 9, 1890.

Blaine Journal (Blaine, WA. Courtesy of Whatcom Genealogical Society), "The Evangel," October 22, 1891.

Blaine Journal (Blaine, WA. Courtesy of Whatcom Genealogical Society), "Ferndale and Mountain View," July 21, 1891.

Blaine Journal (Blaine, WA. Courtesy of Whatcom Genealogical Society), "Ferndale and Mountain View," September 17, 1891.

Blaine Journal (Blaine, WA. Courtesy of Whatcom Genealogical Society), "First Train Ride," August 27, 1891.

Blaine Journal (Blaine, WA. Courtesy of Whatcom Genealogical Society), "Grandma Whitcomb's 90th," August 31, 1894.

Blaine Journal (Blaine, WA. Courtesy of Whatcom Genealogical Society), "Grandpa Whitcomb Ill," April 5, 1888.

Blaine Journal (Blaine, WA. Courtesy of Whatcom Genealogical Society), "Hannah Van Luven Dies," October 25, 1888.

Blaine Journal (Blaine, WA. Courtesy of Whatcom Genealogical Society), "Incorporation Election," May 7, 1891.

Blaine Journal (Blaine, WA. Courtesy of Whatcom Genealogical Society), "Lamp Explosion," August 26, 1886.

Blaine Journal (Blaine, WA. Courtesy of Whatcom Genealogical Society), "Mabel Ray Harvey Death," March 27, 1890.

Blaine Journal (Blaine, WA. Courtesy of Whatcom Genealogical Society), "Mahala Evan's Accident," February 2, 1889.

Blaine Journal (Blaine, WA. Courtesy of Whatcom Genealogical Society), "Mrs. Whitcomb's 88th," September 2, 1892

Blaine Journal (Blaine, WA. Courtesy of Whatcom Genealogical Society), "Mrs. Whitcomb's 95th," August 30, 1898.

Blaine Journal (Blaine, WA. Courtesy of Whatcom Genealogical Society), "Otto Family's Thrilling Experience," June 27, 1889.

Blaine Journal (Blaine, WA. Courtesy of Whatcom Genealogical Society), "Runaway Bride," March 21, 1899.

Blaine Journal (Blaine, WA), "Thomas Bice Obituary," December 2, 1911," December 12, 1911.

Blaine Journal (Blaine, WA. Courtesy of Whatcom Genealogical Society), "Wagon Accident," July 2, 1891.

Blaine Journal-Press (Blaine, WA), "Edward Holtzheimer, One of Earliest Settlers, Goes On," May 3, 1928.

Blaine Journal-Press (Blaine, WA), "Holtzheimer, Edward Obituary," May 3, 1928.

Blaine Journal-Press (Blaine, WA), "Lois A. Boblett, First White Woman Here, Dies," March 19, 1925.

"Bobblet Land Records." Prescott, AZ: Third Book of Deeds, Yavapai County Arizona Recorders Office, n.d.

Boblett, Marlayne. "Boblett Family Photos and Papers." Goodyear, AZ.

Bourasaw, Noel V. "James Frederick Wardner: miner, cat rancher, town boomer, city father, man of leg-end." Skagit River Journal of History & Folklore, 2003. http://www.stumpranchonline.com (accessed March 21, 2008).

Briggs, Tom. *Brigg's Banjo Instructor*. Do They Miss Me At Home? 1855. http://freepages.music.rootsweb.com/~edgmon/.htm
(accessed April 20, 2008).

Brown, Noah. "Letters from Alaska." 1897. Personal Collection of Fern Crothers Kelly, Cashmere, WA.

Caribou Sun, "Two Men Drown," May 10, 1898, Courtesy of Murray Lundberg, Explore North. http://www.explorenorth.com///obit1.htm
(accessed April 15, 2008).

Carleton, J. H. "Special Report of the Mountain Meadows Massacre. U.S.A, 25 May 1859." May 25, 1859. Mountain Meadows Association.
http://www.mtn-meadows-assoc.com (accessed February 5, 2008).

Carpenter, Mary. "Long Meadow Ranch." Prescott Arizona Ranch History. http://www.lmrpoa.org/.htm (accessed February 13, 2008).

Chase, A. W. *Chase's Recipes; or, Information for Everybody: an Invaluable Collection of About Eight Hundred*. Ann Arbor, MI: A.W.
Chase, 1864.

Clark, Dolores. "Boblett Photos and Papers from Personal Collection." Everett, WA.

Cross, Jean. "Williamson Valley's Way Station to the Colorado," *Prescott Daily Courier* (Sharlot Hall Museum, Prescott, AZ), April 18, 1999,
Days Past Archives.

"Custer's Last Stand." Library of Congress, American Memory Archives. http://memory.loc.gov///.html (accessed March 19, 2008).

Daily Central City Register (Courtesy of Gilpin Historical Society), "Gregory Gulch," December 3, 1874, Central City, CO.

The Daily Freeman (Waukesha, WI), "A Half Century Old," June 30, 1890.

The Daily Miner (Butte, MT), "New Gold Excitement, Headwaters of the Coeur d'Alene Glistening With Golden Nuggets," August 3, 1883.

The Daily Revielle (Whatcom-New Whatcom, WA), "Mary E. Dye Visits," November 18, 1891.

Davidson, George. *Coast Pilot of California, Oregon, and Washington Territory, United States Coast and Geodetic Survey. 1869*. Government
Printing Office: Tatoosh Lighthouse Photo courtesy of NOAA Photo Library, n.d.

"E.A. Boblett Land Records, Yavapai County Recorder, SG5-RG113." Archives and Public Records. Arizona State Library, Phoenix, AZ.

Evans, Elwood, comp. *History of the Pacific Northwest: Oregon and Washington*. Portland, OR: North Pacific History Co., 1889.

Fairhaven Herald (Fairhaven, WA), "James F. Wardner Dying in Milwaukee," September 5, 1903.

Fairhaven Herald (Fairhaven, WA. Courtesy of Whatcom Genealogical Society), "New Buildings Now in Course of Erection in this City,"
March 11, 1890.

Fairhaven Herald (Fairhaven, WA.), "Wardner Dying in Milwaukee," September 5, 1903.

Fanning, William H.W. "Pierre-Jean DeSmet." New Advent, The Catholic Encyclopedia. http://www.newadvent.org//.htm (accessed March 10,
2008).

Farish, Thomas Edwin. *History of Arizona Vol. II*. Phoenix/Francisco: Filmer Bros., 1915.

Farish, Thomas Edwin. *History of Arizona Vol. III*. Phoenix/Francisco: Filmer Bros., 1916.

Farish, Thomas Edwin. *History of Arizona Vol. IV*. Phoenix/Francisco: Filmer Bros., 1916.

Farish, Thomas Edwin. *History of Arizona Vol. V*. Phoenix/Francisco: Filmer Bros., 1918.

Farish, Thomas Edwin. *History of Arizona Vol. VIII*. Phoenix/Francisco: Filmer Bros., 1918.

Ferguson, Ann. "Steamboat History." April 2, 2008. Bonner County Museum, ID.

"The Founding of Albuquerque." Friends of Albuquerque's Environmental Story, City of Albuquerque. http://www.cabq.gov///.html (accessed January 31, 2009).

Frank Leslie's Illustrated Magazine, "Man Wants A Wife," March 5, 1859.

Gehling, Richard. "The Pike's Peak Gold Rush." Pike's Peak Gold Rush. http://www.geocities.com////.html (accessed February 11, 2008).

"Goodnight, Charles." Handbook of Texas Online. http://www.tshaonline.org/////.html (accessed January 30, 2009).

Granger, Byrd H. *Arizona Place Names*. Tucson: University of Arizona Press, 1960.

Griffing, James Sayre. "Topeka, Kansas Territory. Letter to Mr. Editor." James Sayre Griffing to William Smyth, July 27, 1859. In *Territorial Kansas Online*. Kansas State Historical Society and University of Kansas. http://www.territorialkansasonline.org (accessed February 6, 2008).

Hackbarth, Linda. "Bayview the Early Years." http://www.bayviewidaho.org/.html (accessed February 20, 2008).

Hambleton, Chalkley J. *A Gold Hunter's Experience*. Chicago: R.R. Donnelly, 1898.

Hanable, William S. "Flattery Light on Tatoosh Island begins operating on December 28, 1857." History Link.org Online Encyclopedia of Washington State History. http://www.historylinkorg/ (accessed February 2, 2008).

Hart, Herbert M. "Historic California Posts, Drum Barracks." The California State Military Museum. http://www.militarymuseum.org/.html (accessed April 6, 2008).

Hartman, Dorothy. "Women's Roles in the Late 19th Century." ConnerPrairie.Org. http://www.connerprairie.org//.html (accessed April 8, 2008).

Hartman, John W. "Interview, September 27, 1938, American Life Histories." Library of Congress, American Memory– Manuscripts from the Federal Writers' Project, 1936-1940. http://memory.loc.gov///.html (accessed June 21, 2008).

Hartnett, Thomas J. "Interview, Oct. 24, 1938, American Life Histories." Library of Congress, American Memory–Manuscripts from the Federal Writers' Project, 1936-1940. http://memory.loc.gov///.html (accessed March 12, 2008).

Highlights of Early Wilmington History. Wilmington, CA: Wilmington Historical Society, 2008.

"History and Culture, The Mission." FYINorthIdaho.Com. http://www.fyinorthidaho.com/Relocation/and-culture.aspx (accessed June 20, 2008).

"History of Rancho Cucamonga." City of Rancho Cucamonga. http://www.citivu.com//.html (accessed February 3, 2008).

Hitchcock, Mary Evelyn. *Two Women in the Klondike: The Story of a Journey to the Gold-fields of Alaska*. New York: Putnam's Sons, 1899.

Hobson, George C. "Gems of Thought and History of Shoshone County." *Kellogg Evening News Press* (Kellogg, ID), July 1940.

Huse, William. *History of Dixon County Nebraska*. Norfolk, NE: Press of the Daily News, 1896.

Idaho Daily Statesman (Boise, ID), "Oldest Coeur D'Alene Claim Has Been Sold," March 30, 1901.

Idaho Sun (Murray, Idaho), "Death of Dream Davis," February 1877.

Idaho Sun (Shoshone, ID), "Shooting of Jack Enright," July 8, 1884.

Johnson, Mabel. *Foods "in prospective" on the Oregon Trail*. Oregon: Mabel Johnson, 1995.

Kay, Theodore. Telephone interview by author, *History of Oakum*, February 4, 2008.

"Kellogg, Idaho–Center of Coeur d'Alene Mining District." History of Murray, Idaho. http://www.murrayidaho.com/ (accessed February 22, 2008).

Kershner, Jim. "Bumpy beginning, but quite a ride." *The Spokesman-Review* (Spokane, WA), May 19, 2007. http://www.spokesmanreview.com//story.asp (accessed February 8, 2008).

Knapp, Martin Wells. *Bible Songs of Salvation and Victory*. Cincinnati, Ohio: W.P. Knapp, 1902.

Larsen, Ellen. "Idaho History Facts." Rathdrum Historical Society, ID.

"List of Klondike Supplies." History and Culture, National Park Service. http://www.nps.gov//////_pioneer2.htm. (accessed February 6, 2008).

Lockwood, Jeffrey A. *Locust: The Devastating Rise and Mysterious Disappearance of the Insect that Shaped the American Frontier*. New York: Basic Books, 2004.

Lockwood, Lizzie. "Interview. Nov. 11, 1938, American Life Histories." Library of Congress, American Memory–Manuscripts from the Federal Writers' Project, 1936-1940. http://memory.loc.gov///.html (accessed March 15, 2008).

Luchetti, Cathy. *Men of the West, Life on the American Frontier*. New York: W.W. Norton & Co., 2004.

Lynam, Bill. "The facts of Virgil Earp's connection to Prescott," *Prescott Daily Courier* (Sharlot Hall Museum, Prescott, AZ), October 14, 2001, Days Past Archives.

Mackay, Emma. "Interview. October 22, 1938. American Life Histories." Library of Congress, American Memory–Manuscripts from the Federal Writers' Project, 1936-1940. http://memory.loc.gov///.html (accessed March 3, 2008).

Maher, T.J. "The Coast Survey of the Pacific Coast." NOAA Pacific History. http://www.history.noaa.gov/_tales/.html (accessed February 14, 2008).

Mather, R.E. *Scandal of the West: Domestic Violence on the Frontier*. Oklahoma City, OK: History West Publishing Co., 1998.

Mayhew, H., and J. Binny. *Criminal Prisons in London and Scenes of Prison Life, 1862*. London ed. Portsmith Asylum, Oakum and Idle Hands. Mystic Seaport Museum, CT: Employees Wildlife Habitat Committee. http://www.rewhc.org/.shtml (accessed March 15, 2008).

McNaught, Lois. "Genealogy Notes from Private Collection." 2008. Hamilton, ON.

Messersmith, Dan W. "Camp Beale's Springs, A Short History." Mohave Museum of History and Arts. www.ctaz.com/~mocohist//.htm (accessed February 6, 2008).

Miners Register (Central City, CO), "Locusts," August 7, 1864.

Mix, Robert W., and Beth Mix. "Boblett History and Photos from Personal Collection." 2008. Pea Ridge, AR.

The Morning Journal (Blaine, WA. Courtesy of Whatcom Genealogical Society), "Return from Mt. Baker," September 26, 1890.

The Morning Journal (Blaine, WA. Courtesy of Whatcom Genealogical Society), "Trip to Mt. Baker," September 11, 1890.

Morning Oregonian (Portland, OR), "Eighty-five Thousand Dollar Fire at Rathdrum, Idaho," September 28, 1884.

Morton, J. Sterling, and Albert Watkins. *History of Nebraska*. Nebraska: Western Publishing and Engraving Co., 1918.

Moulton, Candy. *The Writer's Guide to Everyday Life in the Wild West*. Cincinnati: Writers Digest Books, 1999.

Murphy, Claire Rudolf, and Jane G. Haigh. *Gold Rush Women*. Anchorage: Alaska Northwest Books, 1997.

Nelson, Fred B. "Old Cemetery at Walnut Creek Gives Look Into History." *Prescott Daily Courier* (Sharlot Hall Museum, Prescott, AZ), September 18, 2005, Days Past Archives.

New York Times, "Against H.F. Beecher," July 9, 1899.

New York Times, "The Black Hills – Letter From Lieut. Gen. Sheridan to G. Sherman," March 27, 1875.

New York Times, "The Coeur d'Alene Mines – Over the Trail to the Camps in the Gold Gulch," July 28, 1884.

New York Times, "End of the Buffalo, How The Mighty Herds Have Been Exterminated From The Great Plains," December 26, 1884.

New York Times, "Indian Outrages in Arizona – Arrival of Governor McCormick," February 2, 1868.

New York Times, "Latest from the Mines – Departure of Mr. Greeley – Great Conflagration in the Mountains – Dreadful Loss of Life – Rich Diggings Discovered," July 12, 1859.

New York Times, "Nellie Cashman Dead, Pioneer Miner and 'Champion Woman Musher' Dies at 80," January 8, 1925.

New York Times, "She Selects Klondike Home," February 28, 1904.

Nordstrand, Dorothea. "Maynard: Seattle Pioneer." History Link.org Online Encyclopedia of Washington State History. http://www.historylinkorg/ (accessed February 2, 2008).

Omaha Herald (New Hampshire Historical Society), "Stagecoach Etiquette," Spring 1877.

"Original Session Resolutions & Memorials, First Territorial Legislature of Arizona." 1864. History and Archives Division. Archives and Public Records, Arizona State Library, Phoenix, AZ.

Ott, John S., and Dick Malloy. "The Development of the Tacoma Water Supply System." The Tacoma Public Utilities Story: The First 100 Years, 1893-1993. http://www.prism.washington.edu//y.html (accessed May 15, 2008).

"Our History – Founding and Early Years." Gilpin Historical Society, Central City, CO. http://www.gilpinhistory.org (accessed February 5, 2008).

Parsons, William B. *The New Gold Mines of Western Kansas*. Territorial Kansas Online. Pikes Peak. Ohio: Geo. S. Blanchard, 1859. Kansas State Historical Society and University of Kansas. http://www.territorialkansasoline.org/ (accessed April 22, 2009).

Perkins, Robert P. "John Robert Baylor, The life and times of Arizona's Confederate Governor." Colonel Sherod Hunter Camp 1525, Sons of Confederate Veterans. http://members.tripod.com/~azrebel/page15.html (accessed January 23, 2009).

Peterson, Chuck. *Stories of Wardner*. Wardner, ID: Chuck Peterson, 2003.

Pioneer Stories of Arizona's Verde Valley. Courtesy of the Camp Verde Historical Society, AZ: Verde Valley Pioneers Association, 1954.

Prichard, George J. "A brief outline of the life of Andrew J. Prichard." Eli M. Oboler Library Archives, J.A. Harrington Collection, Box 2, #13. Idaho State University, Pocatello, ID.

Rochester, Junius. "Henry Yesler arrives in Seattle on October 20, 1852." Revised by Walt Crowley, October 17, 2002. History Link.org Online Encyclopedia of Washington State History. http://www.historylink.org/ (accessed February 6, 2008).

Rocky Mountain Gold Reporter and Mountain City Herald (Denver, CO. Courtesy of Gilpin Historical Society), "Mountain City," August 13, 1859.

Rocky Mountain News (Denver, CO. Courtesy of Gilpin County Historical Society, Central City, CO), "Emigration," April 25, 1860.

Rocky Mountain News (Denver, CO. Courtesy of Gilpin Historical Society, Central City, CO), "Value of Gold," December 21, 1859.

Ross, Mrs. "Interview, Oct. 4, 1938, American Life Histories." Library of Congress, American Memory–Manuscripts from the Federal Writers' Project, 1936-1940. http://memory.loc.gov///wpahome.html (accessed February 6, 2008).

San Francisco Examiner Sunday Magazine, "How I Mined for Gold in the Klondike," August 1, 1897.

"Scrapbook of Judge Edmund William Wells, Jr." DB488, f.1. Sharlot Hall Museum and Archives, Prescott, AZ.

Sharp, Dana. "Granite Mountain Stands As A Monument to a Vanished Time," *Prescott Daily Courier-Westward* (Sharlot Hall Museum, Prescott, AZ), October 31, 1975, Days Past Archives, Reprinted Feb. 8, 2004.

Shelly, W.H. "The Shelf Behind the Door." Springfield-Greene County Public Library, Missouri. May 14, 1958. Max E. Hunter Folk Song Collection-Cat. #0099 (MFH #574), http://maxhunter.missouristate.edu//.html (accessed March 5, 2008).

Sheridan, Thomas E. *Arizona, A History*. Tucson, AZ: University of Arizona Press, 2003.

Sinnwell, Mike. "Ghost Town Photos, Maps and Information." Rocky Mountain Profiles. http://www.rockymountainprofiles.com (accessed February 6, 2008).

Skaguay News (Skaguay [Skagway], AK), "When and How to Outfit," December 31, 1897, Alaska State Library, Gold Rush Archives.

Smalley, Eugene V. "The Coeur d'Alene Stampede," *The Century Magazine*, October 1884.

Smith, Lutella. "Woman Wants a Husband," *Blaine Journal* (Blaine, WA. Courtesy of Whatcom Genealogical Society), September 27, 1888.

Spargo, L. Darlene. Flick Family Papers. Wenatchee, WA.

Spargo, L. Darlene, and Judy Artley Sandbloom. *Pioneer Dreams, Histories of Washington Territorial Pioneers*. Kansas: Central Plains Book Manufacturing, 2004.

Speidel, William C. *Sons of the Profits*. Seattle, WA: Nettle Creek Publishing Co., 1967.

The Spokane Falls Review (Spokane Falls, WA), "The Deadly Pistol," June 20, 1884.

The Spokane Falls Review (Spokane Falls, WA), "The Ready Revolver at Eagle City. The Mining Camp the Scene of a Shooting Affair," June 21, 1884.

The Spokane Falls Review (Spokane Falls, WA), "A shooting scrape," April 1884, Vol. 2, pg 1.

Strong, Annie Hall. "From Woman's Standpoint," *The Skaguay News* (Skaguay [Skagway], AK), December 31, 1897, Alaska State Library, Gold Rush Archives.

Taylor, Alan. "Klondike Gold Rush Centennial, 1897-98 to 1997-98." Kokogiak Media. http://www.kokogiak.com (accessed May 23, 2008).

"Testimony in Trials of John D. Lee." Mountain Meadows Association. http://www.mtn-meadows-assoc.com/.htm (accessed February 5, 2008).

Thomas, David M. *Arizona Legislative Manual*. Phoenix, AZ: State of Arizona, 2003. http://www.azleg.state.az.us///.pdf (accessed February 13, 2008).

"Threads of Gold, Women of the Alaska Gold Rush." Golden Opportunity-Gallery of Alaska Exhibit. University of Alaska Museum of the North, Fairbanks, AK.

Truman, Ben C. "A Very Dangerous Trip," *New York Times*, June 1, 1890.

Victoria Daily Times (Victoria, B.C.), "Former Police Matron Dies," December 5, 1930.

Wardner, Jack. *Jack Wardner of Wardner, Idaho*. New York: Anglo-American Publishing Co., 1900.

Warren, James R. "Seattle at 150: Kindly 'Doc' Maynard could not say 'no,'" *Seattle Post-Intelligencer*, October 2, 2001.

Warren, James R. "Ten who shaped Seattle: Henry Yesler struck gold in lumber and real estate," *Seattle Post-Intelligencer*, September 25, 2001.

Waugh, Benjamin. *W.T. Snead: A Life for the People*. London: E. Marlborough & Co., 1885. The W.T. Stead Resource Site. http://www.attackingthedevil.co.uk//imprisonment.php (accessed March 16, 2008).

Weiser, Kathy. "Mountain Meadow's Massacre." Legends of America. http://www.legendsofamerica.com/mountainmeadowshistoricaccounts.html (accessed April 23, 2009).

Wilkeson, Frank. "The Gold mines of Idaho, A Trip to the Coeur d'Alene Mountains – Prospecting holes to deceive investors – A mining town today in all its squalor," *New York Times*, September 11, 1877.

Wright, E.W. *Lewis & Dryden's Marine History of the Pacific Northwest*. Portland, OR: The Lewis and Dryden Printing Co., 1895.

Zetterberg, Kathie M., and Wilma David. "Henry Yesler's Native American daughter Julia is born on June 12, 1855." History Link.org Online Encyclopedia of Washington State History. http://www.historylinkorg/ (accessed February 7, 2009).

Index

A guide to the people, places, and events of Lois's and Ed's lives in the West, *bold italic page numbers* reference Lois's memoir; other page numbers reference research findings in the sidebars. **Chapter headers** from Lois's story are in bold.

L. Darlene Spargo

My passion for history, especially American West history, was fueled by a combination of my upbringing in a post-war military family and the advent of television. As a child, my greatest joy was playing cowgirls and Indians, riding my golden-maned pony through my grandparents' cotton fields with my pearl-handled Annie Oakley cap pistol blazing a trail of wonderfully pungent smoke. Or, I would stick a pigeon feather in my braids and tip-toe through the rows of corn, an Indian armed with a home-made bow and arrow on the look-out for danger. After supper, we children would gather in the yard for a game of "now you see me, now you don't" as we rode our imaginary horses through the firefly studded night, bursting into the squares of light thrown onto the grass by the uncurtained windows and as quickly disappearing into the dark again, accompanied by the theme songs emanating from our wonderful new TV: Rawhide, Gunsmoke, *and* Have Gun, Will Travel.

Well I remember the day my Wild West died. My family stepped into the back yard of our San Antonio home, turned our faces to the sky, and watched Sputnik slip silently over the horizon. Sputnik replaced the past with the present, and I was swept along on the tide of history in the making. At school our tornado drills were replaced by Civil Defense drills. We were taught to stop, drop, and cover, preferably while wearing white. The Cold War dominated the news; one war marched after another. We heard of the Bay of Pigs, buried a president, and put a man on the moon. We watched a wall go up and lived to see it come down. Civil Rights burst upon the scene, and America was forever changed. Computers took us into a world of instant information without boundaries. Time passes so quickly that my life's events are now just "ancient history" to my children and grandchildren.

My husband, Jim, and I live in Wenatchee, Washington, and share four children and six grandchildren. I indulge my love of history, research, and genealogy by participating in the DAR, Native Daughters of Washington Territorial Pioneers, volunteer work with local museums, and cross-country travel visiting historical sites and museums. I enjoy taking pioneer women's stories into nursing and retirement homes, schools, and local club meetings. This is my third history book, and I am always looking for the next great life story.

Darlene Spargo

Cover credits:

Map:
  Henry Lange, 1854. Courtesy of Dave Rumsey, Dave Rumsey Map Collection.

Photos:
  Lois Boblett, circa 1910, courtesy of Robert Mix
  Freight Wagons, Prescott, Arizona, circa 1880, Sharlot Hall Museum and Archives